SICK SOCIETIES

Challenging the Myth
of Primitive Harmony

ROBERT B. EDGERTON

THE FREE PRESS
A Division of Macmillan, Inc.
NEW YORK

Maxwell Macmillan Canada
TORONTO

Maxwell Macmillan International
NEW YORK   OXFORD   SINGAPORE   SYDNEY

The Free Press
A Division of Macmillan, Inc.
866 Third Avenue, New York, N. Y. 10022

Maxwell Macmillan Canada, Inc.
1200 Eglinton Avenue East
Suite 200
Don Mills, Ontario M3C 3N1

Macmillan, Inc. is part of the Maxwell Communication
Group of Companies.

Printed in the United States of America

printing number

1 2 3 4 5 6 7 8 9 10

Library of Congress Cataloging-in-Publication Data

Edgerton, Robert B.,
    Sick societies: challenging the myth of primitive harmony/
Robert B. Edgerton.
        p.   cm.
    Includes bibliographical references and index.
    ISBN 0-02-908925-5
    1. Cultural relativism.   2. Ethnocentrism.   3. Social perception.
    4. Developing countries—Social conditions.   I. Title.
    GN345.5.E34   1992
    302'.12—dc20   92-13948
                                                            CIP

Contents

Acknowledgments   vii

1. Paradise Lost:
   The Myth of Primitive Harmony   1

2. From Relativism to Evaluation   16

3. Maladaptation   46

4. Women and Children First:
   From Inequality to Exploitation   75

5. Sickness, Suffering, and Premature Death   105

6. From Discontent to Rebellion   133

7. The Death of Populations, Societies, and Cultures   160

8. Adaptation Reconsidered   188

Notes   211
Bibliography   229
Index   271

Acknowledgments

Every author owes more debts to others than can be acknowledged, much less repaid. I am grateful for the many challenges posed to me by so many students at UCLA, as well as students and faculty members at Case Western Reserve University and the University of California, San Diego, where I presented abbreviated versions of this book. For their helpful advice, I thank Melford Spiro, Donald Symons, Nadine Peacock, Robert Bailey, Joan Silk, and Theodore Schwartz. For their many comments on various earlier versions of this manuscript, I am grateful to Robert Boyd, L. L. Langness, John Kennedy, Walter Goldschmidt, Jerome Barkow, Thomas Weisner, Douglas Hollan, Jill Korbin, Alex Cohen, and Karen Ito.

For unending and gracious assistance over the years in transforming bits of text into something resembling a book, I thank Susan Wilhite, Tina Tran, Thelma Woods, Esther Rose, Ellen Lodge, and Dana Stulberg. I am also most grateful to Adam Bellow of The Free Press for his sound editorial guidance.

And to all of those people around the world with whom I have lived, I am thankful for the opportunity to have experienced other ways of life, ways that are in some respects better, and in others worse, than those of my own people.

Chapter 1

Paradise Lost

The Myth of Primitive Harmony

All societies are sick, but some are sicker than others. This paraphrase of Orwell's famous quip about the equality of animals calls attention to the existence of traditional beliefs and practices that threaten human health and happiness more in some societies than in others. But it also indicates that there are some customs and social institutions in all societies that compromise human well-being. Even populations that appear to be well-adapted to their environments maintain some beliefs or practices that unnecessarily imperil their well-being or, in some instances, their survival. Populations the world over have not been well served by some of their beliefs such as, for example, those concerning witchcraft, the need for revenge, or male supremacy, and many of their traditional practices involving nutrition, health care, and the treatment of children have been harmful as well. Slavery, infanticide, human sacrifice, torture, female genital mutilation, rape, homicide, feuding, suicide, and environmental pollution have sometimes been needlessly harmful to some or all members of a society and under some circumstances they can threaten social survival.

To Americans besieged by headlines and television reports concerning our endangered environment, homelessness, child abuse, the threat of drugs, AIDS, or gang violence, the idea that some things

1

people do may be harmful to themselves and others will hardly seem controversial. Beliefs that lead to anorexia nervosa or wife beating are likely to be seen as harmful, and beliefs favoring anti-Semitism or male supremacy are also likely to be seen as dangerous. Americans may also believe that if surveys can rate various cities in the United States in terms of their "relative quality of life," the same could be done for foreign cities and, for that matter, foreign countries. Many would surely be troubled by the idea that the political systems of Iraq, Hitler's Germany, or the Khmer Rouge in Cambodia were, or are, as good as those in, say, Norway, Japan, or Switzerland. And they would probably react with disbelief to the assertion that there is no scientific basis for evaluating another society's practice of genocide, judicial torture or human sacrifice, for example, except as the people in that society themselves evaluate these practices. Yet that is exactly what the principle of cultural relativism asserts, and this principle continues to be widely and strongly held.

So too is the belief that "primitive" societies were far more harmonious than societies caught up in the modern world. We know that human misery, fear, loneliness, pain, sickness, and premature death are typical of America's urban ghettos and its homeless people, South Africa's black townships, the starving villages of the Sudan, the slums of Brazil, and the war-ravaged lands of Central America or the Middle East. We also know that people in places such as these are the hapless victims of such forces as governmental neglect, racism, corruption, ethnic, religous and political strife, and economic exploitation, among other kinds of social, cultural, and environmental pressures. However, many prominent scholars believe that this sort of misery is not natural to the human condition, that people in smaller, more homogeneous "folk" societies have historically lived in greater harmony and happiness, and that many small populations continue to do so today. The belief that primitive societies are more harmonious than modern ones, that savages are noble, and that life in the past was more idyllic than life today is not only reflected in the motion pictures and novels of our popular culture (the recently acclaimed film *Dances with Wolves* comes immediately to mind), it is deeply engrained in scholarly discourse as well.

This "community-lost" way of reconstructing history is founded in the romantic belief that the malaise and mayhem of the modern world is not the natural human condition. Instead, human misery is thought to be the product of pervasive social disorganization, divisive ethnic

2

or religious diversity, class conflict, or competing interests that plague large societies, particularly nation states. Because smaller and simpler societies, on the other hand, developed their cultures in response to the demands of their immediate and stable environments, their ways of life must have produced far greater harmony and happiness for their populations. Robin Fox, for example, vividly described the upper Paleolithic environment of big-game hunters as one in which " . . . there was a harmony of our evolved attributes as a species, including our intelligence, our imagination, our violence (and hence our violent imagination), our reason and our passions—a harmony that has been lost."[1] If a small society is found that lacks harmony, many social scientists conclude that this condition must be the result of the disorganizing effects of culture contact, particularly urbanization. This idea, like cultural relativism, has been deeply embedded in Western thought for centuries, and it persists in scholarly thinking today.[2]

In 1947, when Robert Redfield published his well-known folk-urban typology, he did little more than lend the cachet of anthropology to an already ancient distinction.[3] The idea that cities were characterized by crime, disorder, and human suffering of all sorts while small, isolated, and homogeneous folk societies were harmonious communities goes back to Aristophanes, Tacitus, and the Old Testament. The idea was given renewed prominence in nineteenth-century thought by such influential figures as W.H. Morgan, Ferdinand Tönnies, Henry Maine, Fustel de Coulanges, Emile Durkheim, Max Weber, and, not least, Karl Marx in the *Communist Manifesto*. Their writings and those of others led to a consensus that the emotional and moral commitment, personal intimacy, social cohesion, and continuity over time that characterized folk societies were lost in the transition to urban life, where social disorganization and personal pathology prevailed. In the twentieth century, the contrast between folk "community" and urban "society" became one of the most fundamental ideas in all of social science. The idea that large urban societies lost the harmonious sense of community that was thought to be characteristic of folk societies is widespread among social philosophers, political scientists, sociologists, psychiatrists, theologians, novelists, poets, and the educated public in general. Kirkpatrick Sale recently answered criticism of his book *The Conquest of Paradise* (about the European conquest of the native peoples of America) by vigorously insisting that compared to the culture of Europe,

3

the "primal communities" of preconquest America were more "harmonious, peaceful, benign and content."[4]

The contrast between folk harmony and urban conflict is rooted in the evolutionary assumption that while people in folk societies, like the Indians of America, were achieving harmonious ways of living together, they were also developing traditional beliefs and practices that helped them to adapt to their environments without depleting or destroying them. Jean-Jacques Rousseau made the idea of the Noble Savage part of our common parlance, and in one form or another, many modern scholars sustain this viewpoint. There is no shortage of evidence documenting the social pathology that plagues many modern societies, but reliable evidence for primitive harmony is less plentiful. Before we look at what that evidence is like, we should pause to consider how it came into being.

Knowledge of life in folk societies—those small, traditional, and often less complex societies that existed all over the globe before the coming of states, industrialization, and world economic systems—comes primarily from the work of anthropologists. Some useful reports about folk societies have been produced by explorers, traders, missionaries, military men, and even adventurers, but many of these reports have been wildly inaccurate, even fantastic. Some romanticized folk societies so outrageously that Rousseauist illusions of primitive Arcadia resulted, and others were so luridly negative that tribal peoples were caricatured as grotesque subhumans. Humans were often depicted as apes or monsters, and Rousseau actually based his renowned portrait of the Noble Savage on a description of an orangutan.[5] The most accurate descriptions of small-scale societies have usually been written by anthropologists, those men and women who have learned the local languages and whose stock in trade is interviewing, observing, and participating in the lives of people in societies other than their own. Everyone has heard of Margaret Mead, but before she went to Samoa, New Guinea, or Bali, hundreds of anthropologists had described tribal peoples, and later, thousands more would follow. Their many ethnographic accounts provide the bulk of what we know about folk societies.

While theirs is the best available information about life as it has been lived in small-scale societies during the late nineteenth and twentieth centuries, this information is neither entirely complete nor entirely accurate. In the year (or two or three) that an anthropologist typically spends in a small society, he or she can learn only so much

4

and, in the course of a professional career, can write only so much. This means that some aspects of life among small non-Western populations simply cannot be fully described. For a number of reasons that we will discuss below, many anthropologists have chosen not to write about the darker side of life in folk societies, or at least not to write very much about it. Among themselves, over coffee or a cocktail, they may talk freely about the kinds of cruelty, irrationality, and suffering they saw during their field research, but only a relative few have written about such things or about any of the many ways in which people in various folk societies do things that are seemingly harmful to themselves and others. As a result, it is likely that the ethnographic record substantially underreports the amount and kind of human suffering and discontent that has actually existed in the world's small societies, just as it underrepresents the various things that people believe and practice that do not contribute to their well-being.

This may sometimes occur because anthropologists believe that the cruel, harmful, or ineffective practices they see in a folk society are the result of social disorganization brought about by colonialism, something that in fact has often taken place. And certain practices, all anthropologists know, are sometimes not reported because doing so would offend the people being described or discredit them in the eyes of others. For these reasons along with other forms of personal bias, some anthropological monographs, or as they are also called, "ethnographies," are idealized, even romanticized portraits. For example, Jane Belo wrote this about the Balinese: "The babies do not cry, the small boys do not fight, the young girls bear themselves with decorum . . . Everyone carries out his appointed task with respect for his equals and superiors, and gentleness and consideration for his dependents. The people adhere, apparently with ease, to the laws governing the actions, big and small, of their lives."[6] Unfortunately for the authenticity of this idyllic vision, Belo went on—unwittingly, it would seem—to document instances in which men beat their wives, wives ran away from home, children defied their parents, and people rebelled against their customs and laws.

There are many other examples in ethnographic reports of this sort of discrepancy between the ideal and the reality of life. One of the most significant is Robert Redfield's ethnographic account of the Mexican village Tepoztlan, because it is his understanding of this town that informed his development of the folk-urban comparison. Redfield found the people of Tepoztlan to be tranquil and contented, living in

5

almost ideal personal adjustment and social integration. However, when Redfield's former student Oscar Lewis restudied Tepoztlan a few years later, he found widespread social conflict, malicious gossip, mistrust, hatred, and fear.[7] There is some suspicion that Lewis may have exaggerated these negative aspects of life in Tepoztlan, but that Redfield's vision of Tepoztlan was idealized is beyond dispute.

When Elizabeth Marshall Thomas entitled her book about the San (formerly known as Bushmen) of the Kalahari Desert in southern Africa *the Harmless People*, she was giving voice to her perception of these people as being at peace with themselves as well as their environment. Unfortunately for her view of San harmony, it was later shown that these people had an exceptionally high homicide rate and at an earlier time were warlike as well, a correction that was probably missed by much of the general public that read this popular book.[8]

An even more popular book, probably the most widely read ethnography ever written, is *The Forest People*, an account of the Mbuti pygmies of Zaire's Ituri Forest written by Colin M. Turnbull in 1961.[9] Rich in detail and personal observation, Turnbull's gracefully written book describes a people who lived in what he portrays as almost perfect harmony with the forest that provided for all their needs. According to Turnbull, the Mbuti had no homicide, no suicide or rape, no painful initiations or mutilations, and no warfare. Turnbull admitted that the Mbuti were quarrelsome and sometimes fought, that they lied, stole, and sometimes refused to share (and he neglected to mention that men who owned hunting nets exploited men who did not); but no matter—for Turnbull, the Mbuti were a loving, happy people whose culture made them one with their forest world. As seen through Turnbull's eyes, the Mbuti were the very prototype of a folk society. Few of Turnbull's anthropological colleagues challenged the accuracy of his account.

Turnbull was unabashedly enamored of the loving, harmonious way of life that he believed the Mbuti embodied, so much so in fact that a decade later when he studied another small society, he was openly appalled by their loveless existence. As he described them in another very popular book, *The Mountain People*, the Ik, a starving population of some 2,000 people in northern Uganda, had become so horrifically dehumanized, so ruthless about their individual survival, that Turnbull actually proposed to an official of the Ugandan government that they be forcibly rounded up and dispersed throughout the country, not, as one might have thought, to save them from starvation, but to

6

assure that their asocial, loveless culture would die with them, never to corrupt other people.[10] The anthropological reaction was harsh. Turnbull was severely criticized for painting too dismal a picture of Ik culture as well as for unethical conduct.[11]

The truth about the Ik is still in dispute. Formerly a hunting and gathering people with some degree of reliance on cultivation, the Ik had been forced by the government of Uganda to give up hunting and to rely on horticulture. When prolonged drought devastated their crops, the Ik began to starve, and according to Turnbull, all traces of human kindness, caring, and affection disappeared as small children were abandoned to fend for themselves, the old were encouraged to starve, and anyone strong enough to do so literally took food out of the mouths of weaker people. There can be little doubt that those who survived were truly miserable and that as their hunger grew more intense, they thought of survival above all else. Yet this survival behavior was probably adaptive, as Turnbull later came to acknowledge.[12] Just how adaptive it was, and for whom, cannot really be determined without studying them for a period of years, something neither Turnbull nor his critics have done.

That Turnbull may have allowed his Mbuti-like image of what a small-scale society should be like to distort his vision of the Ik became even more apparent when Bernd Heine (a German expert on Kuliak languages, which include Ik) visited them for a brief period in 1983, over fifteen years after Turnbull had completed his field research. He found that despite a recent drought and an epidemic of cholera that had killed many Ik, the population had grown in size and the people were quite sociable. As a result, he raised a number of questions about the accuracy of Turnbull's book. For example, he pointed out that the village Turnbull chose to study (one of twenty) was near a police post, and because of the security that resulted, it contained more non-Ik from neighboring populations than actual Ik. He also observed that Turnbull's use of Ik terms indicated only a minimal grasp of the language, something that Turnbull acknowledged. He added that Lomeja, a man whom Turnbull described as a typical Ik, was in fact not an Ik at all but a Didinga who spoke only "broken Ik." He also challenged various ethnographic facts reported by Turnbull and concluded that the Ik he saw seemed to be "an entirely different people" from the ones Turnbull described.[13] Heine's criticisms have gone largely unnoticed (they appeared in a scientific journal that only scholars interested in Africa are likely to read), however, and for most readers, including some anthropologists, the Mbuti still stand as the very model of a folk society, while the Ik epitomize a people who have lost their sense of community.

In addition to the personal idealism of such as Belo, Redfield, and Turnbull, there has been a benevolent conspiracy on the part of some anthropologists not to betray the trust of a people with whom they have lived and worked (and whom they have often come to like and respect) by writing about their least likable or reasonable practices. Indeed, there is a pervasive assumption among anthropologists that a population's long-standing beliefs and practices—their culture and their social institutions—must play a positive role in their lives or these beliefs and practices would not have persisted. Thus, it is widely thought and written that cannibalism, torture, infanticide, feuding, witchcraft, painful male initiations, female genital mutilation, cermonial rape, headhunting, and other practices that may be abhorrent to many of us must serve some useful function in the societies in which they are traditional practices. Impressed by the wisdom of biological evolution in creating such adaptive miracles as feathers for flight or protective coloration, most scholars have assumed that cultural evolution too has been guided by a process of natural selection that has produced traditional beliefs and practices that meet peoples' needs.

As a result, when a society was encountered that seemed to lack a meaningful system of beliefs or effective institutions, it was usually assumed that the cause must lie in the baneful influence of other peoples—such as colonial officials, soldiers, missionaries, or traders—who had almost always been on the scene before anthropologists were. When a society was encountered whose traditional beliefs and practices appeared to be meaningless or even harmful, the blame was often laid to external disruption. Thus, the conviction has persisted that before the social disorganization and cultural confusion brought about by foreign contact, the lives of traditional populations must have been, if not quite idyllic, then at least harmonious and meaningful.

At one time, that is, even the Ik must have enjoyed love and social harmony (something that Turnbull himself clearly believed). Therefore, rather than report the alienation, violence, or cruelty that sometimes dominated the lives of the people they came to study, some anthropologists tried to reconstruct the people's way of life as they believed it was before it was disrupted by the religious beliefs, taxes, laws, and economic interventions of the colonial powers. Few anthropologists believed that homicide, suicide, rape, and warfare were unknown before folk societies were impacted by external forces, but most of them wrote their ethnographies as if such behaviors were either infrequent or somehow helped these people to adapt to their environmental circumstances. As a consequence, the myth of primitive harmony was inadvertently reinforced, even by anthropologists who knew better.

It is very difficult to be precise about the frequency with which traits that may have been maladaptive occurred in these small societies because the existing corpus of ethnographic accounts so seldom addresses the possibility that some of the beliefs or practices of the people being described might be anything other than adaptive. If one were to select a substantial number of ethnographic monographs more or less at random, probably no more than a handful would contain an analysis of the maladaptive consequences of any particular belief or practice. On the contrary, if seemingly paradoxical, irrational, bizarre, inefficient, or dangerous beliefs or practices are described at all—and very often they are not—they are usually presumed to be adaptive and are treated as if they must serve some useful purpose. For example, even the most extreme forms of penile mutilation— slashing open the urethra, scourging it with abrasive stalks of grass or other plants, mutilating the glans or infibulating it—have typically been analyzed in the ethnographic literature (but not the psychiatric) not as irrational, nonadaptive, or maladaptive practices but in terms of their positive social, cultural, or psychological consequences.[14]

Similarly, the practice of Pharanoic circumcision or female genital infibulation, common in parts of Muslim Northeast Africa, involves slashing away a girl's clitoris and both sets of vaginal labia. The wound is sutured together, leaving an opening the size of a matchstick for the passage of urine and menstrual blood. When young women are married, this small opening must be surgically enlarged to permit sexual intercourse. In addition to inflicting great pain, these procedures carry a considerable risk for infection, infertility, and even death. Nevertheless, anthropologists have commonly chosen to interpret infibulation as an adaptive practice because the people who practice it zealously defend it and because it can readily be seen how it reinforces values of female purity and family honor. That most

9

societies in the world, including most Islamic societies, have managed to cherish female purity and family honor without practicing infibulation is rarely acknowledged.

The cumulative impact of relativistic and adaptivist assumptions has led generations of ethnographers to believe that there simply must be a good social or cultural reason why a long-established belief or practice exists. If it has endured for any length of time, it must be adaptive, or so it has been assumed either implicitly or explicitly by most of the people who have written what we know about the lives of people in small, traditional societies.

But not everyone has made this assumption. Some ecologically oriented ethnographers, for example, have provided descriptions that carefully assess how adaptive a particular population's beliefs or institutions may be. Walter Goldschmidt's ethnography of the Sebei of Uganda is a good example. After analyzing the relatively positive social and cultural adaptations that the Sebei made during their recent history, he described what he referred to as "disequilibria and maladaptation," especially " . . . the failure of the Sebei to establish a social order capable of maintaining their boundaries, and the failure to develop a commitment to a relevant set of moral principles."[15] His analysis went on to specify the changing socioeconomic circumstances that led to these "failures." Similarly, Klaus-Friedrich Koch, writing about the then-unacculturated Jalé who lived in the remote eastern Snow Mountains of Irian Jaya in the mid 1960s before foreign influence had changed their lives, concluded that the disputes and killing which were so common among them, and so divisive, resulted because Jalé methods of conflict management were "very few and very inefficient."[16] However, even ecologically oriented ethnographers have typically paid scant attention to maladaptation.[17] Instead, the emphasis has been placed on showing the adaptive fit between various economic activities and the environment.

When the costs and benefits of a particular belief or institutionalized practice are discussed in ethnographic writing, the result is often vintage Dr. Pangloss. That is, if it is acknowledged that a certain belief system, such as witchcraft, may have costs for a population, it is quickly asserted that it also has benefits that far outweigh them. For example, when Clyde Kluckhohn and Dorothea Leighton wrote their classic ethnography *The Navaho*, they concluded that the pervasive Navaho belief in the existence among them of witches engendered fear, led to violence, and sometimes caused innocent people

10

to suffer "tragically."[18] Nevertheless, they concluded that witchcraft beliefs "keep the core of the society solid" by allowing the Navaho to redirect all the hostility they feel toward relatives and "the hazards of life itself" onto witches, and furthermore, it prevented the rich and ceremonially powerful from attaining too much power and in general served to prevent socially disruptive actions.[19] Kluckhohn and Leighton to the contrary notwithstanding, it is not self-evident that these positive results of Navaho witchcraft beliefs—if they in fact existed—outweighed the fear, violence, and tragic suffering that so many manifestly did exist.

More common still is the practice of providing no explanation at all of the presence of potentially maladaptive behavior. This phenomenon is commonplace in contemporary ethnography as well as in earlier reports, and it is reflected in the writing of some of the most insightful and distinguished ethnographers. For example, the highly esteemed British social anthropologist E. E. Evans-Pritchard wrote in his classic *The Nuer* that these Sudanese men fought with one another frequently, with little provocation, and sometimes with deadly effect. Like the Jalé, the Nuer had no effective means of preventing such violence or the retaliation it evoked. The Nuer themselves, we are told, said that "a feud never ends." It is certainly not implausible that this pattern of internecine violence was maladaptive, but Evans-Pritchard did not address the matter in his book.[20]

Evans-Pritchard also noted that even in normal years, "Nuer do not receive as much nourishment as they require."[21] He then observed that although cattle disease made cattleherding risky, the Nuer nevertheless preferred it to horticulture, which they practiced without rotating, fallowing, or fertilizing, even though good land was in short supply. Moreover, though often hungry, they refused to eat either chicken or eggs, and as fisherman and hunters, we are told with apparent disapproval, "they use little cunning."[22] The Nuer would appear to have employed less than fully efficient subsistence strategies, but Evans-Pritchard offered no analysis that would clarify the issue.

The failure to analyze seemingly maladaptive practices continues to be common. For example, writing of the Mehinaku Indians of Brazil, Thomas Gregor has provided a finely textured, sensitive account of the lives of these fewer than 100 people, who lived together in a single village.[23] His descriptions of their interactional strategies are insightfully drawn, as is his description of their incessant thievery

11

and adultery, which, we are told, had the potential for serious social conflict. Yet Gregor does not discuss why such practices persist nor whether they might indeed be maladaptive. I do not mean to single out Evans-Pritchard and Gregor for criticism, as both wrote excellent ethnographies by most standards. My point is that even the most accomplished ethnographers have often ignored the maladaptive potential of traditional beliefs and practices they encountered in small, simple societies. Indeed, I am reluctant to fire salvos of gunboat criticism at any ethnographer because some years ago I made the same assumptions myself.[24]

Most ethnographers would probably agree with psychologist Donald T. Campbell, who wrote that the assumption of adaptiveness is a good one because no matter how "bizarre" a traditional practice might seem, once it is understood it will make "adaptive sense." Many others would no doubt agree with Marvin Harris's declaration that there is no need to *assume* that beliefs or practices are adaptive because it has already been demonstrated that sociocultural systems are "largely if not exclusively" composed of adaptive traits.[25] To paraphrase Von Ranke, both the assumption that culture is adaptive and the assertion that it has been shown that cultures consist largely or exclusively of adaptive traits are equally far from God. With the partial exception of economic practices, there has been no demonstration of such widespread adaptiveness, and the assumption that culture must be adaptive is therefore unwarranted.

This issue is not of interest only to anthropologists—a tempest confined to an exotic, "primitive" teacup. The implications of the ethnographic record are important for anyone who has an interest in understanding why human societies, including our own, sometimes do not function as well as they might. It is true that some folk societies have been relatively harmonious, and some still are, but life in smaller and simpler societies has not been free of human discontent and suffering. In fact, some small populations have been unable to cope with the demands of their environments, and others have lived in apathy, conflict, fear, hunger, and despair. Nevertheless, the belief persists that small-scale societies are better adapted to their ecological circumstances than we are. The principal burden of this book is to show that some may be, but others decidedly are not.

In a number of small societies, people are chronically hungry and care little about one another's welfare. Consider the Sirionó Indians, who lived in the tropical forest of eastern Bolivia by hunting, fishing, gathering, and planting some crops. Unlike the starving Ik whom Turnbull described, they were not entirely asocial. They loved their children, at least when they were small, had some family bonds, engaged in a few social activities such as drinking parties and wrestling matches, and some people, particularly young lovers, now and then showed affection for one other. Yet Allan R. Holmberg, who lived with the Sirionó in 1941 and 1942 (where he learned about Pearl Harbor three months after the event), wrote that the unconcern of one individual for another, even within the family, "never ceased to amaze" him.[26] To illustrate his point, he recounted an episode, said to have been typical, of a man who was overtaken by darkness on his way back to camp after hunting all day. Lost in the moonless night, he repeatedly called for help. His Sirionó relatives in camp nearby heard his cries but paid no attention. After half an hour his cries ended, and his sister blithely said, " 'A jaguar probably got him.' "[27] In fact, the hunter survived the night by climbing a tree, but when he returned to the camp in the morning, no one welcomed him. Instead, his sister complained bitterly that he gave her only a small portion of his catch.

Holmberg also reported that the Sirionó constantly quarreled about food, accused one another of hoarding it, refused to share it with others, ate alone at night or in the forest, and hid food from family members by, on the part of women, secreting it in their vaginas. For the Sirionó, food was always in short supply, hunger was a constant reality in their lives, and at times, some bands were very close to starvation. In fact, sick or elderly persons who could not keep up with the nomadic round of activities were abandoned, sometimes left pathetically to crawl after the departed band until they collapsed and death came. Grief, like love or caring, was a luxury the Sirionó rarely allowed themselves.

The Sirionó environment was hardly benevolent, it was often cold, wet and windy, and the Sirionó were entirely nude. They did not know how to make fire, and so someone, usually a woman, had to carry a firebrand at all times. Even with fire, their flimsy houses and lack of clothing often left them cold and miserable. They also had no protection against the hosts of mosquitos, gnats, ticks, flies, bees, wasps, and ants that plagued them, nor the snakes, scorpions, spiders, and jaguars that threatened their lives. Hungry, fearful, physically uncomfortable, and without concern for one another, the Sirionó did not live long and did not live well. Few readers of this book would

13

be likely to choose to live as they did, and their neighbors had no desire to emulate them either. We do not know how long the Sirionó lived in this way, but it must have been for a good many years, and unlike the Ik, there had been no recent, catastrophic change in their environment. If anything was to blame for the misery of their lives, it must have been events in the distant past or, perhaps, the Sirionó themselves, because they had not been very successful in meeting their own needs, something they themselves understood. Although their traditional way of life was not threatened by external pressures, when offered Western tools and weapons or the opportunity to work as tenant farmers, many were eager to accept, even though they were badly mistreated. Although some Sirionó have continued to live as forest nomads, most of them were no more committed to their culture than they were to one another.[28]

Unlike the Sirionó, the impoverished Italian farmers of Montegrano in southern Italy were committed to their culture, but that culture directed them to live solely for the benefit of the nuclear family. According to Edward C. Banfield, they did whatever they could to further the short-run interests of their families, and not surprisingly, they believed that everyone else did the same.[29] The people of Montegrano lived with perpetual hunger, fatigue, and anxiety as well as a grim melancholia—known as *la misèria*. They also endured the humiliation that resulted from their unchanging poverty and powerlessness. Yet they were unwilling to take any organized community action on behalf of the village. They badly wanted their children to be better educated because only through education could a family better itself, but they took no action to improve their inadequate local school or even to improve the bus schedule so that their children could attend a better school in a neighboring town. The nearest hospital was five hours away by auto, and ambulance service was inadequate, but they did nothing to remedy that situation either. Banfield concluded that the people of Montegrano were "prisoners" of their family-centered culture that left them incapable of acting for the common good and, incidentally, in their families' own long-term interest.

Sometimes a population like the peasants of Montegrano retains its cherished cultural beliefs even though they are counterproductive. Sometimes a population like the Sirionó that cannot cope effectively with its physical environment develops little commitment to its culture and few social ties. And sometimes a population like the Ik may

14

be overwhelmed by external events. What these three examples suggest is that some small-scale populations do not effectively solve the problems they face, and sometimes the very culture that should sustain them and enhance their well-being instead produces fear, apathy, isolation, and degradation. Populations are sometimes devastated by events beyond their control—floods, epidemics, volcanic eruptions, and military conquest by technologically superior peoples are a few examples. This book is not about the problems that these kinds of catastrophes produce. Instead, it addresses problems that populations might be said to bring on themselves by maintaining traditional beliefs and practices that are inefficient at coping with environmental demands or are harmful to people's health or well-being.

As much as humans in various societies, whether urban or folk, are capable of empathy, kindness, even love and as much as they can sometimes achieve astounding mastery of the challenges posed by their environments, they are also capable of maintaining beliefs, values, and social institutions that result in senseless cruelty, needless suffering, and monumental folly in their relations among themselves and with other societies and the physical environment in which they live. People are not always wise, and the societies and cultures they create are not ideal adaptive mechanisms, perfectly designed to provide for human needs. It is mistaken to maintain, as many scholars do, that if a population has held to a traditional belief or practice for many years, then it must play a useful role in their lives. Traditional beliefs and practices may be useful, may even serve as important adaptive mechanisms, but they may also be inefficient, harmful, and even deadly.

In what follows, I will define what I mean by social and cultural maladaptation, provide examples of the many forms it takes in traditional small-scale societies, and attempt to identify the factors that bring about and maintain maladaptive beliefs and practices.

Chapter 2

From Relativism to Evaluation

Anthropologists have long debated whether their field is or ought to be a science or one of the humanities; some are fond of pronouncing that it must become history or nothing or that biology and psychology have no explanatory power in the study of cultural man. These exchanges, as regular as the seasons, can be entertaining or infuriating, depending on one's tastes, but they do little to advance knowledge. What is needed, I believe, are fewer manifestos about the paradigmatic status of the discipline and better questions for scholars to pursue in whatever fashion they believe will lead to falsifiable answers. I am proposing several questions. First, can we identify valid criteria for determining whether one sociocultural system is more adaptive—or less harmful to its members—than another? Second, do maladaptive or useless beliefs or practices occur even in societies that have survived in the same ecosystem for many years? Finally, if maladaptive beliefs and practices can be identified, why do they occur?

We must first clarify terms such as maladaptive and useless. Even at the simplest level they can have multiple meanings. To illustrate, we could begin with an individual as the focal point. Anything that impaired that person's ability to make the necessary adjustments to the demands of the environment (defer for now questions about what is meant by "environment") would be maladaptive. Although a fear of being caught in an open and unprotected area might have been selected for in our evolutionary past, a fear of open spaces so extreme

16

that it kept a person in seclusion would be maladaptive in most societies. Although people in many societies enjoy alcohol, getting stinking drunk every day would usually be maladaptive, too. A useless belief would be the idea that wearing purple socks would help to win the lottery or that tossing pennies into a wishing well would bring good luck. Unless indulged in excessively, such beliefs would probably not be harmful, only ineffective. A harmful belief or practice would endanger a person's physical or mental health. Smoking tobacco would be one example, fearing that the violation of any one of a hundred taboos might cause death would be another.

If similar practices or beliefs were present among members of a family, kin group, hamlet, or village, they would continue to be useless or harmful, but another issue would arise—the survivability of the group and its sociocultural system. In addition to asking questions about individual well-being and health, we would now ask whether the population can adequately carry out the tasks necessary to meet the needs of its members. And while we will address later the question of what these needs may be, it is sufficient for now to establish the presumably self-evident point that some individuals are unable to adapt to the demands of their environment. Sometimes they are unable to survive. So it is too with some families. And it requires only little more imagination to think of an entire society whose members are so unhealthy, unproductive, and divided against themselves that they inevitably die or are absorbed into another social system. A social system destined to disintegrate could be one, for example, in which only old men were allowed to have sexual access to young women while young men were confined to nonorgasmic sexual relations with aging women. (Aristophanes used such a scenario in one of his comedies.) Knowing only this, one can readily understand that without astonishingly effective systems of inculcating values and powerful means of social control, such a system would be unlikely to thrive.

In reality, there was such a society—the Oneida Community—and it did indeed perish. However, the wonder is not that the Oneida Community ceased to exist but that it lasted as long as it did—some 30 years. From 1848 when it was first organized to 1879 when the community collapsed and its leader, John H. Noyes, fled to Canada to escape prosecution, some 200 communitarians lived together in one large New York house where they engaged in a form of group marriage, prohibited any lasting emotional attachments (including

17

those between mothers and their children), and required all men, except Noyes and a few other leaders, to practice *coitus reservatus*.[1] These remarkable practices were maintained by recruiting only devoted followers to the community and expelling those who did not conform. Regular sessions of group criticism during which any misbehavior was relentlessly exposed and "corrected" also helped maintain compliance with the singular rules of the Oneida Utopia. After the community had achieved a reasonably stable and devoted following, Noyes decreed (and strictly enforced) an edict that because men enjoyed sexual intercourse more (according to him) if they did *not* ejaculate, they would be required to practice *coitus reservatus*. Even *coitus interruptus* was forbidden. Men and women did practice this form of intercourse, and they must have conformed to the rule, at least most of the time, because despite using no mechanical form of contraception there were virtually no unplanned births in the community.[2]

Noyes next declared that henceforth only older men like himself who had achieved spiritual "perfection"—the goal of the community—would be allowed to have sex with young, and as yet "imperfect," women; young men, who were also considered to be "imperfect," could only have sex with postmenopausal women, who were considered to have achieved a degree of perfection similar to that of older men. This time Noyes miscalculated the malleability of the young men: they threatened open rebellion.[3] In an effort to appease them, he reversed himself on the pleasures on nonorgasmic sex and allowed young men to reach orgasm with older women, but he still reserved all the young women for himself and his aging cronies. Somehow the community still managed to avoid disintegration until Noyes finally decided that soon after each young girl experienced her first menses, he would personally initiate her into full sexuality. Other older men of "perfection" who had looked forward to their own right to initiate these girls were so annoyed that they reminded Noyes of the statutory rape laws of the state of New York, and he abruptly decamped for Canada. With his departure, the community collapsed.

Whether we look to a short-lived community like Oneida or, as we shall see later, to well-established societies that have also collapsed, it is evident that some societies do not survive. But there are other societies that do persist, sometimes for many years, even though their members are unhealthy and some of their long-standing practices appear to be maladaptive. The impoverished and embattled populations who live in our inner cities provide an obvious example, and the people who live in rural pockets of poverty are another. For example, the 238 individuals who some 30 years ago lived in Duddie's Branch, an isolated "hollow" in Eastern Kentucky, are an example of a people who were physically unwell, and whose society and culture cannot easily be said to have served them well, but who nevertheless survived and created a world of meaning to which they were committed.

The inhabitants of this remote mountain valley lived in ramshackle wood and tarpaper shacks along a one-mile stretch of a polluted stream. Their houses had no indoor toilets, and only a few had functioning privies. Most people simply defecated on the ground, leaving their feces to be eaten by their emaciated dogs or to be carried into the river by the frequent rains. In addition to human feces, the stream was polluted by all manner of garbage and waste that people threw into it. Nevertheless, it provided the people's only source of water. Except for a handful of men who were employed, mostly in nearby coal mines, everyone lived on welfare. A few people had some chickens and small gardens, but the Duddie's Brancher's survival was dependent on grossly inadequate governmental food allowances. There was little protein available to them; in fact, there was little food of any kind, and most Duddie's Branchers were perpetually hungry. Their children were so malnourished that all were very thin and small. Some six-year-olds had achieved only half the growth that is normal for children their age, many were anemic, and all were chronically ill with endemic diseases.

Although several children and adults slept piled together in the same bed, they were perpetually chilled during the long season of cold weather. Their health was also threatened by the cockroaches, insects, and rats that infested their houses. Their few cooking utensils and bowls were rarely washed, and neither were the tin cans they used as cups; when they were washed, they received only a cursory rinse in contaminated stream water. There was no soap. The Duddie's Branchers, who ate with their fingers, rarely washed themselves either. Their clothes were as dirty as they were ragged, and their hair literally throbbed with lice. Anthropologist Rena Gazaway grew very fond of the people, but nevertheless spoke frankly about the conditions that left them chronically ill with tuberculosis, among other

19

diseases. "With few exceptions, the housekeeping is shocking and the filth defies description. The air is foul with the stifling odor of dried urine, stale cooking, unwashed bodies, dirty clothing."[4]

Although the people of Duddie's Branch tried to reckon kinship—their principal social tie—it was often difficult because sexual relations were indiscriminate (girls began to have sexual intercourse as early as the age of six) and illegitimate births were commonplace. Perhaps as a result, children had little interest in the identity of their fathers. When Gazaway asked one boy if he was not curious about his father, he answered "Hain't worth knowin'," a common sentiment.[5] People were indifferent about marriage, and there were no community groups or formal organizations, not even a church. Indeed, there was very little sociality of any kind. There was little interaction among households, and none at all as an entire community. In fact, even household members communicated with one another only in quite limited fashion. People sometimes shot others' dogs simply because it amused them to do so.

People spoke to one another so infrequently that for some time Gazaway actually thought that many of them were mute. During the course of an ordinary day and evening, a family might not exchange more than half a dozen words with one another. They also had such limited knowledge of the outside world that none knew the name of any president, past or current, or the capital of the United States. One man had heard of the American "king"—someone named Kennedy—but he could not say what a king was. Duddie's Branchers not only could not read, they could not even make change for money—a bill of any denomination was called a "skin"—and they were frequently victimized by shopkeepers as a result. They also had no conception of either clock time or calendar time. Parents opposed formal schooling, and school attendance was not enforced by school authorities. But parents did nothing to educate their children either. Not only could these unschooled children not perform rudimentary tasks of reasoning, when asked to do so they were unable to draw a circle or a square, raise their right or left arms, extend their fingers, or spell their names. Gazaway wrote, "I showed them a series of pictures pasted on cardboard; cat, raccoon, rabbit, otter, rat, squirrel. 'What are they?' I inquired. 'Reckon they's cats,' they decided."[6]

The children could not play simple ball games, learn to whistle, sing, or even hum a simple tune. Older boys could not saw a straight line or hammer nails. And according to Gazaway, neither children nor adults displayed much curiosity about the world in which they lived nor ingenuity in deriving satisfaction from it. The major exception occurred when a few men somehow managed to illegally tap into a passing electric line to bring power into their homes. Gazaway could not explain how this could have been done successfully because she found the men of Duddie's Branch incompetent to make even minor repairs to their houses and completely incapable of repairing their old cars when they broke down.

Here then is—or at least was—a physically unwell population that could not feed itself, that had no apparent social institutions they valued, whose children would seemingly qualify as being mentally retarded, and who were apparently incapable of doing anything to improve their nutrition, health, comfort, or general well-being. Yet this was only part of the reality of Duddie's Branch. Despite the absence of any kind of ritual, ceremony, or community-wide activities, these people were fiercely loyal to their hollow and their way of life. Even those few who could emigrate, like a boy Gazaway took away from the hollow for a brief period of schooling, preferred to remain in Duddie's Branch. They could also express great love for members of their families, and even for an outsider like Gazaway. They had pride, dignity, courage, and generosity. Many populations that have excellent health, good education, and material plenty and have never experienced hunger have shown less commitment to their culture and to one another. If it is a basic human need for people to feel content with themselves and their lives, then that need, if no other, was being met in Duddie's Branch.

Stressing this positive accomplishment of the people of Duddie's Branch is not intended to direct attention away from their harmful practices. Instead, it emphasizes the point that there are several criteria by which social and cultural inadequacy can be measured. One is survival—of the population or its culture—another is the physical well-being of its members, and still another is the members' satisfaction with their lives. The people of Duddie's Branch were satisfied, but their physical health was very poor, and their survival depended on government food allotments.

Any attempt to develop a cross-culturally valid perspective on maladaptation must take into account these and other difficult-to-measure criteria of human biocultural success—a daunting prospect. But before confronting these difficulties by turning to issues of comparison and evaluation, approaches that run counter to the perspectives taken in relativistic or interpretive anthropology, it would be useful to put the contributions of these latter approaches in perspective. Although some comparativists scorn relativists and interpretivists, who produce "nothing" but accounts of particular cultures (arabesques of allusion and allegory, some critics have implied), and some interpretive anthropologists reject all comparative research, these extreme adversarial positions parody the search for human understanding. Both interpretive and comparative approaches have value, both have contributed to anthropology and more generally to human understanding, and they should continue to do so in complementarity.

The principle of cultural relativism is not merely a shibboleth but has helped to counter ethnocentrism and even racism. It has also provided an important corrective to ideas of unilinear evolution, which presumed that all societies passed through the same stages of "progress" until they eventually reached near-perfection; namely, one or another version of Western European "civilization." The relativists' insistence on respect for the values of other people has undoubtedly done more good for human dignity and human rights than it has done harm to science. Even the overheated assertions of the epistemological relativists have been useful, for they remind anyone audacious enough to compare cultures that any sociocultural system is a complex network of meanings that must, indeed, be seen in context and, as much as possible, be understood as its members understand it. What is more, they may be right in arguing that some understandings and emotions are unique to a particular culture. Also, the meanings and functions of some practices may remain permanently beyond the comprehension of outside observers or interpreters of that particular culture.

Relativism, then, has its value, and not just in cautioning comparativists to proceed at their own risk. The admonitions of functionalists to attend carefully to the linkages among beliefs and practices continue to have value as well. When these perspectives—functionalism and relativism—are brought together to produce finely textured protraits of life in other cultures, the result is not the work of the Devil but the essential descriptive material without which neither cultural comparison nor evaluation can take place.

22

Evaluating Cultures

A commony articulated reason for abandoning cross-cultural comparison is that it has yielded no useful generalizations, or "laws." Thus, when Sir Edmund Leach decided that anthropology should be an art rather than a science—"in the natural science sense," as he put it— he did so because "During the hundred years of their existence academic anthropologists have not discovered a single universally valid truth concerning either human culture or human society other than those which are treated as axioms: e.g. that all men have language."[7] Without knowing what else Leach regards as axiomatic and hence, apparently, trivial, this assertion flies in the face of an imposing body of evidence about universals of human society and culture.[8] Not all claims of the many scholars who believe that cross-cultural comparisons have yielded valid generalizations may be correct, but enough are well-documented that it should be obvious that Leach's categorical rejection of anthropology's success in its scientific search for truth is greatly overstated.[9]

To be sure, anthropology's long practice of cross-cultural comparison is not without its many and serious difficulties.[10] (Problems of sampling, equivalency of concepts, inadequate data, coding, and statistical analysis continue to bedevil even the most sophisticated practitioners of this kind of comparison.)[11] But setting technical problems like these aside for the moment, it should be pointed out that even the most particularistic interpretive anthropologists who confine themselves to a single culture and reject all comparison nevertheless implicitly use a comparative perspective as they make their interpretations. Just as social anthropologists could not avoid making psychological assumptions about the people they studied, so epistemological relativists must make comparative assumptions about mind, self, and emotion, for example, in order to talk about them at all. The emotions of another people, to choose only one example, are either the same as ours or different, and either conclusion implies, at the very least, comparisons between the emotions of the interpreter and those of the people being interpreted. When another people's emotions are said to differ from ours, then the comparative dimension is even more overt.

Even though comparison is inescapable, its practice as a systematic scholarly activity is nonetheless demanding, and the most demanding form of comparison involves evaluation. To continue with emotion as

23

our propaedeutic example, it is difficult enough to determine whether people in two cultures experience the same emotions; to evaluate these emotions as more or less adaptive or healthy is even more so. Suspicion, hatred, envy, fear, or rage can be adaptive in some circumstances but maladaptive in others. Devising criteria for such evaluations is a formidable undertaking.

Nevertheless, what I am proposing calls for the evaluation of other cultures, something that challenges the prevailing doctrine of cultural relativism. By asserting that some traditional beliefs and practices are maladaptive because they endanger people's health, happiness, or survival, I am opposing the established tenets of relativism and adaptivism. Any attempt to evaluate another culture is a controversial task that must be undertaken with caution (not unlike scaling Vesuvius on one of its more agitated days) because—in addition to the conventional wisdom in social science, which maintains that virtually all established beliefs and practices are adaptive and that there can be no universally valid criteria for evaluating peoples' cultural beliefs or social institutions—many scholars today believe that it is quite impossible even to *understand* the lives of people in other cultures. Before discussing the doctrines of cultural relativism and adaptivism, the radical epistemological position that people in other cultures are beyond our ken must be examined.

How this understanding—that the conduct of other peoples is inaccessible to scientific comprehension, much less evaluation—came into being has a complex and controversial history, but anyone familiar with the enchanted postmodern era of unstable truths will recognize that scholars today must contend with a world where the possibility of even one human comprehending another is challenged. In a series of influential books, philosopher Richard Rorty has endorsed the views of philosophers no less celebrated than Wittgenstein and Quine that scholars should abandon their quest for objective truth.[12] Like scholars in many other disciplines, anthropologists have been profoundly affected by hermeneutics, poststructuralism, deconstructionism, and other "critical" perspectives that challenge the older epistemologies that once lent a comfortable degree of certainty to Western science. How much matters have changed can be seen in the despairing perspective of British anthropologist Rodney Needham. After many years of passably successful efforts (by prevailing standards of scholarship, at any rate) to understand human beliefs, Needham was struck by ". . . how thoroughly we are induced to

24

misunderstand one another."[13] Referring to Einstein's famous comment that "the eternally incomprehensible fact about the universe is that it is comprehensible," Needham offered this contrary conclusion: "The solitary comprehensible fact about human experience is that it is incomprehensible."[14]

Although Needham's counsel of despair would be considered extreme by most anthropologists, many share his skepticism about the possibility of comparing or evaluating the practices of other peoples, a skepticism that took root long before postmodernism. Most anthropologists have readily, and in many cases fervently, provided a host of reasons why any attempt to evaluate the beliefs or practices of people who live in different societies—in different worlds of meaning—is misguided, trivial, politically dangerous, and not least, scientifically invalid.

Much of this reluctance to evaluate other cultures can be traced to the concept of cultural relativism, one of our most venerable—and, many say, most valuable—principles. This principle, or more correctly, this axiom, states that because there is no universally valid standard by which the beliefs or practices of other cultures can be evaluated, they can only be judged relative to the cultural context in which they occur. This idea did not originate in anthropology, although Franz Boas and his students at Columbia University did much to establish its credibility. Montaigne and Hume sometimes espoused a version of cultural relativism, and to some extent, so did Herodotus and the fifth-century Sophists. But the first explicit formulation of the principle probably came, not from a Greek or an anthropologist, but from an American sociologist, William Graham Sumner, in 1906. It was Sumner who memorably said, "The mores can make anything right, and prevent condemnation of anything," and he meant exactly that. For Sumner, who had never done research in a non-Western society, practices such as religious prostitution, cannibalism, human sacrifice, infanticide, and slavery were perfectly reasonable human adaptations to particular circumstances. Like all practices, they had to be understood in context; there could be no absolute standard for evaluating them.[15]

Because anthropologists made the study of the world's many diverse cultures their professional monopoly, their assertions about cultural relativism came to have a special impact. In the 1920s and 1930s, owing largely to the efforts of Boas' famous students, Ruth Benedict, Margaret Mead, and Melville Herskovits, cultural relativism became so fundamental to anthropological thinking that in 1939 Clyde Kluck-hohn, a prominent Harvard University anthropologist who was destined to become even more influential, could write that this idea was ". . . probably the most meaningful contribution which anthropological studies have made to general knowledge."[16] In fact, cultural relativism soon became a taken-for-granted postulate of modern liberal thought. As British philosopher Martin Hollis and sociologist Steven Lukes put it, "Other minds, other cultures, other languages and other theoretical schemes call for understanding from within. Seen from within, they make us doubt whether there is anything universal under the sun. . . ."[17]

There are some highly vocal scholars who deplore cultural relativism and confidently exalt the superiority of one culture over others, Allan Bloom being a conspicuous example.[18] However, as Bloom, among others, has deploringly observed, the principle is deeply rooted. In general, contemporary American college students so unquestioningly accept cultural relativism that they are quite unwilling to evaluate the customs of other people. In Bloom's example, the custom that students refused to judge was the Hindu practice of suttee, in which a widow, willing or not, was called upon to join her deceased husband by being burned to death. (This practice will be examined in chapter 6.) Their reluctance to evaluate illustrates the deep inroads of cultural relativism, despite the fact that the rise of totalitarianism, the horrors of World War II, and the tensions of the Cold War had weakened many scholars' faith in the concept to such an extent that by the 1950s it had come under increasingly heavy fire.[19] Along with the related concept, functionalism (which in its strongest version has it that all established beliefs and practices have positive social functions), relativism came to be seen as a conserative doctrine opposed to change in Third World countries that were attempting to gain their independence from colonial governments.[20]

Nevertheless, the majority of anthropologists still accepted the basic idea of cultural relativism, and in the 1970s a far more radical version of the concept came into vogue. Propelled into prominence by such distinguished anthropologists as Clifford Geertz and David M. Schneider, this epistemological form of relativism challenges more than one's ability to evaluate other cultures; it contends that cultures cannot even be compared. Cultures, this new relativism insists, are incommensurable; each one can only be understood, or more correctly, interpreted, in its own terms as a unique system of meanings.

What is more, only someone enculturated in that system can comprehend it fully. As Renato Rosaldo put it, "My own group aside, everything human is alien to me."[21]

For these relativists, not only is each culture unique unto itself, but people's thoughts, feelings, and motivations are radically different from one culture to another.[22] It follows then that any attempt to generalize about either culture or human nature must be false or trivial unless it is confined to people who live in a specific cultural system.[23] As these relativists have said, it necessarily follows that if peoples' minds vary so much from one culture to another, Western science is only a culturally specific form of ethnoscience, not a universally valid way of verification or falsification.[24] In this perspective, a person from another culture remains the "Other," forever incomprehensible. Physicist Charles Nissam-Sabat has chided epistemological relativists for adopting this extreme position because "they make the people they study falsely incomprehensible and thus dehumanized".[25]

The same epistemological relativists might also be chided for failing to heed the lessons of the famous Sapir-Whorf hypothesis, which, in its strong version, claimed that the language people spoke had such a profound effect on how they saw the world and thought about it (as Sapir had often declared) they lived in different worlds of meaning. This much-promoted relativistic idea helped to popularize linguistics, and it led generations of students (along with some anthropologists) to believe that language profoundly shaped how people understood the world around them. Benjamin Whorf, a student of Sapir, chose the Hopi language to illustrate this hypothesis. Among other things, he claimed that the Hopi language had no terms for time comparable to ours and also that it had no such tenses as past, present, and future. As a result, he said, the Hopi conceived of time in a manner radically different from and, he added, scientifically more sophisticated than that of speakers of English. Subsequent research proved Whorf wrong on all counts: the Hopi did have tenses and various words for time comparable to those used in English. Also, the Hopi had no difficulty thinking of time in the ways English speakers do.[26] Attempts to show that language had a significant impact on thought in other societies also failed to confirm Whorf's ideas, and his hypothesis has been rejected in linguistics for at least fifteen years.[27] Despite such failed attempts as this, epistemological relativists seem to be gaining ground in numbers and, apparently, in influence as well.[28]

27

This antipositivistic epistemological relativism, as its critic Melford E. Spiro has called it, has sometimes been linked to interpretive anthropology, which attempts to comprehend alien cultures by "reading" their system of meanings as if it were a text, without, however, adopting any standard by which one interpreter's reading should be preferred to a contradictory reading by someone else. Some anthropologists have found nothing of value in this preference for insightful readings, variously referring to the enterprise as absurd, trivial, clairvoyant, and dangerous.[29] Many others, however, have embraced this perspective with enthusiasm. Like the epistemological relativists, interpretive anthropologists usually deny the validity of cultural comparison or attempts to reconstruct social evolution.[30] For them, too, all human beliefs and practices must be understood only in their own context. Indeed, the enterprise of science, particularly positivistic social science, is often rejected altogether. For example, in a Jovian pronouncement (lacking only thunderbolts) Stephen A. Tyler has declared that scientific discourse is "deeply mendacious,"[31] an "archaic mode of consciousness" that has failed in its search for proof, and should be replaced by a postmodern approach to ethnography that seeks to "evoke" what cannot be known discursively and that stands, we are told, "beyond truth and immune to the judgment of performance."[32]

Not all scholars who oppose positivism are as nihilistic as Tyler nor as beguiled by postmodern discourse, but most would probably agree that the postmodern relativists—if we may call them that—are asserting far more than the self-evident point that people in different societies live in somewhat different worlds of meaning. They are claiming that each of these worlds is truly unique—incommensurable and largely incomprehensible—and that the people who inhabit them have different cognitive abilities.[33] In what Dan Sperber has referred to as "cognitive apartheid"[34] and Ernest Gellner has called "cognitive anarchy,"[35] various postmodern relativists and interpretivists postulate fundamental differences from one culture to the next in cognitive processes involving logic, causal inference, and information processing. The existence of such basic cognitive differences has yet to be demonstrated, and if the history of research into human cognition and inter-subjectivity is any guide, it will not be.[36]

To be sure, all anthropologists or other scholars who attempt to understand another culture admit that their success in doing so is only partial. Indeed, long before 1973, when Clifford Geertz wrote

28

his celebrated article about the difficulties anthropologists have in getting to the bottom of another culture's system of meanings, other anthropologists had acknowledged that intercultural understanding could never be perfect.[37] For that matter, long before Geertz, anthropologists (such as A. F. C. Wallace) had argued that even intracultural understanding could never be perfect, because individuals within any given culture never fully share the same world of meaning—husbands and wives, for example.[38] These caveats aside, most anthropologists believe that it is possible to understand many aspects of another culture. As Gellner and Spiro have observed, no ethnographer known to them (or to me) has returned from a stay in another culture to report that the people they encountered were so alien that their beliefs and practices were completely incomprehensible.[39]

Well before Quine's indeterminacy thesis, which held that any one of several translations would fit the language or belief system of an alien people equally well, no one believed that one language could be perfectly translated into another.[40] Indeed, as Wittgenstein was fond of reminding us, at one level language serves to promote misunderstanding more than understanding. But ethnographers and linguists have without exception found ways to translate foreign languages into their own language well enough to establish workable communication with all peoples yet studied. True enough, there are thoughts that cannot adequately be translated even from one Indo-European language to another—from Russian "aspect" to English "tense," for example—but there is no known language that cannot be translated well enough to permit a reasonably complete exchange of ideas between speakers of that language and any other known language.[41] Indeed, one would have thought that radical claims of cognitive relativism might have ceased over twenty years ago when Brent Berlin and Paul Kay showed that people in different cultures did not divide the color spectrum in arbitrary and untranslatable ways from one society to another, as was then thought to be the case. Instead, Berlin and Kay showed that basic color terms are universally translatable because eleven psychophysiologically defined colors serve as the focal points of *all* the basic color terms in *all* the languages of the world.[42]

Though the adversarial tone and mannered literary style of some of the interpretive anthropologists and postmodern relativists have perturbed a number of anthropologists[43] and the continuing claims of cultural and cognitive uniqueness seem burlesque to others,[44] nevertheless various aspects of this approach have drawn support from some of the most acclaimed scholars in the field. Marshall Sahlins has argued for the determinative power of culture as radically as anyone possibly could and has also declared that anthropology is metaphysics, not science.[45] Similarly, both E. E. Evans-Pritchard and Sir Edmund Leach, two of the most important figures in the history of British social anthropology, have concluded that anthropology should abandon its scientific pretensions and declare itself an art form or a humanistic enterprise.[46] Many able younger scholars on both sides of the Atlantic have also embraced epistemological relativism as the only true path to valid cultural understanding.

Although what I have referred to as interpretive anthropologists and epistemological or postmodern relativists are the most determined opponents of cross-cultural comparison, they are not alone in rejecting the legitimacy of cultural evaluation. For example, distinguished anthropologist Marvin Harris, whose cultural materialism (in some ways similar to Marxism) is as far from interpretive anthropology as any approach could reasonably be, also opposes cultural evaluation. Even before the emergence of interpretive anthropology or epistemological relativism, Harris wrote, "As a result of the cultural relativistic critique, anthropologists no longer believe that the study of cultural evolution will provide a scientific basis for judging which cultures are aesthetically, ethically, or politically superior."[48] Harris was right about the impact of relativism, but there is another reason why anthropologists have typically refused to evaluate the customs of other peoples. That reason is the long-held assumption that culture is an adaptive mechanism, and thus the beliefs and practices of any established culture must serve some useful purpose, a position that is explicitly stated in many contemporary introductory anthropology textbooks.[49] Few contemporary anthropologists have made this assumption more often or more vigorously than Harris himself. In his recent book, *Good to Eat*, Harris insists that eating patterns that seem "impractical, irrational, useless or harmful" are in reality the utilitarian result of human attempts to maximize benefits and minimize costs, an argument he has previously advanced with regard to many other kinds of seemingly irrational beliefs and practices.[50]

The assumption that human practices and beliefs are adaptive is also present in other scientific fields. When Donald T. Campbell gave his presidential address to the American Psychological Association in 1975, he declared that culture should be regarded as adaptive. He noted that when an evolutionary biologist encounters some seemingly ludicrous or bizarre form of animal life, he approaches it with awe, ". . . certain that behind the bizarre form lies a functional wisdom that he has yet to understand."[51] Campbell urged psychologists and other social scientists to adopt the same sense of awe ". . . when considering an apparently bizarre, incomprehensible feature of their own or another culture . . . expecting that when eventually understood, when our theories have caught up with it, that seemingly bizarre supersitition will turn out to make adaptive sense." Campbell later amended this comment by saying that instead of awe, the proper approach should be "grudging, skeptical respect," but his belief in the adaptiveness of culture was unshaken.[52]

In the late nineteenth century, when the scholarly study of small non-Western societies began in earnest, many anthropologists accepted neither cultural relativism nor the belief that all customs are adaptive. John Lubbock (later Baron Avebury), an influential British anthropologist who was eventually elected to Parliament, was frankly ethnocentric and sometimes racist; he approved of the Eskimo because they had kin terms for aunt and uncle like those used in English, but he regarded the Hawaiians as savages because they did not. Clark Wissler, a student of Boas and one of the most distinguished figures in early American anthropology, was an unabashed racist who believed in the superiority of "Nordics."[53] E. B. Tylor, perhaps the most influential of the nineteenth-century anthropologists, often referred to what he called "survivals," or customs that may once have served a useful social purpose but no longer do so, as "absurd" or "foolish."[54] The belief that some traditional beliefs and practices were useless survivals lasted until it was supplanted by the emerging concept of functionalism, especially as developed by Bronislaw Malinowski in the 1920s and 1930s. According to Malinowski, ". . . in every type of civilization, every custom, material object, idea and belief fulfills some vital function, has some task to accomplish, represents an indispensable part within a working whole."[55]

Malinowski's British rival in the development of functionalist theory, A. R. Radcliffe-Brown, once held a position that was quite similar to that of Malinowski[56] but later ridiculed his ". . . quite impossible view that all customs and institutions of any society are right and good. . . ."[57] But the idea that every custom had a positive function, whether manifest or latent, soon took hold in both anthropology and sociology, and neofunctionalist ideas continue to exert an influence

31

today.[58] Marvin Harris summarized the conventional wisdom as it existed in 1960: "Countless studies of extant socio-cultural systems and bio-organisms have been made to discover the functional status of socio-cultural and bio-morphic structures. In both realms the results of these studies indicate that bio-organisms and socio-cultural systems are largely if not exclusively composed of positive-functioned, that is, useful traits."[59]

Despite Harris's enthusiasm, functionalism lost much of its credibility in the early 1960s until V. C. Wynne-Edwards published a book about "group selection" that gave it new life. Wynne-Edwards's hypothesis was that organisms had evolved the ability to regulate population growth and therefore "naturally" avoided overexploitation of food and other resources. Thus, individuals naturally cooperated to conserve resources, refrained from reproduction and even intentionally sacrificed themselves to maintain a stable ecosystem.[60] Before other investigators showed that this kind of group population regulation was illusory, the hypothesis was widely adopted in the social sciences, especially cultural ecology, where all manner of human practices, including ritual cycles, warfare, and infanticide, were interpreted as means of bringing about population equilibrium.[61] For example, Roy Rappaport's *Pigs for the Ancestors*, which offered such a functional interpretation, became one of the most influential books in the field of cultural ecology soon after it was published in 1968.[62]

Marvin Harris to the contrary notwithstanding, it has never been demonstrated that all human customs or institutions, or even most of them, have adaptive value,[63] but the assumption that this is so is still commonplace among scholars who study human evolution.[64] In 1990, Richard A. Alexander, a leading evolutionary biologist (or sociobiologist to some) wrote that "any human attribute that is too elaborate to be accidental" should be considered adaptive.[65] The idea that every known society is well adapted to its environment, or that all of the beliefs and practices of that population contribute to the society's adaptation, is, on its face, tantamount to arguing that all living humans are equally healthy simply because they are alive and seemingly able to carry out their required tasks. Nevertheless, despite various disclaimers, the prevailing assumption in anthropology continues to be that any custom or practice that has survived for any length of time is adaptive until proven otherwise, an assumption that Stephen Jay Gould has likened to Dr. Pangloss's declaration that the nose exists

32

to support the eyeglasses. Despite the strength of this assumption, not everyone in anthropology has accepted it.

In earlier times anthropologists interested in cultural evolution tried to evaluate all manner of social institutions from kinship to legal systems as well as beliefs from food taboos to the etiology of disease, but their conclusions were for the most part arrantly ethnocentric. The first relatively viable evaluative comparisons had to do with technology. Several scholars observed that technology tended to evolve through stages from simple to complex.[66] Moreover, it was obvious that some tools and weapons were better than others.[67] A sinew-backed bow is more powerful than a slingshot, a rifle is a better weapon than a musket, a repeating rifle is better still, and for many purposes a machine gun is even better.[68] As all populations yet discovered have agreed, a steel axe is better than a stone one. Alexander Goldenweiser took pains to point out that some oars were more efficient than others and that there were a limited number of ways to make an efficient one.[69] Later, Thomas Gladwin showed that knowledge about technology could also be evaluated when he compared Polynesian navigational systems.[70] Even archrelativist Melville Herskovits admitted that forms of technology could be evaluated in terms of their efficiency.[71] Others pointed out that for various purposes certain systems of writing, money, or counting were more efficient than others.

Surprisingly, even the most zealous proponents of cultural relativism sometimes made evaluative judgments about other cultures. In her phenomenal two-million-copy, 1934 best-seller *Patterns of Culture*, Ruth Benedict proclaimed that all ways of life were of equal value and that all standards of behavior were relative. She praised cannibalism and often went to great lengths to put seemingly maladaptive institutions in a positive light.[72] For example, she referred to the kinship system of the Kurnai of Australia as a "social liability" because the Kurnai classified so many women as one's "sister" or "mother" that it was virtually impossible for a man to marry without committing incest, thereby quite literally risking death.[73] Yet Benedict went on to write approvingly about a "subterfuge" the Kurnai employed to "avoid extinction." It seems that young couples could choose to "elope" to a nearby island, and if they succeeded in reaching it without being overtaken and killed by outraged pursuers, they were given sanctuary. If the couple could then manage to survive long

33

enough to bear a child, they were permitted to return to society, but only after running a gauntlet and being pummeled before they were allowed to live as a married couple. Instead of adhering to her initial view that this extraordinarily cumbersome institution of marriage was a social liability, Benedict chose to see it as a clever social adjustment that permitted people to find a spouse despite violating the Kurnai role against incest.[74] Even Clifford Geertz, no foe of cultural relativism, was perturbed by Benedict's contorted version of the principle, saying that her position that ". . . anything one group of people is inclined toward doing is worthy of respect by another . . ." was a "strange conclusion."[75]

Elsewhere in her book, Benedict compared three tribes—the Zuni, Dobu, and Kwakiutl—with what can only be described as bald evaluation. First, she left no doubt that she preferred the peaceful Zuni to more violent societies (it may not be coincidental that she omitted from her account a sizable body of evidence describing Zuni violence). When she then characterized the Dobuans of Melanesia as "paranoid" and the Kwakiutl of America's northwest coast as "megalomanic," not only was she suggesting that terms for individual psychopathology could be used to characterize an entire society, but she inspired a spate of similar characterizations of other societies as "sick." In what might stand as the culmination of this practice, Weston LaBarre wrote that the Japanese were ". . . the most compulsive people in the world ethnological museum."[76]

Benedict did not acknowledge Freud, but the imputing of psychopathology to entire populations drew its "scientific" warrant from *Civilization and Its Discontents*, where Freud argued that it was possible for a society to conflict so markedly with the needs of its members that entire populations could become neurotic.[77] The terms used by Benedict, LaBarre, and others seemed to imply an even greater severity of psychopathology than neurosis, and anthropologists such as Anthony F. C. Wallace, Irving Hallowell, and Marvin Opler denounced the use of psychiatric terms to typify a population. When Erich Fromm wrote *The Sane Society* in 1955, he rejected this criticism as one based on what he described as the postulate that "each society is normal inasmuch as it functions." He insisted that there could be "sick" societies—as well as sane ones—because, as Freud had directed, some societies were more successful than others in meeting human needs.

Sharp criticism of the practice of imputing psychopathology to en-

34

tire societies brought this sort of cultural evaluation to an end, but several of the world's most respected anthropologists, all of whom had earlier endorsed the principle of cultural relativism, eventually published critical evaluations of "primitive" societies, as folk societies were often referred to at that time. For example, in 1948 Alfred Kroeber, then the doyen of American anthropology, not only rejected relativism but declared that as societies "progressed" from simple to more complex, they became more "humane," and he asserted—in language calculated to make present-day anthropologists' hair stand on end—that ". . . the mentally unwell in modern advanced cultures tend to correspond to the well and influential in ancient and retarded cultures."[78] Furthermore, "progress," as Kroeber referred to cultural evolution, not only involved advances in technology and science but also entailed the abandonment of practices such as ritual prostitution, segregating women at parturition or menstruation, torture, sacrifice, and belief in magic or superstition. In 1950 Ralph Linton, another leading anthropologist, who possessed perhaps the most encyclopedic understanding of world ethnography of anyone then alive, wrote that there could be universal ethical standards,[79] a position that Clyde Kluckhohn, by then no longer a committed relativist, endorsed five years later.[80]

Robert Redfield, a distinguished anthropologist at the University of Chicago, agreed with Kroeber by declaring that primitive societies were less "decent" and "humane" than more "advanced civilizations": ". . . on the whole the human race has come to develop a more decent and humane measure of goodness—there has been a transformation of ethical judgment which makes us look at non-civilized people, not as equals, but as people on a different level of human experience."[81] In a paper presented in 1960, George Peter Murdock, then the leading figure in comparative studies in the world, said that Benedict's relativistic idea that a cultural element has no meaning except in its context was "nonsense" and that Herskovits's assertion that all cultures must be accorded equal dignity and value was "not only nonsense but sentimental nonsense."[82] He added that it was an "absurdity" to assert that cannibalism, slavery, magical therapy, and killing the aged should be accorded the same "dignity" or "validity" as old age security, scientific medicine, and metal artifacts.[83] All people, Murdock continued, prefer Western technology and would rather be able to feed their children and elderly than kill them. Furthermore, he said, primitive peoples readily relinquish such practices as can-

35

nibalism and headhunting ". . . when colonial governments demonstrate the material advantages of peace."[84]

The strong antirelativistic sentiments of Kroeber, Linton, Kluckhohn, Redfield, and Murdock—anthropology's equivalent of the 1927 New York Yankees—were not accepted by the majority of anthropologists, who continued to reject the idea that civilized societies were ethically superior to primitive ones. Indeed, they deplored even the use of terms such as "civilized" or "primitive." With relatively few exceptions, they continued to call for every culture to be respected in its own context, and they chose to interpret established beliefs and practices as adaptive. What Marvin Harris wrote in 1960, when he said that there was no scientific standard by which ethics, aesthetics, or politics could be measured, was the consensual view then, and it has continued to be.

Nevertheless, a few anthropologists have rejected this position. In the early 1960s Edward Norbeck rejected the received view of witchcraft as a benign and natural belief system with numerous socially positive functions; instead, he made much of witchcraft's socially harmful consequences.[85] Similarly, Melford Spiro interpreted the Burmese belief in witches as a form of psychological projection that led to cognitive distortion,[86] and in 1974 Theodore Schwartz pointed out the dysfunctional effects of what he called the "paranoid ethos."[87] Schwartz speculated that a paranoid belief system was ". . . the bedrock psychopathology of mankind"[88] that has persisted "over the span of human history as a substratum of potential pathology in all societies."[89] Schwartz believed that in Melanesian societies, especially Dobu, paranoid ideation with its extreme suspiciousness and hostility was so deeply entrenched that ". . . existence is at least uncomfortable, possibly highly stressful, and undoubtedly anxious."[90]

Even earlier, John G. Kennedy launched a direct attack on the prevailing relativistic doctrine that all beliefs and practices have positive social functions. Taking issue with scholars such as E. E. Evans-Pritchard, Clyde Kluckhohn, M. G. Marwick, and Beatrice Whiting, all of whom had argued that a belief in witchcraft can have socially positive consequences, Kennedy asserted that witchcraft beliefs were "irrational and dysfunctional." Stressing the paranoid character of witchcraft beliefs as well as the fear and aggression that such beliefs produce, Kennedy proposed that belief in witchcraft was "institutionalized irrationality."[91] The conclusion he offered was controversial then and it still is: ". . . we should seriously entertain the possibility

36

of the existence of 'sick societies' or pathological institutions and culture patterns, rather than making the a priori relativistic assumption that all groups automatically find a healthy, balanced level of functioning."[92]

A decade later, Arthur Hippler scolded anthropologists for adhering to cultural relativism, accusing them of regarding ". . . anything and everything done in or by some non-Western culture . . . as good or at least neutral [while] everything done in or by Western society is seen as bad."[93] The charge that some anthropologists have been quick to criticize Western culture while steadfastly withholding criticism about non-Western cultures has been made many times before.[94] Indeed, Herskovits once wrote about a critic of cultural relativism who defined an anthropologist as "a person who respects every culture-pattern but his own."[95] Even Marvin Harris, who has endorsed relativism and offered positive functionalist explanations for the seemingly "irrational and harmful" around the world, wrote a book, *America Now*, that purported to explain what has gone wrong with American culture.[96] More recently, Washburn has attributed the "continuing power" of cultural relativism to anthropologists' hostility to the values of their own society and a preference for those of others.[97] This bias may be subtle, but it is often there.

Echoing Murdock, Hippler also asserted that Western culture was superior and that most "primitives" find it irresistible. What is more, echoing Freud, he concluded that cultures such as the Yolngu of Australia institutionalize "immature defenses and coping mechanisms."[98] Hippler also concluded that the Yolngu have a limited capacity for reality testing, and that they are ". . . self-evidently to me, not a terribly advanced group."[99] He saw nothing unusual in their lack of "advancement," because, as he said, entire populations can exist at ". . . very low levels of cognitive development. All they have to do is reproduce."[100] It will come as no surprise that Hippler's conclusions provoked a flurry of critical comment.[101] Another controversial evaluation was recently offered by C. R. Hallpike. First, as a result of his ethnographic field research among the Tauade, a small population of Papua New Guinea, Hallpike concluded that their practice of warfare was not adaptive.[102] Hallpike also believed that it was maladaptive for the Tauade to raise huge herds of pigs that "devastated" their gardens and led to "innumerable quarrels and even homicides," only to be slaughtered in such large numbers that they could not be eaten. He also saw no adaptive advantage to the Tauade

37

in keeping rotting corpses in their villages. He observed acerbically, that "No doubt, the Tauade had survived to be studied, but their major institutions and practices seemed to have very little to do with this fact."[103] In an earlier ethnography of the Konso of Ethiopia, Hallpike concluded that the Konso did not need their elaborate age-grading system.[104] "Primitive societies are not," he concluded, "beautifully adapted little organisms put together like watches, in which every component functions for the well-being and survival of the whole."[105]

Another noteworthy approach to cultural evaluation was taken by Raoul Naroll in his book *The Moral Order*.[106] Naroll was concerned that suicide, divorce, child abuse, mental illness, excessive use of alcohol and drugs, and crime, among other things, were weakening the basic human primary group that he called the "moralnet." Comparing statistical data from various countries about these "social ills," as he called them, he found that when moralnets were weakened, the result was a reduction in physical and mental health, as well as a higher mortality rate. Comparing only European countries where the data were most comparable on variables he named physical health, mental health, brotherhood, progress, peace, order, and variety, Naroll found that Norway had the highest quality of life with an index value of 550. The United States scored 483, and Israel had the lowest index at 440, just behind Spain.[107] Recently, Benjamin Colby has taken the quantification of quality of life, or well-being, a step further by proposing to measure a person's adaptive potential defined as adaptivity, altruism, and creativity. Colby hopes to be able to develop a universal theory of well-being defined in terms of physical health, satisfaction and happiness.[108]

While these cultural anthropologists were discussing the possibility of evaluating cultural dysfunction or pathology, parallel developments were taking place in evolutionary biology, or as some prefer to call it, sociobiology. Until quite recently, most evolutionary biologists also assumed that existing cultural practices were adaptive[109] and attempted to explain these traits by matching them to reproductive fitness optimization models,[110] but this assumption is no longer universally held. Scholars from fields such as ecology, biology, psychology, anthropology, and even sociology have argued that there is no a priori reason to assume that any given cultural practice is adaptive.[111] Moreover, various scholars have identified mechanisms that could lead to and perpetuate maladaptation.[112]

In their influential book *Culture and the Evolutionary Process*, Robert Boyd and Peter J. Richerson rejected Sahlins's contention that Darwinian theories of evolution must result in adaptive or functional hypotheses about human behavior: "Nonadaptive, or even frankly maladaptive, cultural variants can spread in a population under the influence of indirect bias, even in the face of selection and direct bias favoring more adaptive variants."[113] Although his model differs from that of Boyd and Richerson, Alan Rogers agrees that natural selection can produce mechanisms of cultural transmission that are not adaptive.[114] In another significant book, *Darwin, Sex and Status*, Jerome H. Barkow has suggested that maladaptive cultural traits can be produced by such factors as environmental changes to which a population fails to respond effectively, short-sighted practices of the population that lead to ecological ruin, and the tendency of powerful elites to favor traits that serve their interests at the expense of the majority of the population.[115]

This brief review of some approaches to the evaluation of other cultures should be sufficient to demonstrate that despite the tenacity of cultural relativism and the prevalent assumption that all, or nearly all, existing cultural practices are adaptive, some scholars of quite varied backgrounds and theoretical persuasions have had their doubts about those assumptions, and with the passage of time, those who believe that cultural maladaptation exists have grown in numbers and sophistication. Today, various scholars are beginning to agree that cultural practices can be maladaptive, and a few have gone so far as to say that entire societies can become pathogenic. This is not to suggest that most anthropologists share these views. It is impossible to be certain, but it seems likely that the majority of anthropologists would reject the idea that cultural maladaptation is common, and some vigorously reject the idea that it occurs at all. And it is almost certain that a large majority would not accept the assertion that entire societies can legitimately be thought of as sick. One major reason for this, it is said, is the absence of a universally valid and measurable set of criteria for maladaptation.

Defining Maladaptation

One reason why defining maladaptation is so difficult is that there is a multiplicity of levels at which it can be said to occur. It can involve a single gene or a number of genes that in combination may predispose an individual to depression, schizophrenia, or panic. Maladaptation can also be defined in terms of a single individual's ill health or lack of reproductive success, a group of related individuals' refusal to engage in altruistic behaviors, or the absence of well-being among cooperating groups of people engaged in warfare or big-game hunting. The focus can also legitimately fall on categories or corporate groups of people who share common interests and risks because of their age, gender, class, ethnicity, race, occupational specialty, or some other characteristic, or it can encompass an entire society, a kingdom, an empire, or a confederation. For some purposes, maladaptation may be conceptualized in terms of the well-being or survival of all people on earth.

Maladaptation can also be defined in terms of Darwinian selection, as sociobiologists have done. The early and generic sociobiological approach began by assuming that at some point in the evolutionary past there was genetic variation within our species (or some subgroup of us) concerning some trait such as aggressiveness, bravery, passivity, timidity, or the like. Individuals with genes that favored, say, bravery and aggressiveness would have more offspring than those whose genes made them passive or timid. As Lewontin, Rose, and Kamin, among others, have pointed out, this approach is based on some as yet unsubstantiated assumptions.[116] First, it assumes that complex human behaviors like bravery, cooperation, and empathy are products of genes of high heritability. Until such genes have been demonstrated to exist and to be highly heritable, it may be more reasonable to assume that human behaviors such as those named are produced by a complex of interacting genes, and that it may not be highly heritable. The approach also suffered from arbitrariness in assigning a reproductive advantage to certain behavioral traits. It is not at all difficult to imagine scenarios in which bravery, perseverance, empathy, or virtually any other behavioral trait might have yielded a reproductive advantage under certain conditions, but these scenarios are usually so unverifiable that critics have referred to the imaginative process of creating them as a version of "let's pretend" or a Kiplingesque *Just So Story.*[117]

Consider, for example, the fact that men cannot detect when a woman is ovulating, even though such an ability would surely be valuable in increasing the reproductive success of a male who possessed it.[118] Darwinists would argue, one must presume, that no heritable genes for this ability existed. But it has been proposed that some women might well once have had the ability to detect their own ovulation. Instead of using this knowledge to increase their fecundity, they chose to restrict it because pregnancy and childbirth were unpleasant. The result was selection for the inability to detect one's own ovulation.[119] The possibilities surrounding this kind of question are as numerous as they are speculative.

Problems such as these have led a number of evolutionary biologists or psychologists to reject sociobiology as a useful paradigm for the study of human evolution. Donald Symons has concluded that sociobiology, or "Darwinian social science" as he prefers to call the approach, is an "inefficient and ambiguous way to illuminate adaptation."[120] For Symons, understanding the evolution of human behavior requires elucidation of the psychological mechanisms or designs that underlie it. And Charles J. Lumsden, co-author of *Genes, Mind and Culture* with sociobiologist E. O. Wilson, has also found the sociobiological approach of limited value for the study of human behavior "because of its assumption of direct causal links between genes and social phenomena, and for its adherence to the standard fitness optimization models of classical evolution."[121] Instead, Lumsden, along with Symons and others, believes that attention should be turned to the human psychological mechanisms that both generate and change culture.[122] They call for an evolutionary psychology that will provide knowledge of the innate psychological mechanisms that actually constrain and produce human behavior, a position that Jerome Barkow took as early as 1973.[123] According to John Tooby and Leda Cosmides, the goal of this new discipline is identifying the adaptive problems that organisms must be able to solve and discovering the information-processing mechanisms that have evolved to solve them.[124] When it comes to the study of contemporary human societies rather than the long span of human evolution, a Darwinian emphasis on reproductive success has its limitations. It cannot be denied that certain individuals, such as big men, chiefs, clan leaders, or great warriors—that is, the powerful and wealthy—may outreproduce others, and it is possible that their offspring may therefore more often share a certain gene or set of interacting genes than the offspring of other people. Indeed, Paul W. Turke continues to insist that in studies of small, traditional societies, people of wealth and power consistently outreproduce others.[125] He notes a telling example of this pattern that comes from Monique Borgerhoff Mulder's research

41

with the Kipsigis of Kenya.[126] Yet D. R. Vining finds no general support for the rich outreproducing the poor,[127] and Alan R. Rogers has found that the rich only outreproduce the poor in societies in which large numbers of children are valued.[128] Neither Turke nor other evolutionary biologists who believe that reproductive success is the ultimate measure of evolution maintain that humans consciously attempt to outreproduce others. Instead, humans are said to crave wealth, power, and prestige, and it is these activities that, if attained, lead to greater reproductive success.

However, the rich and powerful may choose not to reproduce. For example, like some other despots, King Shaka Zulu refused to allow any of his possible offspring to live for fear that they would attempt to overthrow him. And although differently motivated, the wealthiest and most powerful members of modern societies tend to have fewer children than lower-class people.[129] The Japanese elite did so over the past century,[130] and as Barbara Miller has shown, during the nineteenth century the high-ranking military and land-owning castes of northern India killed all of their female offspring even though they were more than affluent enough to raise daughters as well as sons.[131] Rather than achieve reproductive success, they chose to reduce the numbers of children who could claim inheritance.

Instead of assessing individuals as evolutionary biologists have done, social scientists have typically preferred to concentrate on the well-being of a social system. From Saint-Simon, Comte, and Durkheim to British functionalists like Malinowski and Radcliffe-Brown or to Talcott Parsons and the contemporary neofunctionalists, the question has been what is required to hold a society together, to maintain its "social solidarity." Conflict theorists ask what conditions lead to social collapse. Either perspective can be translated into a description of a society as either well- or maladapted.

In an attempt to be specific about what they called the functional prerequisites of society, several sociologists joined with anthropologist David F. Aberle to specify the conditions that would terminate the existence of a society. They proposed four: (1) the biological extinction or physical dispersion of its members, (2) apathy of the members, defined as loss of motivation to survive, (3) the war of all against all, and (4) the absorption of the society into another one.[132] To avoid the occurrence of one or more of these self-evidently terminal conditions, Aberle and his colleagues proposed that a society must provide for the following functional prerequisites: adequate "relationship" to the environment; sexual recruitment; role differentiation and assignment; communication; a shared, articulated set of goals; the normative regulation of means and affective expression; socialization; and the control of disruptive behavior. Walter Goldschmidt later offered a somewhat different set of prerequisites that he called "social imperatives," or those elements necessary to the organization of every society. These imperatives are groups, values, status and role, authority, and ideology.[133] In 1986, Hallpike suggested that there are seven areas of a society's organization where problems are likely to be encountered: leadership, social organization, division of labor, systems for allocating and controlling scarce resources and property, reciprocity and cooperation, dispute settlement, and the regulation of relations with the supernatural and other communities, including recruitment.[134] A serious problem in any of these areas would presumably constitute maladaptation.

Emphasizing group selection is another way of focusing on group maladaptation. Although, as we have noted, Wynne-Edwards's hypothesis that some species automatically control their population to maintain homeostasis has not fared well when applied to humans, there may yet be an advantage in examining group selection, as Donald T. Campbell argued when he wrote that social evolution has had to counter selfish individualism, like that of the Sirionó, and familism, like that in Montegrano, with "self-sacrificial altruism."[135] In this view a society can become maladapted if it cannot socialize at least some of its members to sacrifice their individual interests for others or the society as a whole by sharing scarce goods, engaging in patriotic military action, or accepting undesirable social roles that contribute to the group's survival.

Turning from the group once again to individuals, it is also possible to define maladaptation as the failure of a society to meet its members' creature needs, as Malinowski did in his now-famous attempt to attribute elements of culture to physiological needs as basic as metabolism, reproduction, and health.[136] Such an approach is still viable, of course, since any population whose needs for food, water, shelter, and the like are not met will not survive, whatever other virtues its culture may possess; but it is also simplistic.[137] Other scholars, such as Henry A. Murray, preferred to define human needs in terms of higher-order abstractions like achievement, affection, autonomy, dominance, nurturance, order, play, and understanding, among others. After reviewing various theories of human nature, Christopher

Boehm has suggested that the needs of humans are best understood in terms of ambivalences in human nature, some of which may be brought about by the contrasts and contradictions between humans; psychobiological inheritance and their enculturation.[138] What the study of adaptation must not include, yet sometimes has, is gratuitous value judgments. For example, however much one may dislike aggression, it can be a highly adaptive attribute. Indeed, a population whose men are not aggressive enough to defend themselves may not survive. As repugnant as one may find warfare, it can sometimes confer a significant advantage on populations that are skilled in its use.

The concept of inclusive fitness, or the differential reproductive success of individuals, may have value for understanding certain kinds of biologically constrained behaviors,[139] but as was mentioned earlier, it has more limited value for scholars interested in the maladaptation of human societies who may prefer to assess the relative satisfaction that people have with their lives.[140] People's dissatisfaction with their life circumstances or with specific aspects of their social institutions or culture may take such forms as apathy, alienation, dysphoria, vocal protest and open rebellion. The measurement of life satisfaction has a long history in the West, and discussion of the concept in anthropology goes back at least to Edward Sapir, who in the 1920s wrote that some societies had "genuine" cultures that were "inherently harmonious, balanced, self-satisfactory."[141] But it is only in the last decade or so that systematic attempts to study the satisfaction of non-Western peoples have appeared.[142]

These two criteria—population growth and personal satisfaction—are the Scylla and Charybdis of cultural adaptation. Biological evolution takes place as a result of differential reproductive success—that is a given—but unrestrained population growth can be ruinous if the carrying capacity of the environment is exceeded. Malthus's apocalyptic vision of population increase has not always been realized, but small societies have struggled to control their population growth with mixed success, and in much of the world, populations are increasing so rapidly that social survival is threatened.[143] Today, the population of the world increases at the astounding rate of 10,000 people per hour, and most of the increase occurs in societies unable to feed their existing populations. If population growth is the ultimate criterion of adaptation, as many have argued,[144] then Japan and the Western world are maladapted because they are losing the baby race. Yet if people in those societies chose to maximize the number of

44

offspring they produced, they could match if not exceed the rate of fertility in the developing world, and they could keep a much greater percentage of these children alive. For Japan and the West, the search for happiness and well-being does not include population proliferation. But surely, no one would seriously propose that these nations are less well adapted than the rapidly increasing populations of Bangladesh or Sudan.

If population growth is not a universally valid criterion of adaptive success, then what is the alternative? The most obvious answer would be people's own subjective assessment of their happiness or well-being. Nothing could be more plain than the fact that people try to enhance their own well-being, yet as a criterion of adaptiveness, this once again opens the door to cultural relativism. If we use only this measure of societal success, we may be left with nothing more illuminating to say than that whatever people find satisfying—headhunting, feuding, enslaving others, or torturing them—must be adaptive so long as that society has been able to survive. However, *dis*satisfaction with one's culture can certainly be maladaptive, because if enough people are seriously disaffected, their society can be endangered.

As we have seen, and as any good *bricoleur* would attest, there are many potential criteria of maladaptation, each with a claim to legitimacy for certain purposes. I have chosen to rely on the most self-evident of these. I shall first define it as the failure of a population or its culture to survive because of the inadequacy or harmfulness of one or more of its beliefs or institutions. Second, maladaptation will be said to exist when enough members of a population are sufficiently dissatisfied with one or more of their social institutions or cultural beliefs that the viability of their society is threatened. Finally, it will be considered to be maladaptive when a population maintains beliefs or practices that so seriously impair the physical or mental health of its members that they cannot adequately meet their own needs or maintain their social and cultural system. Defined in these three ways, I will contend that maladaptation is common among the world's societies, and what is more, it is inevitable.

Chapter 3

Maladaptation

There are many reasons why traditional beliefs and practices may become maladaptive. Some traditional practices that evolved early in human history must have been relatively inefficient solutions to environmental demands, but without rigorous competition from other populations or other belief systems, such practices tend to persist. Besides, because humans do not always make rational adaptive decisions, some of their beliefs and practices may have been maladaptive from the beginning. What is more, when environmental change occurs, practices that once were adaptive may become maladaptive, just as practices that may be adaptive over the short term can have long-term costs. Cultures may also create needs in people that become so imperative that they can become destructive when environmental change occurs. Even when the need for change is clear, human populations, especially small traditional ones, have seldom been sufficiently innovative to improve their cultural patterns. Even if potentially more adaptive innovations are introduced, they may not be accepted because populations tend to be so conservative that without severe pressure from other populations, their traditional beliefs and practices will be retained. Finally, and in some respects most important of all, some of the beliefs and practices that become established in a population are not adaptive responses to environmental demands at all but are reflections of human genetic predispositions to think, feel, or behave in certain ways. Before illustrating each of

46

these points, it may be helpful to describe a small society where all appear to have played a role, the now-extinct aboriginal culture of Tasmania.[1]

The Tasmanians

People are known to have lived on Tasmania, an island about the size of Ireland, for over 20,000 years, and for the last 10,000 to 12,000 years of their cultural existence these people were totally isolated from all other human populations because the rapidly melting glacial ice cap flooded the land bridge that had previously connected Tasmania to Australia. No other society that survived until modern times was so completely isolated for such a long period.[2] As a result, the Tasmanians are a unique example of people who were allowed to adapt to their surroundings without pressure or competition from other populations.

When Europeans first made contact with them in the eighteenth century, the approximately 4,000 Tasmanians then living had the simplest technology ever reported for any human society. Men relied on one-piece wooden spears and wooden clubs that they threw, along with stones, usually with great accuracy. Women used simple wooden digging sticks to prise up roots, wooden chisels to pry shellfish off rocks, short grass ropes to climb trees, and woven grass bags to carry the fruits of their efforts. In addition to two types of temporary huts or windbreaks, the Tasmanians made pouches of animal skin and kelp, used abalone shells as drinking vessels, wore kangaroo skins slung over their shoulders for warmth, and fashioned a few ornaments. In all, the entire Tasmanian inventory of manufactured goods came to no more than two dozen items.[3] This paleolithic technology had been replaced on the Australian mainland where the Tasmanians had once lived by a substantially more complex array of tools, weapons, and other artifacts long before European contact. In short, these Tasmanians put the lie to the myth of *Homo Faber*.

The Tasmanians lived in bands of forty to fifty people led by an accomplished warrior (in one band, the leader was a woman). Each band claimed exclusive hunting and foraging rights over a territory of some 200 to 300 square miles stretching inland from a coastal strip to the wooded and mountainous interior. They subsisted on shellfish (mostly mussels, oysters, whelk, and abalone), seals, marsupials (possums, wallabies, and kangaroos), and birds and their eggs, as well as various vegetables. In all, they ate sixty species of animals and seventy species of vegetables.[4] Moving continually in search of food, each of the Tasmanian bands apparently had an adequate diet for much of the year, but during the frigid winter months, food shortages could become so extreme that they were reduced to eating kangaroo skins.[5]

What is known about the Tasmanians is based on observations not only by sundry explorers, missionaries, and settlers but also by Francois Péron, the first person ever officially called an anthropologist, who visited Tasmania in 1802 under the auspices of the world's first anthropological research group.[6] The resulting ethnographic record, while spotty, is sufficient to suggest that all of the sources of maladaptation listed at the beginning of this chapter played a part in Tasmanian life. First, some of their basic economic practices appear to have been inefficient. For example, men clearly dominated women and benefited disproportionately from their labor and risk. Yet with the possible exception of spearing kangaroos and wallabies, a task at which men arguably would be more efficient than women, either sex could, in principle, have carried out any of the necessary subsistence activities. In reality, however, almost all of these activities, including the potentially most dangerous ones, fell exclusively or primarily to women. While men often remained in camp resting or talking (early European observers called them "indolent"[7]), women fetched water and firewood and gathered vegetable products. They alone collected shellfish, the dietary staple, by diving deep into coastal waters where sharp rocks, unpredictable currents, and stingrays were dangerous hazards. More remarkable still, the job of climbing eucalyptus trees (to a height of as much as ninety feet!) to club possums to death also fell to women. And it was women who swam and crept up on sleeping seals to club them to death.

It is likely that Tasmanian women took more risks in the food quest than women have in any other folk society. Conversely, men took virtually no risks in their subsistence activities. For example, men appear to have excluded women from hunting kangaroos and wallabies not because this activity was dangerous, but because to them hunting was enjoyable while other forms of foraging were not. Despite the risks that women took and their crucial role in the economy, Tasmanian women appear to have been treated harshly by men[8] and to have been denied access to the choicest foods.[9] That Tasmanian women were not content with their lot was evident from the fact that they frequently complained to early European visitors about their husbands' mistreatment of them. It is true that this Tasmanian economic system functioned well enough to maintain the population at a more or less steady state, but a set of food-getting practices that exposed women to so many hazards while men contributed so little would hardly seem to be optimal, especially not if, as was the case, women were disaffected as a result and the population nearly starved every winter.

Like their technology, Tasmanian social institutions were undeniably simple. When the paleolithic technology that the Tasmanians relied on was replaced on the Australian mainland by more complex tools and weapons, the aborigines of Australia were able to provide for their subsistence needs far more quickly, allowing much more time for the elaboration of social and cultural forms, particularly their remarkably complex systems of art, religion, and kinship. Unlike the Australians, the Tasmanians had no initiation rituals, only rudimentary religious conceptions and rituals, and no elaborated forms of social organization.[10] Their beliefs and practices were adequate to maintain a small population in a large and diverse environment, but similar ways of doing things did not persist among the ancestral Australian population. It must be concluded that like people in many other societies, the Tasmanians persisted in their traditional practices even if they were only tolerably efficient ways of getting food, maintaining social harmony, or satisfying human needs.

There were other aspects of Tasmanian culture that appear to have been frankly maladaptive. As Rhys Jones has trenchantly pointed out, the Tasmanians either lost or abandoned some seemingly useful forms of the technology they originally brought to the island.[11] They once had bone tools, wooden boomerangs, barbed spears, hafted stone tools, and edge-ground axes, but all these were gone long before the Europeans arrived.[12] Most Tasmanian groups also lost the ability to make rafts or catamarans, even though these watercraft would have been useful in reaching nearby islands with rich food resources.[13] And inexplicably, the Tasmanians also gave up fishing. Until approximately 4,000 years ago, fish were an important food source for them, but after that time fish disappeared from the archeological record. By the time the Europeans arrived, the Tasmanians had no fishhooks, fish spears, or nets, and when they were offered cooked fish by European visitors, they rejected it with revulsion. For a population that spent most of its time seeking food, ate virtually every other food source on the island, and were desperately hungry during winter months, to reject fish as a source of food borders on the bizarre. The same fish that they routinely ate in early times were still abundant in the shallow coastal waters of the sea, as well as the many rivers and lakes of the interior. It is true that one species of fish (out of hundreds) was poisonous, but bones of this fish do not appear in archeological sites,[14] and if the Tasmanians gave up fish as a food because one, easily identifiable, fish was poisonous, this was not a rational adaptive strategy, especially because fish were plentiful during the winter months of famine. Most coastal Australian aborigines made fish a staple of their diet, and they were incredulous when told that the Tasmanians did not do the same.

The Tasmanians were far from being an innovative people, but there is no reason to suspect them of deficient intellect. When first contacted by Europeans, they played quite effective practical jokes on them, and when their children were sent to European schools, they performed as well as European children except in grammar and arithmetic, and in both of these subjects the grammatically quite different Tasmanian language, which was limited to only five number terms, probably placed them at a disadvantage. Despite their apparent intelligence, the Tasmanians did not replace the items of material culture that they lost with anything better or even as efficient. It would be too much to ask them to have invented the bow and arrow or agriculture—few people have been that inventive—but despite the bitterly cold winters the Tasmanians had to endure, they apparently made no effort even to fashion clothing. They simply threw a kangaroo skin over their shoulders or smeared themselves with animal fat. As a result, during the winter months people were forced to huddle around fires all day for warmth, and their ability to procure food was much restricted.

What is more, they could not make fire by any of the methods known on the Australian mainland; each Tasmanian band had to carry a burning firebrand at all times or risk having no fire at all for warmth or cooking. Tasmanians often fell ill, particularly during the coldest periods, but their principal medical treatment consisted of slashing the patient with deep cuts until the victim was covered with blood, and visibly weakened. If the Tasmanians had any effective herbal preparations, they were not reported by European visitors, some of whom remained with Tasmanian patients throughout their serious illnesses until death.[16] Instead of creating new and better forms of hunting, fishing, or medical treatment, the Tasmanians lived on, generation after generation, actually abandoning previously useful practices without creating new ones. As Rhys Jones, perhaps the foremost student of Tasmanian ethnoarcheology rather dyspeptically put it, 4,000 years of isolation apparently led not to more adaptive cultural forms but to a "slow strangulation of the mind."[17]

After millennia without any exposure to external forces for change, in the eighteenth century the Tasmanians found themselves exposed to European exploration. Long before the onset of newly introduced epidemic disease or European efforts to exterminate the aborigines by warfare, the Tasmanians responded to this new set of environmental changes with a remarkable, but not self-evidently adaptive, vitality. The European seal fishermen, who formed the bulk of the newcomers, introduced dogs to Tasmania where previously no such potentially valuable adjunct to hunting had existed, and the Tasmanians quite literally could not get enough of them. Without delay, and apparently without much thought for the consequences, they gave the Europeans exactly what they wanted for dogs—namely, young women. As we have already noted, hunting was far from being the mainstay of the Tasmanian economy, and although the acquisition of dogs made hunting more efficient, it was still a less vital source of food than women's foraging or diving for shellfish. By trading young women for dogs, Tasmanian men managed, in a singularly ill-advised choice, both to reduce their food supply and to exacerbate the most glaring problem in their society, interband fighting over women.[18]

Given the relative abundance of food resources in the Tasmanian environment, there is no obvious reason why their bands of people could not have lived amicably with each other. As we have seen, each band had foraging rights within a territory that provided adequate sustenance except in winter, and few of these territories were markedly richer or poorer in resources than any other. There was no economic need for conflict, then, and because their practice of band exogamy forced men to find wives in bands other than their own, there was an additional reason for Tasmanian bands to live in peace with one another. Yet they did not. Each band claimed exclusive foraging rights to its territory, making any trespasser subject to death and the killers subject to retaliatory raids. But trespass was not the only cause of hostility or of death, nor even the major one. Raids to capture women were the main cause of death, and these raids were commonplace.[19] To avoid deadly retaliation, bands were obliged to circumscribe their foraging movements, and people lived in a climate of fear.[20]

It is difficult to understand how this pattern of raid, counterraid, and pervasive fear could have been adaptive for the Tasmanians. It seems more probable that this pattern is not an adaptive response to some environmental demand at all but rather a reflection of human predispositions, especially those having to do with male competition for women and dominance over them. There were no social or economic imperatives that drove Tasmanian men to treat their wives badly, to require them to carry out dangerous tasks, or to kill other men in pursuit of more wives, but there may well have been psychological imperatives that in the absence of social or cultural constraints led men to behave in these ways. Like many other small societies, Tasmanians failed to devise social and cultural mechanisms to control their destructive tendencies. Grasping for an explanation of Tasmanian fighting over women, one might argue that it was a population control mechanism, but infanticide would surely have been a far less destructive and more efficient solution to overpopulation (if indeed that was a problem, and there is no indication that it was).

The Tasmanians have not been singled out for discussion because they were a profoundly maladapted population. On the contrary, compared to many societies that will be discussed in subsequent chapters, they were relatively well adapted at least by the criterion of maintaining their population over thousands of years. But their way of life was hardly ideal. Their feuding was deadly, disruptive, and purposeless, their food supply was at times inadequate, and their women were discontented. The population also maintained practices that could have proven to be maladaptive if the Tasmanians had been challenged by competing societies with better tools or weapons, more compelling religious beliefs, or more efficient economies. When the Europeans arrived, Tasmanian society quickly collapsed. Until then, the Tasmanians had the luxury of muddling through the centuries because they were wholly isolated from other populations and different cultures. Most societies had no such good fortune.

Adaptation—Optimal or Tolerable?

Some years ago, primatologist Hans Kummer criticized what he saw as a tendency on the part of behavioral scientists to interpret every existing social practice as adaptive because, as he put it, "all we can say with certainty is that it must be tolerable, since it did not lead to extinction."[21] Because few populations die out, everything a population does or believes must, by this definition, be considered adaptive.

Nevertheless, Kummer's argument that practices may become entrenched for long periods even though they are merely tolerable makes a useful point by calling attention to the possibility that human beliefs and practices may persist even though they serve individual or social needs rather badly. Without strong selective pressure from other populations or a rapidly changing environment, that is exactly what one would expect unless populations' early solutions to the demands of their environments were remarkably efficient. The Tasmanian design for living suggests that this was not the case for them, and it is likely, as C. R. Hallpike has argued, that "mediocre" practices and beliefs have quite commonly survived in small-scale societies, even though they were simple or inefficient to begin with, because there were too few selective pressures to force change.[22]

Weston LaBarre has provided compelling evidence that the antiquity of a belief is no assurance of its "tested truth," as he put it, nor does its survival demonstrate that it serves any positive purpose.[23] To illustrate these points, LaBarre refers to the ancient and widespread idea that the fundamental source of semen, and thus fertility and life, is the brain. After documenting the importance of this belief from its origin during the Paleolithic to modern times, LaBarre shows that it led countless populations throughout the world to become headhunters in order to eat the brains of others because it was thought that doing so would enhance their own life essence and fertility. The great antiquity and virtual ubiquity of this demonstrably false belief and lethal practice led LaBarre to coin the term "group archosis" to refer to "nonsense and misinformation so ancient and pervasive as to be seemingly inextricable from our thinking."[24] He concluded, "A frightening proportion of all culture is arguably archosis, more especially sacred culture."[25] French anthropologist Dan Sperber has taken a similar position by asserting that while some mental dispositions have been selected for in the process of biological evolution, others are mere "side effects" that have only marginal adaptive value. Provocatively, Sperber concluded that religion is one of these side effects of evolution.[26]

Another example of an ancient practice that is still widespread, was once probably universal, yet has dubious adaptive value is divination. The belief that one or another form of divination—searching for cracks in a heated scapula, flipping sandals into the air, poisoning chickens, or whatever—could provide answers to questions about what caused illness, where to hunt, when to make war, whether it would rain, and other important matters may have been reassuring; as Evans-Pritchard pointed out after his stay with the Azande in the Sudan, for some highly indeterminate activities, such as running a large household, divination may be as efficient a basis for decision making as any other. But when more accurate means of forecasting or controlling events such as weather satellites, insecticides, and immunization become available, divination declines in importance.[27] For example, many small-scale societies relied on divination to tell them when and where to conduct raids against their enemies, but it is difficult to believe that sound intelligence and skillful scouting would not have been more efficient. While divination is not entirely absent in modern warfare—Hitler's reliance on astrology is one example—military leaders who rely on it in their war planning today would be at a decided disadvantage.

It has nevertheless been seriously proposed that divination can be adaptive. A classic adaptive interpretation of divination was offered by Omar Kayyam Moore, who purported to show that the Montagnais-Naskapi Indians, who subsisted primarily by hunting caribou on the Labrador peninsula, used divination to maintain the ecological equilibrium between themselves and the caribou.[28] Basing his analysis on data recorded earlier by Frank Speck, Moore argued that the Montagnais-Naskapi use of scapulimancy to tell them where to hunt for caribou (they interpreted the cracks and breaks that appeared in an animal scapula after it was exposed to fire) was highly adaptive. Moore believed that because this procedure resulted in randomizing the areas where hunters searched for game, it prevented them from being so successful in finding caribou that they would overhunt and deplete the caribou herds. Moore's paper soon became widely cited as an example of the adaptive value of divination.[29]

But as a recent reexamination of Moore's analysis has shown, he was wrong on many essential counts. First, according to Vollweiler and Sanchez, he badly misstated Speck's data. Of the thirty-four cases of scapulimancy Speck discussed, only one approximated what Moore claimed was a general practice.[30] Moore also misunderstood how the Naskapi actually searched for game, and he falsely assumed that caribou respond to human predation by changing their location. Finally, he asserted that the use of divination was commonly used by hunters in other societies to locate game. In fact, divination has rarely been used for this purpose.[31]

One might also call into question the adaptive value of primitive warfare, which, though widespread, was not self-evidently of benefit to most of the populations that have practiced it. Challenging the view of Vayda and others that primitive warfare can be adaptive, R. B. Ferguson has argued that any benefits warfare may bring to a population can also be achieved without war, and that the presence of warfare limits the number of people who can live in the affected area. He concluded that "life is worse for war."[32] Many others have concluded that life is also worse as a result of the need that people in many small-scale societies feel to seek vengeance in feuds that never end.

A similar question can be raised about the universal existence of ethnocentrism in human society. Ethnocentrism may once have been adaptive by reinforcing in-group commitment, solidarity, and cooperation or by preserving scarce economic resources. Some scholars have made such arguments, but others have wondered if ethnocentrism might not be an example of a belief system that arose by chance and has always been maladaptive.[33] Whether it arose by chance cannot be known, but like a paranoid ethos, ethnocentrism is probably rooted in quite basic, if not necessarily adaptive, attributes of the human mind—fear and mistrust of strangers. From our postnuclear perspective, we can readily see the need to eradicate ethnocentrism if the world is to survive, but as events the world over so dramatically demonstrate, ethnocentrism is as widespread and virulent today as at any time in history.

As British anthropologist Roy Ellen has suggested, another reason why early human beliefs and practices were not highly adaptive is that humans are not consistently rational. He wrote, "Cultural adaptations are seldom the best of all possible solutions and never entirely rational."[34] Although Ellen did not use this example, we might note that one reason for this is that people tend to make faulty causal inferences. This limitation has led them to blame one another rather than bacteria or viruses for ill health. It has led them to conclude that some people possess the evil eye or that performing various rituals will bring rain, improve hunting success, increase fertility, or ward off death. To be sure, once established, almost any human practice, including divination, feuding, or accusing other people of being witches, can develop some positive social functions for at least some members of a population. But beliefs and practices like these are usually not the most efficient ones on which to found a society. The development of scientific medicine, effective means of adjudicating disputes, and peaceful relations with neighbors, to suggest a few examples, are likely to be more adaptive in the long run.

For some specific examples of less than fully rational beliefs and practices, let us turn to the Bena Bena of highland Papua New Guinea as described by L. L. Langness. Many Bena Bena quite clearly loved their children, and they sought to protect them against harm by making sure that they never visited neighboring villages where malevolent sorcerers were thought to live. Yet these same concerned parents allowed their small children to play with very sharp knives, sometimes cutting themselves, and they permitted them to sleep unattended next to the fire. As a result, a number of children burned themselves seriously. Langness reports that it was not uncommon to see children who had lost a toe to burns, and some were crippled by even more severe burns. A similarly nonrational and apparently maladaptive Bena Bena practice concerned food. Although chemically short of protein, the Bena Bena would eat neither chicken nor eggs because, they said, chickens ate feces. Yet their favorite food source, pigs, also ate feces.[35]

It must be noted, of course, that the Bena Bena are not uniquely nonrational. As Melford Spiro among others has pointed out, other populations, including our own, cling to beliefs and practices that are equally nonrational.[36] Research has shown that American parents, for example, like their Bena Bena counterparts, are frequently more concerned with protecting their children against rarely occurring and relatively benign threats to their health than with more serious risks.[37] (I will return to this discussion in the concluding chapter.)

Another, often overlooked, reason why the practices of small, traditional societies may not be adaptive solutions to the challenges of their environments is that some of them were never humanly contrived solutions at all. Instead, they are expressions of human biological predispositions that populations have failed to control through social mechanisms or cultural beliefs. Men's competition for nubile women, their sexual jealousy, and the resulting lethal bloodshed and feuding have occurred not only in Tasmania but among the !Kung San, Inuit (Eskimo), Yanomamo, and many other small societies.[38] To take a single example, in the 1920s the San (or Bushmen as they then were called) were anything but peaceful, as I noted earlier. Much like the Tasmanians, each band claimed exclusive hunting rights to a territory, and trespass almost invariably led to bloodshed.[39] Bands also raided one another, killing all men and boys in fights that were conducted with "great bitterness."[40] Any killing, even by accident, triggered retaliation, and if the killer could not be found, his wife, relatives, or children were killed. But if these reasons for violence were not enough, there were also lethal fights over women. Men often attempted to capture women from other bands to marry, and they were met by "violent resistance."[41] Is fighting like this, especially fighting over women, an adaptive practice or merely a tolerable one because most societies that engage in it nevertheless manage to survive? Or is it instead a maladaptive practice that results from the inability of small-scale societies to create effective social and cultural restraints on biologically driven male sexual competition and jealousy? We will return to this question later in this chapter.

The Persistence of Maladaptation

From time to time over the course of human history, rigorous selective forces have compelled societies to change, and those that could not were absorbed by other populations or, sometimes, became extinct. But more often there has not been enough competition among societies to bring about major social or cultural change.[42] In the absence of strong competition, there is little motivation for change. Just as people very often do not rationally calculate how each of their beliefs or customs might better serve their needs, neither do they very often rationally calculate how best to change their ways in order to survive whatever the future can reasonably be expected to bring. As the Tasmanians illustrated, people in small traditional societies are neither consistently rational maximizers of their well-being nor highly innovative. The history of small societies is one of little change even in the realm of technology, where so much as a minor improvement— a feathered arrow, a hafted axe, a spear thrower, a weighted digging stick—is a rare occurrence. Even when innovations are proposed, the population may resist their adoption.

Psychologist Donald Campbell has suggested that this may be so because people have evolved to be conservative, to respect established ways and responsible leaders; for Campbell, conservatism is a survival mechanism.[43] Similarly, sociologist Joseph Lopreato was so impressed by the human predilection for conforming to rules and forcing others to do likewise that he posited a genetic need for conformity.[44] Whatever the truth of these speculations, it is clear that most populations are reluctant to change their traditional beliefs and practices. With the exception of self-evidently more efficient tools such as steel axes, the majority of populations resist innovation.[45] For this reason, even a quite ineffective or actually harmful belief or practice may persist because most people are reluctant to change it. Their reluctance may occasionally be based on a rational argument for the adaptiveness of the belief or practice in question, but more often it is not. With the partial exception of subsistence activities, for every man or woman in a folk society who has been able to explain why something believed or done is beneficial, there have been thousands (in some societies this includes everyone) who provide no more by way of explanation than "it is our custom" or "we've always done it this way." And indeed, when an answer is offered such as "we do not eat eggs because to do so would anger a terrestrial spirit" or "we sacrifice children because the moon god demands it," anthropologists are almost certain to dismiss such explanations and search for one of their own based on their preferred understanding of how such a practice might have an adaptive basis.[46]

Consider the Ijaw of Nigeria, who above all else wanted to have more children but nevertheless killed all twins of either sex, even after British rule declared such actions to be homicide. When Philip E. Leis asked them why they did so, they answered that it was because "our ancestors did it this way."[47] For Leis, the Ijaw practice of killing twins was "nonfunctional," a "remnant of the past," and he felt obliged to caution scholars against finding a positive function that twin killing performed. He apparently believed that such a cautionary note was necessary because, as he put it, anthropologists took great satisfaction in finding meaningful explanation for the exotic and seemingly irrational. As Ernest Gellner had written a few years earlier, anthropologists have found little sense of accomplishment in concluding that an apparently pointless ritual was, after all, pointless.[48]

Of course, humans can modify their beliefs or practices to accommodate to change, and they sometimes do so,[49] but more often they refuse to change or are unable to do so, and often they fail to understand the implications of changing conditions, believing that the lessons of the past will continue to serve them well in the future. Just as many generals were slow to recognize how drastically the machine gun, the tank, or air power would change the nature of warfare, some populations overlook economic or political changes as they steadfastly believe that the future will mirror the past. For example, the Tapirapé and Tenetehara Indians of Brazil were economically similar societies that responded quite differently to the changes brought about by European contact. The Tenetehara were sociopolitically flexible enough to change, and as a result their population remained steady despite 300 years of colonial influence. The Tapirapé did not change, and after only 40 years of much less intense colonial pressure, they were decimated.[50]

Populations may also find that initially productive practices have long-term costs. The destruction of wooded areas can bring short-term benefits, but in the long run deforestation may result. Goats may become prized because they are wholly self-sufficient yet provide highly desirable meat, but in large numbers, omnivorously grazing goats can contribute to desertification. Swidden agriculture can produce high yields, but in time it can lead to deterioration of the soil, development of diseases, and topsoil erosion. A grain may be replaced by a root crop that provides more calories for less effort, but in the long run the reduction in protein can be harmful. Industrial growth may benefit millions before people discover that the resulting pollution may endanger even larger numbers.[51] In this regard, so-called environmentalists tell us on a daily basis, our own lack of foresight may soon prove to be catastrophic.

To take an example from the past, for over two hundred years before 1000 A.D., Norse settlers occupied the islands of the North Atlantic: Iceland and Greenland, the Shetlands, Faroes, Hebrides, and Orkneys. These Norse colonists were keen observers of their new habitats, but they were unwilling to sacrifice short-term personal advantage for long-term common benefit. They were also unable to recognize subtle differences between their homelands and these new territories, so that their traditional practices of overstocking domestic animals, fuel collection, and construction activity so badly depleted the trees, shrubs, and pasture land that severe soil erosion resulted. The degradation of these new environments was a product of human error, and although this error came about for understandable reasons, it was error nonetheless.[52] It also seems likely that the collapse of the classic Mayan state was related to urban demands for wood fuel that

59

led to deforestation and soil erosion.[53] Archeologist Arthur M. Demarist believes that he has found evidence to show that the ultimate cause of the destruction of the Mayan state was large-scale warfare. When besieged populations fortified themselves in towns and cities, their need for wood as fuel eventually became impossible to fulfill.[54]

There are many reasons, then, why traditional beliefs and practices—culture, if you prefer—can become maladaptive and remain so. Even if one were to make the untenable assumption that humans are remorselessly rational beings who unfailingly devote themselves to optimizing their adaptation in every way possible, the vagaries of human social living and of ecological constraints would often thwart their best efforts. But humans are not utterly rational, nor are they very much given to optimizing the well-being of their fellows. They sometimes seek to better their own ways of living, of course, and they can sometimes do so with remarkable ingenuity, as Inuit technology so vividly illustrates. Yet as ingenious as Inuit groups were in solving some of their technological problems, they maintained some markedly maladaptive beliefs. There can be no doubt that Inuit technology exemplified rational, even ingenious, "applied science": houses of wood and ice blocks that kept them warm in arctic winters, clothing that was both waterproof and warm, efficient bird and animal traps, snow goggles that anticipated modern designs, sleds, kayaks, and complex harpoons, to mention only a few of their most obvious achievements. But at the same time, they imbued their environment with an appallingly large assemblage of aggressively evil entities: mermaids that enticed and then killed people, giant birds able to carry off and kill caribou and people alike, giant lake fish able to swallow a man with a single bite, and all manner of invisible ghosts and spirits capable of causing illness or death.

These fearsome entities forced the Inuit to employ elaborate means of protection that were a poor use of their time and energy. The presumed existence of these entities also created such anxiety that the Inuit chose to alter their hunting and fishing strategies in order to avoid them. For example, they avoided lakes that they admitted offered superior fishing and hunting because they were thought to be inhabited by monstrous man-eating fish, and they avoided excellent campsites in order to avoid malevolent ghosts and spirits. Good hunting and fishing areas could not be visited at night for fear of "wild babies"—creatures resembling human infants—that were thought to devour people like wolves or, more remarkable still, tickle them to

60

death.[55] Neither needlessly living in fear of culturally created super-natural entities nor limiting subsistence activities because of them is a rational adaptive strategy, as the early European visitors proved when they hunted and fished with great success in areas the Inuit feared to enter. The Inuit were also far from successful in solving their social problems, especially those having to do with male competition for women.

Biological Predispositions and Maladaptation

Humans have not devoted themselves exclusively or consistently to solving the problems they face; instead, while populations sometimes seek solutions to pressing problems or to better meeting their collective needs, they also create problems by engaging in behaviors that appear to be rooted in their biological predispositions. Their psychobiological inheritance—their evolved "nature"—includes far more than the predispositions selected for during the relatively brief period of time since humans have become fully cultural creatures. A part of our genetic inheritance was established much earlier than that, and at times it makes us unruly, difficult, and self-serving—the beast within us, as some have said. Whether one looks to Freud, Norman O. Brown, Donald T. Campbell, or some other scholar who has attempted to illuminate the conflicts that humans bring upon themselves, the perduring message is the same: if humans are to succeed in adapting to one another and to the environments in which they live, they must devise social and cultural mechanisms to control certain aspects of their biological nature. It is self-evident that no population has yet done so with complete success.

Because the role of genetic factors in human behavior is poorly understood by many in the general public as well as by many scholars, some of whom steadfastly reject any assertion that genes produce behavior, it will be necessary to provide some background. It is generally agreed that human beings evolved in our present form during the Pleistocene and that few significant changes in the human genotype have taken place since then.[56] It is also generally agreed that the human genotype and culture evolved at the same time and that this process of dual evolution involved reciprocal influences between culture and human genetic predispositions. But the nature and intensity of the influence that culture had on the hominid genotype

61

that evolved into humankind during the Pleistocene is in dispute. Some, like P. D. MacLean, who coined the term "triune brain," have conceived of reptilian and mammalian brains overlain by newly evolved cortical capacities. In this view, the cerebral cortex was greatly influenced by the challenges of the Pleistocene environment, including the cultures (or culture) that developed at that time, but the earlier genetic hominid predispositions, although to some degree modified, were not wholly transformed. Adherents of this view believe that biology imposes powerful constraints on human thought and behavior. Others disagree, vehemently insisting that biological constraints are so weak that they play no significant role in determining human behavior.[57]

Probably the most influential spokesman for this latter view is Princeton's Clifford Geertz, who holds that culture as a system of symbols and meanings played such a fundamental role during the evolution of *Homo sapiens* that without it humans would be "unworkable monstrosities with very few useful instincts, fewer recognizable sentiments, and no intellect: mental basket cases."[58] For Geertz, ". . . there is no such thing as a human nature independent of culture."[59] He believes that because our central nervous system, especially the neocortex, developed in interaction with culture, ". . . it is incapable of directing our behavior or organizing our experienc without the guidance provided by systems of significant symbols."[60] We are, concludes Geertz, "incomplete" animals who complete ourselves through culture, more exactly through the highly particular form of culture in which we are raised.

Those who find Geertz's *tabula rasa* position persuasive have the formidable task of explaining how it came to pass that early hominids were able to evolve into true humans solely by means of culture without becoming different creatures—*Homo Javanese, Homo Hopi, or Homo Tasmanian*. If it is culture that shaped our nature, why are we one species with differing cultures instead of different beings altogether? Some scholars, as we saw in chapter 2, write as if they believe that such a culturally determined division of humankind has taken place, but most anthropologists and evolutionary biologists reject this cultural deterministic position, preferring to believe that although the acquisition of language and culture greatly affected the developing neocortex and may have modified older parts of the brain as well, human psychobiology is the same everywhere. How people think and behave is a product of their genetic predispositions acting under the influence of various environmental factors that include but are not limited to their culture. These scholars also assume that the Pleistocene environment—including human culture—in which humans evolved was sufficiently homogeneous that various small bands of people evolved virtually identical genotypes.

Exactly what that Pleistocene environment was like is a matter for speculation. Based on what is known about the early hominids, it is likely that men and women had to learn to cooperate in hunting and gathering and, indeed, that they developed a division of labor. They must have been nomadic, at least most of the time. They probably felt close ties for family members, and practiced considerable sharing and mutual aid. Some evolutionary biologists believe that what mattered most during the Pleistocene and what has given all modern humans the same psychobiology was their need to understand and manipulate other people. Some of the demands of social living must have called for affection, companionship, even skills at entertainment, but others would have involved more onerous demands for sharing, assistance, or self-sacrifice, and at times the demands must have called for effective displays of hostility, intimidation, deception, and aggression. There have been many ingenious speculations about what Pleistocene life must have been like for modern humans to have evolved as we did, but these are largely unverifiable because the archeological record has not yet told us enough about the selective forces that shaped us and we cannot infer that any contemporary hunter-gatherer societies have retained that Pleistocene way of life.

Nevertheless, we can make some assumptions that bear on the development of maladaptive behavior in modern populations. First, and most obvious, whatever the human genotype was that evolved during the Pleistocene, some aspects of it were selected for that particular environment. In the radically different environments faced by modern populations, some aspects of our genetic inheritance could prove to be "pathological," as Robert Boyd and Peter J. Richardson bluntly put it.[61] For example, it is quite possible, as various evolutionary biologists have suggested, that the cravings of modern humans for fat, salt, and sugar were selected for during the Pleistocene when these substances were scarce. A craving that might once have been adaptive became harmful when fat, salt, and sugar became as readily available as they have been in recent times. It is also important to note that there is no reason to assume, as evolutionary biologists often do, that Pleistocene hunter-gatherers were optimally adapted to their environment. It seems much more likely that some of their beliefs and behaviors were as harmful or inefficient as those of modern men and that some of these cognitive and behavioral tendencies would in all likelihood persist in modern populations. The belief that semen resides in the brain is an example, as LaBarre has pointed out. What is more, because of a phenomenon known as pleiotropy, a desirable trait like endurance or physical strength that was selected for during the Pleistocene may have been genetically linked with an undesirable one such as low intelligence; hence, selection for an adaptive trait may bring with it a maladaptive one. And finally, many hominid predispositions, such as selfishness or competition for mates, that can make social living problematic appear to have survived largely unmodified despite centuries of Pleistocene evolution.

We will turn to a consideration of the potentially maladaptive character of some aspects of human nature in a moment, but first it is important to acknowledge the power of culture to shape how people think, feel, and behave and to point out how this too can lead to maladaptation. As anyone with a passing knowledge of advances in the cognitive and neurosciences knows, Geertz's belief that human psychobiology cannot shape behavior independently of culture is mistaken, even though his insistence on the importance of culture—of systems of meaning—for human existence is axiomatic. However, in some hands the concept of culture has been used as the explanation for all behavior. For example, if human nature is rejected as a causal factor in how we behave, then when men in all societies behave more violently than women, it follows that it must be a result of their culture. It should be obvious that this kind of explanation is as vacuous as it is circular. Nevertheless, the power of human beings to teach one another how to feel, think, and behave is undeniably profound.

In spite of power of culture, no society yet discovered has succeeded completely in making all its members want to do all the things they have to do for the society to prosper—to share, for example, to avoid envy or to speak no evil of others. But most societies have nevertheless managed to do well enough in the process of socializing themselves and their young to create populations with culturally constituted needs that can become as powerful as they are, independent of genetic predispositons. Conceptions of trust, beauty, valor, honor, prestige, decency, achievement, and the like are the stuff of human existence. Often these conceptions fit well with the needs of a people to cope with their environment, and when they do, successful adaptation can be greatly enhanced. But these conceptions, often thought of by those who embrace them as the defining characteristics of everything that is desirable and proper, can become so deeply embedded, so over-determined by an onslaught of symbols, rituals, and everyday rein-forcements, that they are difficult to change when change becomes necessary. Thus, for the Dakota Indians to exalt the manly virtues of the warrior as strongly as they did helped them to survive in com-petition with other Indian societies that were equally warlike. But when warfare was suppressed after United States military conquest, these Dakota could not easily adapt to a life without the thrills and honors of warriorhood, and, as Gordon McGregor documented in *Warriors Without Weapons*, they became apathetic and depressed.[62] So did the warlike people of Eddystone Island in the Pacific when the British abolished the practice of head-hunting to which they had been devoted.[63]

Culturally constituted needs can lead toward maladaptation even when there is no dramatic environmental change like the one that unmanned the Dakota and the Eddystone Islanders. A cultural value on the accumulation of wealth can lead people not only to avaricious-ness but to accusations of witchcraft and deadly forms of competition. Inculcating a profound love of place can be helpful in uniting a com-munity and in encouraging positive forms of cooperation, but if that love of a particular place causes people to return again and again to an area that has been ravaged by earthquakes or volcanic eruptions, as has happened in Italy, then what would otherwise be a virtue can become a threat to a population's survival.[64] The individualism that Tocqueville saw in the 1830s and feared might eventually isolate Americans from one another is another example. As Robert Bellah and his colleagues have shown in their book *Habits of the Heart*, our cultural commitment to individualism rather than collective achieve-ment has enhanced our self-reliance, a virtue that was probably adap-tive earlier in American history but that has also brought about such a loss of community that the consequences now threaten our common well-being.[65]

Assessing Human Nature

Scholars from various backgrounds, disciplines, and political persua-sions have sought to discover the nature of human nature by such wondrously diverse strategies as, referring to what they believed to be natural law, studying our primate "relatives," and extrapolating from cultural universals to presumed biological causes. They have also examined how infants behave before they are "socialized" (or how strongly they resist certain kinds of efforts to socialize them). Other scholars have invoked such basic physiological needs as hunger and creature comforts and have examined the functioning of the central nervous system. Still others have studied behavior genetics or modeled presumed evolutionary processes such as parental investment strategies. Very often, one suspects, introspection is the method of choice.[66]

Some of the resulting catalogues of human nature consist of dismayingly short lists of genetic predispositions that are thought to exercise relatively little constraint over human behavior. For example, Marvin Harris's search for the smallest number of what he called "pan-human psychobiological drives" capable of accounting for human behavior led him to identify only four—the "need to eat" and a tendency to choose more rather than less nutritious diets; a preference for carrying out tasks by using less rather than more energy; finding pleasure in sexual intercourse; and craving love and attention.[67] This seemingly arbitrary assessment of human nature is even more abbreviated than Malinowski's earlier and much-derided conception of human nature, which was defined exclusively in terms of physiological needs such as reproduction, health, and metabolism. As many have commented, if human nature is reduced to such self-evident and trivial "drives" as these, it is unlikely to provide much that is of value for the explanation of either human evolution or contemporary behavior.[68]

Fortunately, there have been other, more provocative contributions to the study of human genetic predispositions.[69] Some of these formulations, like the one offered by Robin Fox, are based on the arguable assumption that practices that occur in all societies must have a genetic basis. Taking a cue from the supposed experiments of Pharaoh Psammetichus and King James IV of Scotland, both of whom are said to have raised some children in total isolation from adults to see what language they would speak, Fox concluded that if children were reared in isolation from their elders they would eventually produce a society with rules about incest and marriage, beliefs about the supernatural, initiation ceremonies for young men (an odd conclusion, because such ceremonies are *not* universal), gambling, dancing, myths, legends, and everything else that appears to occur everywhere and hence be the product of human nature.[70] Others have chosen to infer human nature from behaviors shared by both humans and primates. Thus, Kent G. Bailey has suggested that genetic predispositions control a host of behaviors from predation and food seeking through courtship behavior and parenting to patterns of play and friendship.[71] Melvin Konner, on the other hand, has emphasized the biological grounding of human rage, fear, joy, lust, love, grief, and gluttony, many of which, it seems obvious, would make social living problematic.[72]

Sometimes theories of human nature are based on suppositions concerning the adaptive value of certain interpersonal strategies. For example, various forms of deception, including lying, occur in all human populations as people attempt to gain an advantage over others. Someone who can deceive others successfully may gain a significant advantage, as did the Kapauku headman described by Leo Pospisil, who admitted that he lied to his fellow tribesmen in order to acquire a comely new wife. "The people are like that," he said. "One has to tell them lies."[73] As La Rochefoucault put it in his famous maxim, "Hypocrisy is the homage vice pays to virtue," but lying successfully is no easy matter, especially in small societies where people know so much about one another, and being caught out in a lie can have unpleasant consequences. Thus, the best guarantee of successful deception might well be self-deception, that is, a lack of awareness that one is lying at all, because a person who did not realize he was lying would likely be more convincing than one who knew he was distorting the truth. So, various theorists have concluded, one might suppose that if there were a heritable gene or set of genes that enhanced successful deception, this skill might be selected for too. This idea has led to a large literature on the adaptive advantages of self-deception, including related psychoanalytic concepts such as repression and denial.[74] Anxiety may be reduced if one can deceive oneself about some menacing aspects of reality, and so may depression. The denial of death is an example. But if self-deception goes too far, reality may be distorted to such an extent that survival may be endangered. Despite this risk, there is evidence that self-deception occurs in lower organisms as well as humans and may therefore actually have a genetic basis.[75]

The most recent and in some respect most promising approaches to human nature involve the search for specific psychological mechanisms that evolved in response to specific environmental demands. Unlike earlier approaches to learning that assumed the evolution of generalized cognitive abilities of learning or information processing, these approaches argue that humans evolved specific psychological abilities to solve specific problems.[76] That the brain is, indeed, organized into discrete modules of cognitive abilities has been confirmed by neurosurgical research.[77]

As an example of the search for specific psychological mechanisms, David Marr has developed a model that specifies how an organism is able to reconstruct three-dimensional objects from a two-dimensional retinal display.[78] In another approach, Thomas Wynn analyzed the tools made over a span of evolutionary time from almost two million years ago to 300,000 years ago in an attempt to determine what spatial abilities were required to produce them. Wynn found that the hominids that made tools two million years ago possessed concepts of proximity, separation, pairs, and order, but their tools were neither aesthetically pleasing nor symmetrical, and the cutting edges were not straight. However, the tools made 300,000 years ago showed an essentially modern intelligence, including an understanding of Euclidian space.[79] Other developments in cognitive science have brought us closer to an understanding of human thought and problem solving, including limitations in our ability to process information.[80]

The view that human cognitive abilities evolved as discrete modules in response to problems posed by specific environments, combined with increasingly persuasive evidence that humans possess not one generalized intelligence, as previously thought, but multiple intelligences that are also largely independent, requires a more complex conception of human cognition and problem solving.[81] It also raises the possibility that just as individuals differ in cognitive abilities, populations that evolved in somewhat different Pleistocene environments may have developed correspondingly different cognitive abilities. The study of population or racial differences, to use an imprecise gloss, is in its infancy, where perhaps it will remain due to its racist implications and the possibility that gene flow since the Pleistocene would have eliminated any such population differences. However, at least one serious scholar has reported that he has found strong differences in temperament between Euro-American children and their Chinese-American and Navaho counterparts. If these differences are in fact genetic, as psychologist Daniel G. Freedman believes, it would follow that some cultural practices that were adaptive for the more genetically quiescent Navaho children—the use of a cradleboard, for example—would be maladaptive for more active Euro-American children.[82]

In addition to these proposed group differences in temperament, any population, no matter how small, will contain individuals who further test the capacity of any set of traditional beliefs or practices to meet human needs. Inborn differences in temperament can make some people more aggressive, depressed, or irritable than others, just as individuals differ in intelligence, creativity, strength, beauty, endurance, and other heritable characteristics. Idiosyncratic experience in childhood may leave some individuals timid and fearful, others hostile and mistrustful, still others unusually affectionate or empathic. One person may have great charisma, another a capacity for ecstatic experience, yet another a tendency toward paranoia. As a result, every population will contain some unusual, difficult, disputatious, and dangerous people who sometimes challenge or disrupt the beliefs and practices that adequately meet the needs of the majority. They may also make it more difficult for the population to cope effectively with the challenges posed by its environment.

Human Nature Versus Society

Not all human genetic predispositions pose challenges to social living. Indeed, it is likely that some predispositions help people to live with one another. For example, humans are clearly predisposed to enjoy the company of other humans, to cooperate (at least in some activities), and, as several scholars have suggested, we very likely have a need for recognition or positive affect as well.[83] Indeed, as mentioned earlier, some scholars believe that humans have a genetic predisposition to conform. E. O. Wilson has hypothesized the evolution of "censor genes" which inhibit the action of other genes—an authentically biological superego.[84] However, the primary concern is not with genetic predispositions that support society and enhance human well-being but with those that must be controlled if a society is to survive. In *Culture Against Man*, Jules Henry wrote that man's "ultimate problem" was "learning to live with himself" while wringing satisfaction out of culture.[85] In *Beyond Culture*, Lionel Trilling expressed this perspective on human nature as well as anyone: ". . . there is a hard,

69

irreducible, stubborn core of biological urgency, and biological necessity, and biological *reason*, that culture cannot reach and that reserves the right, which sooner or later it will exercise, to judge the culture and revise it."[86] Humans are forever betwixt and between, required (as Jules Henry put it) to "wring" satisfaction from a culture that represses many aspects of human nature, yet still dependent on that culture for all that gives meaning to life.

Many of the predispositions that are commonly believed to exist in humans have the capacity to threaten society and resist the efforts of culture to constrain them. The list is a long and familiar one. Donald T. Campbell has argued that if a society is to survive, it must develop means to curb human greed, pride, dishonesty, covetousness, cowardice, lust, wrath, gluttony, envy, thievery, promiscuity, stubbornness, disobedience, and blasphemy.[87] Ten commandments plus four. R. L. Trivers has added gossip, backbiting, and scolding to the list, one that few would agree was complete without mention of selfishness or egocentrism, probably the most commonly proposed attribute of human nature.[88] All sociocultural systems attempt to control most of these predispositions or to redirect them into culturally acceptable forms, but none, as I observed earlier, has had complete success in doing so. Nowhere have adults found it necessary to teach their children to be selfish, greedy, angry, stubborn, envious, or disobedient; instead, they search everywhere for means to limit or eliminate these characteristics in their children. Many small-scale societies are remarkably indulgent with their children when they are small, but as these children grow older, adults attempt to bring their selfishness, temper tantrums, disobedience, and the like under cultural control.[89]

Although many socially divisive behaviors may have their roots in our common genetic inheritance, not all destructive practices necessarily have a genetic origin. Whether warfare has its roots in genetic predisposition is a matter of continuing debate, but it is likely that some kinds of warfare are the result of conscious choice rather than human psychobiology. The ethnographic record shows that most societies engaged in warfare prior to their pacification. For some the decision to go to war led to tangible gains in arable land, livestock, hunting territory, captives, and other resources. But for most societies these gains were ephemeral and outweighed by the costs of retaliation and irresolvable violence. For example, the Mae Enga of highland Papua New Guinea fought incessantly to gain and hold arable land, but the price they paid for meager advantage was high.[90] Twenty-five percent of all male deaths were the result of warfare, and anxiety was endemic. Elsewhere in highland Papua New Guinea the percentage of male deaths due to warfare was even higher.[91] For a modern state to have, year after year, 25 or 30 percent of its male deaths result from warfare would be almost unthinkable. For some societies in highland Papua New Guinea and for others in Amazonia, warfare with its terrible casualties was virtually unending. Initially, at least, many of these wars were probably seen by those who planned them as the best available solution to a perceived problem,[92] but if they calculated the long-term costs at all, they did not do so accurately.

However, for another common kind of killing, there appears to have been no rational calculus of cost and benefit, but instead a seemingly irresistible predilection on the part of men to fight over nubile women. There is no doubt that men everywhere prefer nubile women, and as Donald Symons has argued, this very likely is a preference that was strongly selected for during the course of human evolution.[93] Various small, relatively peaceful societies like the San fight over women; in fact, almost all San fights in recent times in which deaths have occurred have been over women. So it was for the Tasmanians, the Inuit, and, as we shall see later, the Kaiadilt of Australia, who were close to extinction as a result of their raids to capture women.[94] It is evident that until societies develop adequate mechanisms to control such violence, they are endangered. When the fighting is over the control of tangible resources, it is possible that people are doing their best to enhance their collective welfare, but when men kill other men over sexually attractive women, their goal is not social well-being but personal satisfaction. The result is deadly retaliation by those who feel wronged. Adding a woman to a band or a kin group may sometimes add to its foraging success, and her sons may help to protect them in the future; but these benefits, if they occurred at all, were not intended. The Kaiadilt, for example, explicitly denied that that was why they fought over women, and so have men in such other societies as the Yanomamo, who emphatically said that the reason they fought one another was to possess women, not to enhance their resources.[95]

For a final example of apparent genetic predispositions that can lead to maladaptive beliefs and practices, consider the ubiquitous presence of beliefs in witchcraft (or other forms of human malevolence, such as sorcery or the evil eye) by people throughout the world. As earlier stated, anthropologists have frequently asserted that these

71

beliefs serve a useful purpose; for example, by identifying the cause of illness or misfortune or by giving victims a means of coping with their dilemma through, in some societies, confessing their own wrongdoing or, in others, employing a specialist to take protective or retaliatory measures against the presumed witch. Witchcraft beliefs can also promote social solidarity by redirecting attributions of malevolence away from the family, clan, or village onto more distant people with whom close cooperation is not necessary. It is likely that these and other positive functions of witchcraft do exist, but as we heard from several scholars, the negative consequences of beliefs in witchcraft appear to outweigh the positive ones, often by a large margin. Witchcraft has created fear and led to deaths; in some instances, the virtual annihilation of entire populations. If the costs of believing in witchcraft outweigh the benefits, why has it been so widespread?

The answer would appear to be that it is a product of several related and quite basic characteristics of human thought.[96] First, we are now (and were even more so in earlier, more credulous times) prone to accept correlated events as being causally linked, so that the presumed enmity of another person and the death of a child become conflated. Second, humans are predisposed to paranoid ideation, which leads them to suspect the worst of others. And third, we project our own hostility onto others: if we wish harm to others, surely others must wish the same for us.[97]

The source of witchcraft beliefs, then, may derive more from genetically determined characteristics of the human mind than from a collective desire to explain or control misfortune or redirect aggression away from people who must cooperate with one another. If this view is correct, then beliefs in witchcraft are natural to humans, and if they are to be controlled or eradicated, that must be done by social and cultural means. Such means have often been required over the course of history because of the fear and the killing that witchcraft engenders. Witchcraft may also be maladaptive because as long as such a belief system is uncritically accepted by a society, there is little need to search for more rational explanations for crop failure, infant mortality, adult illness, or other misfortune.

Finally, the success of culture in constraining socially threatening aspects of human nature—or more correctly, the efforts of people to find social and cultural mechanisms to control unwanted aspects of their nature—has never been more than partial. This is no doubt so because some human genetic predispositions are implacable, but there is another reason as well—namely, that some genetic predispositions may be contradictory. Thus, there is reason to believe that we have a predisposition not only to be selfish but also to be altruistic, not only to compete but also to cooperate, to be curious but to fear the unknown, and to be self-assertive yet submissive.[98] There may also be conflict between, for example, biological needs for food and for comfort or sociability. As a result, people may come to feel ambivalent about certain choices they must make in life, leaving them less than fully committed to the goals and values of their cultures— timid warriors, reluctant food sharers, lazy hunters, squeamish cannibals, disrespectful wives, disillusioned children. At a still more basic level, people have a need for variety. Humans tend to prefer variety in all sensory modalities, and they find boredom so unpleasant that they frequently take dangerous risks to escape it. A need for variety may lead to creativity, as Ralph Linton believed, but it can also lead to socially disruptive, deviant behavior as people violate what they experience as stifling cultural restraints.[99]

Of all the causes of maladaptation, none is as controversial as human nature. Yet the controversy among most scientists today is not about whether humans possess genetic predispositions to think, feel, and behave in certain ways but rather about the specification of these predispositions and how modifiable they are by experience. In *A Treatise on Human Nature*, written in 1739 and 1740, David Hume wrote, " 'Tis evident that all the sciences have a relation, greater or less, to human nature; and that however wide any of them may seem to run from it, they will return back by one passage or another." If there is to be a scientific study of human maladaptation, it too will find it necessary to return to the study of human nature, for as much as we are the products of our cultures, we are human animals with genetic predispositions. We are, in that sense, all too human. Our needs are not easily served by the cultures that we have created and that in return have created still more needs in us.

There is ample reason, then, to predict that some traditional beliefs and practices will be maladaptive. But are these harmful practices uncommon and largely inconsequential, or do they significantly endanger people's health, leave them seriously discontented, or actually lead to population extinction? I will attempt to show that dangerously

73

maladaptive beliefs and practices are commonplace in folk societies, as they are in our own, but before doing so, we need to examine another source of maladaptation. That source is inequality, and its universal presence in human societies both small and large makes it inevitable that ways of doing things that may serve the needs of some people in a society will be harmful to others.

Chapter *4*

Women and Children First

From Inequality to Exploitation

Rarely are cultural practices equally adaptive for all members of a society. Because no society yet described is completely lacking in social differentiation, the interests of all members of a society are seldom identical. Even in the smallest societies, family and multi-family groups' competing interests often cause bands or camps to break up into still smaller groups or individual families.[1] Until quite recently, all societies placed the well-being of adults above that of children, especially the very young, and with few exceptions men have put their interests above those of women. Even among the relatively egalitarian Aka, Mbuti, and Efe pygmies of Zaire, men ate a higher-protein diet than women, who subsisted primarily on starchy plant food and consequently were in poorer health than men. And like other such societies, these African pygmies distinguished "leaders" from "nonleaders," and these men enjoyed better health.[2] As societies have grown larger and more complex over the course of human history, ever more kinds of inequality have appeared, and since the emergence of the state, a small ruling elite has often been able to further its own interests against those of the great majority of people. For all these reasons, any inquiry into the adaptiveness of certain beliefs or practices must specify whose needs are being served and whose are not.

Until a few thousand years ago, there were no states; today, virtually every person on earth is subject to the authority of one state or another and influenced by still others. The paradox inherent in this rapid process of state formation is that while a minority has typically benefited greatly from the perquisites of power, most people subject to a state's authority have experienced exploitation and even tyranny. As we know only too well, many states have not only neglected and exploited most of their own people, they have polluted and degraded their physical environments. The most powerful of them—those with great military forces—have dominated, conquered, or destroyed neighboring societies. Most states, including many modern ones, have perverted Jeremy Bentham's principled plea for "the greatest happiness for the greatest number" by providing the greatest misery for the greatest number while reserving happiness for a privileged few.

When we think of tyranny, we are inclined to conjure up an image of a despotic autocratic ruler or a small military elite, but there are many other absolute forms of inequality. When parents in a small-scale society choose to practice infanticide, we may regard their decision as an adaptive necessity for people who fear they cannot adequately support another child. But the decision of adults in a society to enhance their well-being or assure their survival by killing some of their infants may not be qualitatively distinct from the desire of a small minority within a militarily powerful state to advance its interests by exploiting or destroying many other people. Successful human adaptation is often achieved by some at the expense of others— children, women, the very old, the less powerful.

Many European scholars, including Rousseau, Schmoller, and Marx, believed that there had once been a period when all people in a society were equal and that it was only with the coming of "civilization" that inequality developed. Anthropologists often agree that there is equality among people in small-scale societies, but by equality (or egalitarianism, as they are likely to call it) they mean the absence of significant distinctions among people except for those based on sex, age, and ability.[3] These distinctions are universal. In addition, some very small societies also make distinctions based on wealth, power, or kinship. As we saw in chapter 1, Mbuti men who owned hunting nets "rented" them to men who did not.

Nevertheless, some economic anthropologists believe that people in small societies had no motive to exploit one another because for such people the economic necessities of life were in ample supply. In his influential book, *Stone Age Economics*, Marshall Sahlins even argued that a lack of exploitation was also typical of some more complex societies such as small chiefdoms, because the even-handed manner in which chiefs redistributed goods and services resulted in society-wide reciprocity, not inequality.[4] Subsequent research has shown that Sahlins's egalitarian vision was idealized. In many small chiefdoms, indeed probably in most of them, chiefs advanced their own interests at the expense of lower-status people. To take a single example, Ifaluk Atoll in the Western Carolines was populated by fewer than 500 people, a small-scale society by any standard. Yet clan chiefs on Ifaluk had a decided advantage over people of lower status. As Laura Betzig has pointed out, chiefs took home almost twice as much fish after a communal catch as others did, and they regularly received food from distantly related person.[5] Instead of redistributing this food among the population, they gave a disproportionate amount to their close kin, from whom they received various goods and services in return. Chiefs were so favored by their positions of power that they spent only about one half as much time in physical labor as other men of the same age, and they were able to have more children than other men as well.[6]

Most modern sociologists have been anything but romantic about social equality. With few exceptions, they have believed that inequality is ubiquitous. Kingsley Davis and several other followers of Talcott Parsons argued that inequality is inevitable because all societies must have social differentiation. For Davis and other functionalists the presence of inequality was a functional necessity because the roles that must be played in a society are not equally rewarding, and therefore some must have a higher ranking than others. Janitors and judges, for example. This phenomenon may actually occur to some extent in all societies, but in an influential essay, Rolf Dahrendorf argued that the root cause of inequality was not the inevitability of social differentiation but the fact that all societies have rules that are enforced by sanctions. People who break those rules lose prestige and their claim to equality with persons who conform to the rules.[7] This happened to a man named Cephu among the Mbuti pygmies. He broke an important hunting rule by setting up his net in front of other peoples' nets in a futile attempt to kill more game. He lost considerable prestige and dignity as a result. Rule violators may indeed lose prestige, or their lives, just as people who assiduously follow important rules, such as those calling for sharing, bravery, piety, respect, and the like, may gain prestige and, with it, power.

However, Dahrendorf did not acknowledge the extent to which individual differences also make inequality inevitable. Individuals vary in attributes, such as intelligence and strength, that are valued in all societies and others, such as a calm temperament, that may be valued in some societies but not in others. Those who suffer serious physical injury or illness may be treated by others as social inferiors, and as we acknowledged earlier, no society could conceivably treat the very young as the equals of adults (sometimes this applies to the elderly as well). And although women are not nearly as incapable of engaging in hunting, warfare, or other physically demanding activities as has traditionally been thought—Agta women in the Philippines were able hunters, and Dahomean women in Benin made excellent soldiers—their relative lack of physical strength and the demands of pregnancy and nursing have also contributed to the universal phenomenon of sexual inequality.[8] So, I should note, has the widespred practice in small, traditional societies of men's deciding whom women should marry and then forcing them to remain in marriages as subordinates to their husbands.[9]

Finally, it may also be the case that humans are predisposed to seek advantages based on inequality. It was once thought that small bands of people who lived solely by hunting and gathering—people who may have lived as our Pleistocene ancestors did—made no distinction among themselves in terms of privilege or advantage, but there is growing evidence that (like the Mbuti of Zaire and the San of the Kalahari) even those populations that emphasize egalitarianism recognize some people as leaders, and when the available resources become more abundant, people tend to make even more distinctions among themselves in terms of wealth and authority, including hereditary authority. For example, the Chumash Indians, who lived on the Channel Islands off the southern California coast and on the adjacent mainland, were the first California Indians to be contacted by Spanish explorers. These people practiced no agriculture but lived entirely by hunting, gathering, and fishing. Although they made ocean-worthy canoes, their technology was otherwise not greatly developed. They lived in rude huts, and despite the often chilly temperatures of winter and spring, the women wore nothing more than a flimsy skirt and the men went entirely nude. Nevertheless, they

78

had clamshell money, which they avidly sought to accumulate, and their society was dominated by an upper class of people whose power was based on the wealth this money represented. The Chumash also had lower classes, and they kept slaves, as did some other tribes in California, none of which grew any crops. These small societies recognized chiefs who exercized considerable power, they often had social classes, and they all possessed money.[10] "Primitive" egalitarianism, like "primitive" harmony, is often more illusion than reality.

Despite the presence of various social and cultural mechanism to create equality, or the appearance of equality, social inequality is a universal reality of human existence; it leads to competing interests within a society, interests that can generate conflict and exploitation alike. However, when and for whom exploitation may be maladaptive are complex questions. I discussed earlier why adults may practice infanticide in an effort to enhance their well-being. Although this survival strategy serves the interests of adults at the expense of children, it can, under circumstances of food shortage, be a perfectly rational one. If the population is to survive, young adults must live to reproduce again. However callous it may seem to an outsider, children can be replaced. The same argument can be made for the practice of killing the elderly.

Infanticide, however, can be purely selfish. Napoleon Chagnon's vivid descriptions of the ferocious Yanomamo Indians of Venezuela's tropical forest have made them one of the best known small societies in the world. According to Chagnon, a woman was forbidden to have intercourse with her husband from the time that she first discovered she was pregnant until she weaned her child. Rather than endure prolonged celibacy, some young couples chose to kill their infants.[11] Similarly, the torture of animals—which occurs widely in a great many societies, including our own—has no evident adaptive value unless one wishes to argue that people derive some psychological benefit by redirecting aggression from their fellow men (something that could be socially disruptive) to wild or domestic animals. Nelson Graburn has observed that Inuit adults, who prized emotional equanimity and nonviolence, nevertheless encouraged children to torture small animals and birds to death, and he "often" saw men laugh at or strike mortally wounded animals.[12] Almost 100 years earlier, Lucien Turner similarly reported seeing Inuit hunters "mock" mortally wounded animals.[13] If this behavior served to deflect aggression from humans onto animals, as adaptivists might claim, it was not notably successful, because the Inuit were prone to outbursts of lethal violence and in fact killed one another at a very high rate.[14]

Even more difficult to explain in adaptive terms than the practice of torturing wild animals was the cruelty the Inuit inflicted on their invaluable sled dogs. Perhaps because they were economically important, dogs were usually not maltreated, but sometimes men whipped or kicked them, and if a dog were injured so that it could not pull its weight on a dogsled, it might be "beaten mercilessly" and left behind to starve.[15] One can easily make an argument for leaving a lame dog behind, but why should it be beaten mercilessly? The Inuit were not unique in this. The Mbuti, who relied on their dogs for hunting, acording to Colin Turnbull nevertheless ". . . kicked them mercilessly from the day they are born to the day they die."[16] Turnbull does not explain why such behavior was adaptive for the Mbuti. In fact, he was puzzled and dismayed by the pleasure they derived from watching wounded animals suffer agonizing pain. Like outbursts of violence, the practice of torturing domestic animals should not be considered adaptive simply because people enjoy doing it. For example, men among the Machiguenga Indians of the Peruvian Amazon were not particularly warlike or aggressive, and Machiguenga women and children were seldom subjected to capricious violence, yet Machiguenga men sometimes treated their hunting dogs with callous cruelty. According to Michael Baksh, they rubbed hot chili peppers in their dog's mouth and forced them to swallow ". . . more for the entertainment of watching the animals howl, run crazily, and writhe in agony than to prepare them for hunting."[17]

In most of the world's societies, large as well as small, adults have sometimes aborted fetuses and abandoned or killed infants and children. As sad and exploitive as these practices are, they can often be explained as rational expedients for individuals or societies whose resources would not permit them to rear more children. But severe child abuse is much more difficult to portray as an adaptive practice. The practices of abandoning, beating, burning, starving, imprisoning, and murdering children are not confined to Western, urbanized societies, although they are more common in such societies than in smaller, less complex ones. Still, similar forms of severe child abuse have occurred in small, non-Western societies,[18] and they are increasing in brutality and frequency in many parts of the world.[19] Child abuse is often a nonrational behavior, and if any case can be made for child abuse as an adaptive behavior, it could only be that adults are serving their own idiosyncratic need to brutalize a helpless child. This, clearly would be a stark form of exploitation. It would also be a form of psychopathology, not socially adaptive conduct. The exploitation of children in prostitution, industry, or agriculture has also been cruel and exploitive, but at least these kinds of exploitation occasionally had economic advantages for the families involved.

Male Dominance

Men's subjugation of women is another common but potentially counterproductive adaptive strategy. The extent to which women are subordinate to men varies among societies. In some places, men's dominance over women is slight and may in fact be nonexistent, but in a great many societies, including some small-scale foraging populations, women's conduct has been largely controlled by men, women have been considered by men to be their spiritual, moral, and intellectual inferiors, and they have been excluded from the equal exercise of religious or political power.[20] In Europe during the Middle Ages, women were excluded from all political activity, and their legal rights were minimal compared to those of men. Among the many sins attributed to them were vanity, pride, greed, promiscuity, gluttony, drunkenness, bad temper, and fickleness.[21] Many other societies, both small and large, have treated women similarly; but it should go without saying that women have always had some legitimate rights and powers, and along with their considerable informal powers of suasion, these rights have sometimes allowed women to impose their will on men, especially in domestic affairs. Nevertheless, men dominate public affairs, and they typically use their physical strength (or the threat of it) to control women; in doing so, they leave no doubt about whose interests are being served. Men have approved wife beating in virtually every folk society.[22]

In many such societies, choice, desirable foods were denied to women simply because men reserved them for themselves. In his review of food taboos, Frederick Simoons reported that after women among the Chukchee of Siberia had done all the work of slaughtering, butchering, and cooking reindeer, Chukchee men ate their fill, leaving only scraps and bones for the women. These men left no doubt about how they felt when they said, "Being women, eat crumbs."[23] The Chukchee were hardly unique. Peter Freuchen observed that

81

for the Hudson Bay Inuit, boiled meat was "man's food, too good for women to have."[24] Similarly, in many parts of aboriginal Australia, women were not allowed access to food that men were especially fond of; instead, the men ate alone, then "threw" what they could not eat to the women.[25]

These practices do more than signal male dominance. The impoverished diets of women in these and many other societies can have harmful health consequences. In societies in places as culturally different as India, West Africa, Morocco, and South America, women continue to be so regularly deprived of animal protein and fat that they and their children are more vulnerable than adult men to disease and death.[26] A particularly macabre example comes from the Fore of highland Papua New Guinea, where men so monopolized access to animal flesh that women and children sought to supplement their diets by eating the flesh of deceased relatives. As a consequence, they contracted kuru, a deadly neurological disease caused by a slow virus communicated through cannibalism.[27] In these societies and many others where men denied choice food to women, they sometimes sought to justify their actions by referring to religious ideology, taboos, or women's health, but very often their were no justifications, only a transparent sense of their superiority and their lack of concern for women's welfare. This same unconcern sometimes underlay practices such as foot binding, female genital mutilation, selling daughters into prostitution, gang rape, and wife beating.

The division of labor between men and women has not usually been equitable, either. In many small societies around the world, women were required to carry extremely heavy loads on their backs, heads, or foreheads by means of tumplines. It was not at all uncommon for women to carry loads of wood, water, and other valuables that were in excess of their own body weight. Carrying these heavy loads was mandatory because, men frequently said, it was imperative for men to carry weapons to defend women against enemy raiders. However, women very often caried heavy loads when men were far away guarding nothing and were, in fact, idle. What is more, after colonial governments curtailed warfare to such an extent that there were no more raids by enemies and hence there could be no imperative reason for men to carry weapons, men still did not carry water, wood, or other heavy loads. There is no direct evidence that these practices reduced women's fertility or the risk of miscarriage or, for that matter, they they increased birth spacing where that was desirable. But these practices certainly reflect men's dominance over women and their lack of concern for their welfare. For example, men among Efe pygmies of the Ituri forest in Zaire were relatively considerate of their women, but on those rare occasions that men killed a large animal, they did not carry it back to camp; instead, they returned to camp empty-handed, and then required the women to fetch the game and carry it back.[28]

Societies with cults that separated men from women, such as predominated in Melanesia and South America, were particularly blatant about men's superiority to women.[29] In highland Papua New Guniea, for example, men confidently asserted that they were superior to women in every way, and women often said that they agreed.[30] But women's acceptance of men's superiority has by no means been universal. Women have considerable power in some European peasant societies,[31] and in many other societies, arrogant expressions of male dominance result in divisive antagonism between men and women. Among the Kamba of Kenya, women bitterly resented it when men told them that they had "small, smooth brains" and could not think for themselves or openly boasted "we buy them, we give them orders, they are not like men."[32] And the frequent threats by Mehinaku Indian men to gang-rape women reaffirmed male dominace but left women not only fearful but angry.[33] Although all societies have sanctions against many forms of rape, including gang rape, prohibited types of rape nevertheless appear to have occurred in all societies.

Is there an adaptive advantage to a society for men so ruthlessly to assert their superiority over women? Perhaps it helps men to maintain or enhance their aggressive self-confidence, masculine solidarity, or separateness from women. But these qualities have not been shown incontrovertibly to be adaptive either for men or for the societies in which they live. And even if, for the sake of argument, we were to agree that these are socially positive attributes, the socially negative consequences of male dominance would appear to be both more numerous and more damaging. That is so because in all societies, especially small-scale ones, there are important services that men want and need women to perform, such as engaging in satisfying sexual relations with them, giving birth to children, providing child care, gathering wild foods, cultivating, fetching water and wood, and preparing meals, to mention only some elementary roles that women are typically expected to play. If the antagonism between men and women becomes extreme, women may refuse to provide some of

83

these services, may delay in doing so, or may choose to do so inefficiently. In addition, the resulting atmosphere of hostility and fear may interfere with men's lives in many ways and may even endanger their health and threaten their survival.[34]

To illustrate how badly things can go wrong between men and women, let us consider the Gusii of western Kenya. A large, horticultural population near Lake Victoria, the Gusii lived in clans that were territorially separated from other clan territories by areas of uninhabited bush. Because these clans were exogamous, men had to seek wives from neighboring clans. Many societies have chosen marriage partners in the same way without social conflict, but Gusii clans were so hostile to one another that most had feuded in the past, and animosities continued to run high. A Gusii proverb said, "Those whom we marry are those whom we fight."[35] This presented the Gusii with a dilema, but instead of attempting to soothe these tensions as other societies with a similar form of marriage have done, the Gusii made matters worse.[36]

According to Robert LeVine, although the Gusii attempted to prevent open hostilities between the groom's relatives and the relatives of the bride from an alien clan, they nevertheless inflamed an already tense situation in many ways. When the groom first visited the bride's home before the wedding ceremony, he was accosted by a crowd of highly vocal women who colorfully criticized his appearance and taunted him by declaring that his penis was too small, adding that he would be impotent on the wedding night in any event. When the bride visited the groom's relatives, she found the door to her future mother-in-law's house barred by a crowd of hostile women who, not to be outdone, screamed insults at her, mocked and pinched her, and sometimes even smeared dung on her lips before allowing her inside.[37]

Receptions like these could not be expected to herald a tranquil and loving marriage, and neither could the events of the wedding night. Starting matters off on the worst possible foot, the bride refused to disrobe or go to bed, and then she did everything in her considerable power (including tying her pubic hair over her vagina) to prevent her husband from achieving penetration. This behavior was traditional; girls were taught to resist their husbands in such ways, including a practice called *ogotega* in which the vaginal muscles were kept so tense that penetration was said to be impossible.[38] It was also said that a "fierce" bride might prevent her husband from successfully

84

achieving sexual intercourse for as long as a week, but more commonly, young male friends of the groom (who waited outside the nuptial house) intervened and helped the groom by holding the bride's legs apart, a practice that no doubt did nothing to lessen her hostility. Once intercourse finally took place, the husband was obligated to repeat it as often as possible that night (six times was the minimally respectable number) and in the process to cause his bride as much pain as possible.

Interclan hostility contributed to this extraordinary antagonism, but Gusii culture was pervaded by sexual hostility even among members of the same clan. For example, in a custom known as *ogosonia*, when adolescent boys were recuperating from the effects of being circumcised, adolescent girls from the same clan came to the hut where the boys were secluded. Maliciously, they disrobed, danced provocatively, challenged them to have intercourse, and made disparaging comments about their genitals. The girls were triumphant if their actions resulted in erections that caused the boys intense pain when their partly healed incisions burst open.[39]

Both before and after marriage, Gusii men were said to have been so frustrated sexually that they resorted to rape. Whether sexual frustration was the cause or not, the fact is that the Gusii committed rape almost four times as often as the average rate in the United States. In 1937, there were so many rapes that the British colonial government had to threaten military action, and in 1950 there were so many convictions for rape that there were not enough prison facilities to hold the offenders.[40] Not surprisingly, married life itself was always distant and often hostile.[41] The antagonism between Gusii men and women clearly caused considerable stress, and if it served any useful social purpose, it has yet to be identified.

That Gusii women were often depressed by the conditions of their lives is unremarkable. In most non-Western societies, women suffer from depression more often than men do, and as we saw in the last chapter, women also react to the dominance of men by sometimes engaging in social protest or becoming possessed. But they may take more direct action, too, action that can create serious problems for men. The Pokot women who so brazenly and defiantly berated and beat an errant husband in the practice of *kilipat* (described in chapter 6) were almost certainly permitted to do so by Pokot men because they feared that otherwise the women would take recourse to more lethal steps such as witchcraft or poisoning. Many Pokot men refused to eat any food cooked by one of their wives for fear of being poisoned (only a mother or sister might be trusted enough to prepare food), and many others said that their wives were attempting to kill them with witchcraft. A number of thoroughly disgruntled wives openly admitted that their husbands' suspicions were warranted. With the help of their sons, these women said that they were doing their best to kill their husbands through either witchcraft or the use of poison. One woman told me that she had succeeded. A comparable level of sexual antagonism and fear existed among the Kamba, and to a somewhat lesser extent, the Sebei of Uganda.[42] As Walter Goldschmidt put it, male domination among the Sebei was "deeply institutionalized and internalized" and as a result, "the relationships between the sexes are overwhelmingly manipulative, lacking in trust, and hostile."[43] It is unclear what positive social functions these hostile relationships might serve, but it is obvious that an atmosphere in which men demean and beat women who in turn try to kill their husbands is quite literally poisoned.

It would seem that both individual well-being and social stability would be better served by fostering affection, cooperation, and a spirit of shared interests between men and women. Of course, some societies have done exactly that. Men and women among the Mbuti were often affectionate, cooperated economically, and with the exception of one, albeit important, religious ceremony, men generally treated women with respect and consideration. Mbuti men did beat their wives now and then, but women were expected to fight back, and sometimes they did so with intimidating success.[44] Among the Cheyenne Indians, men were clearly dominant, but they treated women with respect, romantic love was not uncommon, and many husbands and wives often remained devoted to each other throughout life.[45] Societies like the Mbuti and Cheyenne—and there have been many others—that join men and women in cooperation rather than hostility would appear to have been at an adaptive advantage over neighboring societies that were divided by sexual hatred.

Political Exploitation

For every Samuel who warned against despotism or every Solon who refused to become a tyrant when given the chance, there have been untold numbers of despots. It is no surprise, then, that when common people the world over have written about their rulers they have so often deplored their selfishness, and in turn, rulers have complained about the ungovernability and ungratefulness of the unruly masses. The prosperity of the few at the expense of the many has been an unending concern of humanity. Recently, the same concern has appeared in the works of scholars interested in cultural adaptation. So, for example, after assessing the relative health of hunter-gatherers, horticulturalists, and urban civilizations, Mark Nathan Cohen concluded that civilized states are superior to all other forms of political organizations because they can absorb or destroy nonstate systems but that they do so at the expense of many of their own people.[46] Jerome Barkow has similarly concluded that one of the reasons why maladaptive cultural traits exist is the tendency of powerful elites to favor practices that are in their interests, not those of the bulk of the population, even when they have come to power as a consequence of revolutions that were intended to achieve equality.[47]

These ideas, so self-evident to most scholars, can be troubling to students of human evolution because they suggest that the culmination of our social and cultural history is an increase not in the well-being of most humans but in that of the powerful few and the social institutions they control. A few simple facts should be sufficient to illustrate this point. The malnourished adolescent poor of London in the late eighteenth century were so short that only two of eighty-one ethnic groups for which comparable data exist are known to have been shorter—two badly malnourished populations in New Guinea.[48] In 1840 in Manchester, England, the average age at death for gentlemen was 38, for traders 20, and for unskilled laborers, 17. In Sheffield in the 1860s, the upper class lived on average to be almost 50, while the lower classes lived to an average of less than 30.[49] In 1901 the average life expectancy at birth for all of England was sixty years for the upper class and only half of that for the lowest class.[50] Class differences like these were hardly lost on Karl Marx, who lived in London from 1849 until his death in 1883. There is no need to detail the wretchedness of the lives of the poor relative to the comforts and good health of the wealthy in the past, nor presumably is there a need to remind readers that large numbers of poor continue to suffer in modern states. The infant mortality rate for blacks in the United States is still twice that of white babies[51]—and much higher in certain especially poor areas[52]—while the lowest-income Americans continue to have higher rates of both physical and mental illness than Americans with higher incomes.

Before the advent of republics and democracies, most large states were largely or entirely despotic. The Romanov dynasty was an egregious example of tyranny. While the Russian nobility lived in great luxury, over 90 percent of the population lived in conditions that gave rise to clichés like "abject poverty." The state was maintained by a vast apparatus of secret police and a loyal military.[53] Later, and in the interest of equality, Stalin would rule by an even more concerted use of terror, but inequality did not vanish. Still later, states like Romania and East Germany would do the same. Just before its collapse in 1990, the East German Ministry for State Security—the infamous Stasi— employed over 34,000 full-time secret police, 6,000 of whom did nothing but monitor phone calls. In addition, the Stasi used many part-time informants.[54] Still, the use of so many secret police and the concerted use of terror, including torture, was not enough to ensure the survival of the East German government or that of many other despotic states. Every annual report by Amnesty International documents the practice of state terror by a depressingly large number of governments, many of which probably would not be able to survive without it. As commonplace as terror has been as an instrument of power in archaic as well as modern industrial states, it is not unique to societies as complex as states. Elman Service has insisted that most nascent states did not rely on repressive controls based on force,[55] but in fact, although some small states did minimize the use of repressive force, many did not, and the roots of political coercion by a ruling minority over the majority can be found even in small-scale societies.[56]

The use of coercive force by an individual or kin group against the rest of a society sometimes occurs even in small hunting and gathering societies. There are also accounts of a highly aggressive man or several related men attempting to dominate a hunting and gathering band in societies as diverse as the Inuit, Hadza, Australians, and San. However, these attempts to dominate are typically short-lived, as the remainder of the band either exiles the potential tyrant or kills him. Religious specialists such as prophets or shamans were sometimes able to exercise power over a majority of the society for longer periods. A prophet among the Kikuyu of Kenya could achieve a dominant

88

position of authority for a period of years, as could a particularly successful shaman among the Inuit and some Siberian tribes.[57]

To take another example, warfare occurred in the western highlands of Papua New Guinea, but it was intermittent enough to allow the development of large populations that produced surpluses of pigs and agricultural products. Political leaders in this region, known as big men, were specialists in controlling the exchange of these surpluses. Big men might grow wealthy as a result, but when they were successful their people benefited as well, and if these leaders were not successful, they could be replaced. But in the eastern highlands, warfare was as vicious and unremitting as it has been anywhere on earth. All other human activities, including providing food, paled into insignificance. Indeed, so much time and energy were devoted to warfare that both agriculture and pig husbandry suffered. Subsistence was made even more difficult because people were forced to live in palisaded villages chosen for defense, not for their proximity to agricultural land or pig pasturage.

Warfare among these societies was so ferocious that entire populations were sometimes annihilated. In order to survive, a society needed a great war leader who could rally his own warriors to battle and recruit the survivors of decimated populations as allies. In this climate of unending warfare, political leaders became despots who ruled by ruthless intimidation. Such men took other men's wives and killed anyone who objected. Capable of every moral outrage, they were usually beyond the reach of public opinion because their people needed them. Some of these despots ruled for over twenty years, and although they ran roughshod over the people they led, they also defended them against their enemies in a world where death in war was an ever-present threat.[58] Such warrior leaders not only gave an adaptive advantage to the populations they led, they were a vital necessity for them. But the system of warfare that prevailed in this region was clearly not adaptive for the area as a whole. Even those societies that survived the endless attacks of their neighbors lost many lives and lived under needlessly deprived economic circumstances.

In other small-scale societies, a kin group such as a clan, might attempt to impose its will on the rest of the society by force, and so might a secret society. Sometimes a powerful political leader could consolidate his power through the support of a clan or a secret society, and together they could thoroughly tyrannize the rest of the people in their society. Audrey Richards observed that a chief among the Bemba of Rhodesia ". . . practices savage mutilations" on those who offended him or injured his interests. Bemba chiefs came from the ruling crocodile clan, which was so named, it was said, because like crocodiles, they seized the common people with their teeth and tore them "to bits."[59] Sometimes the tyranny of chiefs like these was restrained by a council of elders or wealthy and powerful men (as sometimes happened among the Bemba), but from Africa to Polynesia, chiefs, their families, and retainers often ruled over the great majority of the population through the use of force. These political systems—to call them reigns of terror would not be far wrong—were sometimes replaced by more moderate political systems or developed into pro-tostates headed by monarchs who levied taxes, impressed labor, ruled armies, and exercised increasingly absolute power. It is in these larger state systems—managed by bureaucrats, supported by priesthoods and human sacrifice—that social stratification and political oppression became truly institutionalized.

Yet social stratification developed in some small-scale societies that lacked not only bureaucracies and priesthoods but cultivation as well. This was true of many pastoral, nomadic societies, and we have earlier mentioned the small, nonagricultural California Indians who were organized into social classes based on wealth. So were the Kwakiutl Indians of Vancouver Island, who were mentioned in chapter 2 because Ruth Benedict was criticized for characterizing them as megalomanic. They have long generated controversy. Like Benedict, Franz Boas, who studied them for many years, was puzzled by their potlatches in which men gave away or destroyed their wealth simply, it seemed, to gain prestige by dominating and humiliating other men who could not afford to destroy or give away as many valuables as they could. Boas did not refer to this practice as a form of social pathology (although there were times when he appeared to have thought of it in those terms), but Benedict did, as we have seen. Some years after Boas did his research among the Kwakiutl, other anthropologists reinterpreted the potlatch as an adaptive cultural system that equalized food consumption among local groups that were subject to periodic food shortages, thereby benefiting the entire population.[60] Seen from this perspective, potlatching was, as Marvin Harris so charmingly mistook it, ". . . a system, explicable in scientific terms, where previously there was nothing but the unintelligible ravings of megalomaniacs."[61]

This interpretation was based on the erroneous belief that the Kwakiutl were a classless society. Although there were never more than a few thousand of these Indians and they lived by hunting and fishing without practicing agriculture, they were nevertheless socially stratified. A closer look at the Kwakiutl, at least during the period before they were depopulated and disorganized by European contact, strongly suggests that the benefits of potlatching accrued primarily to Kwakiutl chiefs, not the entire population. As Ernest E. Ruyle has argued (and others have concurred), Kwakiutl society was dominated by a chiefly class that controllled wealth along with supernatural and political power. Chiefs owned all of the food resources available to the population, while most of the population were consumers who were obliged to contribute as much as one half of their food production to the chiefs. The chiefs then redistributed most of this food (and other wealth) to the commoners but retained some of it for themselves, and in the process of redistribution, they gained the continuing support and dependency of common people who, in essence, labored largely for the benefit of their chief.

The Kwakiutl also possessed large numbers of slaves—perhaps 15 percent of the population—who were owned by chiefs. These people were an important economic asset to chiefly families, who for all practical purposes lived by the labor of their slaves and the contributions of the commoners. Although the potlatch may have helped to equalize the availability of food during times of shortage, the chiefs always ate well, while commoners and slaves sometimes went hungry. Here, then, was a small society in which a chiefly minority lived well at the expense of the majority. Moreover, because many of the chief's slaves were obtained by making war against neighboring societies, it might also be said that they posed a threat to their weaker neighbors.[62]

The Aztec Empire is a more extreme example of the success a small elite had in using religion and military power to defeat neighboring societies (many of whom were enslaved and then eaten) without sharing the spoils of conquest with the general population. The powerful armies of the Aztecs and their allies were usually successful in battle. Like other victorious armies they exacted tribute in the form of gold, food, and other valuables, but they also demanded slaves who, along with prisoners captured in battle, were returned to the Aztec homelands where they were sacrificed before being eaten. Almost all of the wealth taken in battle, including the flesh from the sacrificed victims, went to the Aztec elite—the king, nobles, and priests.

Michael Harner and Marvin Harris have argued that this "cannibal kingdom" developed because population growth along with progressive degradation of the always limited sources of wild and domestic animals (mostly turkeys, wildfowl, deer, rabbits, dogs, and other small animals) in the Valley of Mexico left the Aztecs critically deprived of animal protein.[63] Their nutritional interpretation of Aztec cannibalism has not escaped criticism,[64] but there is no doubt that the Aztecs scarificed large numbers of people every year—estimates range from a low of 15,000 to as many as 250,000 per year—and that they ate almost all of them. There is also no doubt that human flesh was a delicacy that was highly prized. To be sure, Aztec human sacrifice was justified as a religious imperative demanded by their seemingly insatiable gods, but the people who were sacrificed atop Aztec temples by having their hearts torn out need not have been eaten to placate the gods, and if the gods somehow required that the victims' flesh be consumed, one might have expected it to have been done with elaborate ritual preparations and perhaps even some trepidation on the part of the population.

This was not the case. Sacrificed bodies were rolled down the temple stairs (probably made as steep as they were to facilitate the process) to waiting men who carved them up as adroitly and dispassionately as any butcher might deal with a side of beef before the various parts were carried away to be seasoned, cooked, eaten, and hugely enjoyed. The desire for human flesh was so great that many wars were fought for no other reason than the capture of prisoners, and military operations against neighboring societies were virutally unceasing.[65] It need hardly be added that the societies that were victimized by Aztec armies regarded the Aztec Empire as a scourge, and when the opportunity came to fight against them as allies of Cortés, many were eager to do so.

Not only were the Aztecs a menace to their neighbors, their ruling elite reserved most of the benefits of their conquests for themselves. Except for priests, who chose poverty, the Aztec rulers lived in grand houses and provided themselves with luxuries that Cortés and his men thought stupendous. Cortés found Montezuma's palace in Tenochtitlán so beautiful and magnificent that he said it was indescribable and declared that there was "nothing like it in Spain."[66] Little is known about the life of Aztec commoners, but it is clear that they did not share in their rulers' luxury. Free men gladly served in the army, as it was a potential means to honor and prestige, but they served at a distinct disadvantage. The nobles who formed the elite of the Aztec army wore helmets and body armor and used shields. Commoners were unprotected, and as a result they suffered disproportionately in battle.[67] Commoners also lived modestly. Poorer still were landless peasants, and below them were slaves, many of whom were Aztecs who sold themselves into slavery because they could not otherwise provide for themselves.[68] The splendors of Aztec culture cannot be denied, but they were achieved at great cost by the many largely for the benefit of the ruling few. There are many other examples of the same phenomenon.

The rapid development of the Zulu Empire under Shaka dramatically illustrates the ability of one ruthless man to establish absolute rule over half a million people. It also illustrates the difficulties of sustaining such a despotic rule of terror. Around 1800 the Zulus were one of several dozen small Nguni-speaking groups in and around what is now Natal in southeast Africa. Usually led by a petty chief with limited powers, these people herded cattle and goats and cultivated crops, sometimes shifting their territory every few years. The idea of stronger chieftainships was in the air among the Nguni at that time, as it was with many other Bantu-speaking people. Some stronger chiefs had the power to use force against wrongdoers and to collect taxes, but they redistributed much of this wealth, and their power was constrained by clan elders, the interests of young men who formed military-age sets, and persons who possessed wealth or supernatural power.

Around this time, a chief's son from the Mthethwa (a tribe perhaps twice as large as the Zulus) fled for his life after being accused of intriguing against his father. Now calling himself Dingiswayo ("he who was caused to wander"), the outcast returned in 1805 to find his father dead and wrested political control from his brother. Warfare at this time was a relatively bloodless affair that seldom lasted over a day. In what is now a well-known story, Dingiswayo reorganized his warriors into regiments and demanded a disciplined performance, attacking in a crescent formation that allowed them to envelop their enemies. It has often been assumed that these changes in military organization must have been produced by knowledge of European practices acquired by Dingiswayo during his wanderings, but in fact the changes he made had clear precedents in Nguni culture.[69] Whatever their provenance, Dingiswayo's men used these new tactics to conquer some thirty small chiefdoms. As long as these people agreed to pay tribute, Dingiswayo left them to manage their own affairs and while his conquests led to some bloodshed, his rule changed relatively few lives.

Shaka was also the son of a chief who sent him away, along with his mother, presumably because of an offense on her part. Shaka joined Dingiswayo's army, where he became an officer and made further innovations in tactics. When his father died in 1816, Shaka returned to claim power, killing his brother in the process. Two years later, Dingiswayo died, and Shaka began his campaign to rule his own empire. With an army that initially numbered only a few hundred men, he built a force of over 100,000 that defeated over thirty tribes and established his suzerainty over half a million people. Unlike Dingiswayo, Shaka was not a magnanimous conqueror. Often his armies killed everyone who resisted them—women and children as well as men—and the numbers of dead were appalling. For example, in 1826 Shaka ordered visiting British traders to join his army of 50,000 in a campaign against his most truculent enemy, the Ndwandwe. Henry Fynn, who took part in the battle, reported that it took no longer than ninety minutes for the Zulu army to destroy the Ndwandwe, leaving some 40,000 men, women, and children dead on the field.

Shaka's army was aided by excellent intelligence, but it relied on terror to destroy the fighting spirit of any potential enemy. So many populations fled from his terror that huge areas around Zululand were uninhabited, a circumstance that Shaka turned to his advantage by maintaining these areas as a buffer zone around his empire. Some chiefs who fled Shaka's terror created kingdoms of their own based on the Zulu model. One that was established in Zambia controlled over 500,000 square miles.

Shaka did not rule his empire solely by terror. He created allies by awarding honors and gifts to his armies and redistributed war booty (especially cattle) to his rich and powerful supporters. He also killed those who opposed him, especially those who were thought to possess supernatural power, and he developed his own reputation for knowledge of divination and magic. But most of all he relied on terror, not because he was a madman, as Max Gluckman mistakenly wrote, but because he was an astute, calculating ruler, who believed that only the use of terror would permit him to control the unruly clans and tribes in his domain.[70] Few despots have used terror more effectively to intimidate a people. Followed everywhere by his royal executioners, Shaka needed only to point a finger or nod his head for someone whom he had singled out to be killed. The victim would be bashed on the head or have his or her neck broken before the body was beaten almost to a pulp, and then left for all to see with a sharpened stake driven up the anus, while vultures pecked at the corpse.[71] Fynn, who spent a great many days with Shaka, once saw him order the deaths of sixty boys under the age of 12 before he sat down to eat breakfast. When Fynn's comrade Nathaniel Isaacs joined him at Shaka's court, he saw the same daily killings, but unlike Fynn, who was by then somewhat inured to them, he could not bear to watch.[72]

After ten years of tyrannical rule, Shaka's terror (which included the deaths of some 7,000 people after his mother died) became so intolerable that the Zulu people rebelled, and Shaka was assassinated by two of his half-brothers. One of them, Dingane, became the new king. After promising to put an end to the terror, Dingane renewed it with such vigor that with the partial exception of some of his kinsman and his wealthy councillors, everyone in the empire lived in fear. A few grew very wealthy and powerful, and this elite gradually expressed its power in the Great Council that sat next to the new King, Mpande and, as a parliament might, greatly circumscribed his power. Mpande reigned from 1840 to 1872, when he was succeeded by one of his sons, Cetshwayo. Over his three-decade rule, the use of state terror lessened greatly, although it never ceased altogether, and the Zulu people prospered as never before. The great councillors and their families became virtual feudal barons (British visitors who saw them at this time compared them to English lords) who controlled vast lands and herds of cattle and commanded the loyalty of thousands of retainers.

Yet as the king and the wealthy men redistributed some of their wealth, many commoners prospered too, and their loyalty to the Zulu king grew stronger. When British troops invaded Zululand in 1879, loyal Zulus fought against them with such reckless courage that the British concluded they did not fear death. They feared death—inordinately so—but thirty years after the end of the terror, thousands were willing to risk death for their king when the British invaded their territory.[73] Time and circumstance changed not only the exploitation of the Zulu elite but the commitment of Zulu commoners to their culture and political system.

By the end of the eighteenth century, the Asante Empire (previously written Ashanti) in what is now Ghana was incomparably the greatest military power in West Africa, probably in all of Africa.

Thanks to military conquests, Asante kings ruled over an area the size of the state of Wyoming—or England, Wales, and Scotland combined—for perhaps two centuries. By all accounts, the empire was enormously wealthy, perhaps the wealthiest one ever to exist in Africa. Asante wealth came primarily from gold, and wealthy Asante may have held more gold than existed in all the other West African kingdoms combined.[74] Asante gold was known to the Portuguese as early as 1471, and by 1900 over fourteen million ounces of gold had been produced by as many as 40,000 Asante mines.[75] The royal treasury held at least £1,500,000 in the mid 1800s (a huge sum for that time), and it was not uncommon for a member of the royal administration to possess well over £100,000 in gold, a good deal more money than most upper-class British families had at that time.[76]

The hub of the empire was Kumase, a city of about 30,000 permanent residents. There stood the royal palace, the treasury, and enough government offices to house a large, efficient, and officious bureaucracy. Roads for military and commerical traffic spun out from Kumase in all directions. Guarded by special highway police, these roads were usually well maintained despite the constant encroachment of tropical vegetation. Kumase itself was built around huge, tree-shaded avenues that were 50 to 100 yards wide. Now and then wheeled carriages could be seen, pulled by people because there were no horses. Painted in brilliant red and white, well-constructed ornate buildings, some two-stories tall, served as residences, shops, and offices. The streets were swept daily, courtyards were clean, and markets were full of produce.[77]

One of the first Europeans to write about his experiences in Kumase was T. E. Bowditch, who arrived with three other Britons in 1817. They were greeted—or more nearly engulfed—by more than 5,000 people, most of whom were warriors who fired their muskets in the air so often that it quickly became difficult for the awe-struck visitors to see their welcomers through the smoke. But they could not fail to hear the deafening cacophony of drums, horns, rattles, and gongs played with what Bowditch called "a zeal bordering on phrensy.[78] For half an hour the throng continued its welcoming dance, led by officers whose dress excited the wonder of the white men. Each officer wore an immense cap with gilded ram's horns thrusting out from the forehead and topped by three-foot-long plumes of eagle feathers. On their chests they wore red cloth vests covered with amulets of gold and silver, as well as various small bells, shells, and knives that jangled as they moved. Three or four animals' tails dangled down their backs, covering a small bow. A quiver of poisoned arrows hung from their right wrists, and each man brandished a small spear covered with red cloth and silk tassels in his left hand. They wore loose cotton trousers that were stuffed into soft, red leather boots that reached to midthigh, where they were attached by small chains to cartridge belts worn around the waist.

When the welcoming ceased, the British visitors moved on to deposit their supplies and gifts in a large house assigned to them. As they did, they were serenaded by various bands melodiously playing horns and flutes in concert. They were soon ordered to proceed toward the King's palace, while much of the population of Kumase gathered around to stare at them. On the way, they witnessed the disconcerting spectacle of a man being tortured prior to his execution. He was made to walk with his hands tied behind his back, a knife passed through his cheeks; one ear was cut off and carried before him while the other hung by a small piece of skin. His bare back was gashed and bleeding, and knives had been thrust up under each shoulder blade. The man was being led along by a cord that had been passed through his nose. The English visitors needed no further convincing that this kindgom was as cruel as it was grand.

After this unfortunate man had been led away, the four Englishmen and their interpreters were led down a very broad street toward the marketplace, where they were stunned by the "magnificence and novelty" of the next scene that "burst"upon them, as Bowditch put it.[79] They had to avert their eyes to escape the blinding glare of the sun reflected off masses of gold ornaments worn and carried by the King, his court and attendants, and thousands of soldiers. As the Englishmen stared in amazement at the display of gold, no fewer than 100 bands began to play, alternating between drums and horn on the one hand and softer, more melodic tunes from long flutes and instruments that resembled bagpipes on the other. As the music continued, at least 100 huge umbrellas, each large enough to provide shade for thirty people, sprung open, adding bright splashes of scarlet and yellow to the scene.

The dazzled Englishmen were invited to come forward to take the hand of each captain, chief, noble, and important figure in the King's court. Most of these men wore heavy silks thrown over one shoulder like a Roman toga, and they displayed so much gold and silver that the visitors were stunned. Some Asante had attached to their wrists gold ornaments so heavy they had to be supported by boy attendants. Others had solid gold, life-size wolves' or rams' heads suspended from their gold-handled swords. Bowditch noted that the swords were apparently not reserved for ceremonies because their blades were crusted with blood. Large numbers of young soldiers bedecked in leopard skins, wearing elephant-hide cartridge boxes encrusted with gold, silver, blue agate, and shells, and carrying gold-handled swords and long Danish muskets, also ornamented with gold, sat on the ground.

Before they could reach the King, the visitors met the royal executioner, a huge man wearing a gold breastplate and holding before him the execution stool, which was clotted in blood and nearly covered by a caul of human fat. Four of the King's spokesmen came next, and then the keeper of the treasury, who ostentatiously displayed the boxes, scales, and weights of his office, all made of solid gold. Finally the white men reached the King, Osei Bonsu, who courteously extended his hand. About forty years old and heavy-set, the King was every inch a monarch. His dress was magnificent but restrained; he wore a rich green silk robe, and his many gold ornaments were of the finest workmanship. Even his white leather sandals were delicately ornamented with gold and silver. He wore gold castanets on his finger and thumb, which he clapped to enforce silence.

After the king greeted the Englishmen, they were passed on to meet handsome female attendants, small boys holding elephant tails whose job was to clean up the King's spit, eunuchs who oversaw his harem, and hundreds of wives. Prominently displayed by itself under its protective umbrella was a golden stool—symbol of the Asante state—entirely encased in gold. As they moved farther from the King and his retinue, they were greeted by older men of rank who were carried by their slaves, as well as by the children of chiefs and noblemen who were so weighed down by their golden jewelry that they too had to be carried. As the Englishmen were escorted to their quarters, they were entertained by royal dancers, mimics, and buffoons. The mimics were remarkably talented, being able to repeat English phrases and even sentences that they had heard only once before. At eight that evening, the King paid a visit to the Englishmen, asked their names for a second time, and wished them a good night. The Englishmen could not agree on how many people they had seen in Kumase, but they all estimated the number of soldiers alone at 30,000.

Later, the King invited the Englishmen to dinner, where they were treated to a lavish meal of pork, duck, lamb stew, soups, vegetables, oranges, and pineapples, elegantly presented on silver service. The meal was washed down by port, madeira, Dutch cordials, and gin. Bowditch wrote "We never saw a dinner more handsomely served, and never ate better."[80] Astonished by the opulence of the royal court, the Englishmen were almost as impressed by the lifestyle of Asante chiefs. Bowditch observed that ". . . the chiefs are fed bountifully by the labours of their slaves" and that they possessed a large surplus of income that accumulated daily.[81] He also noted that their great wealth was a result of the tribute paid them by conquered people. He did not mention that their slaves also came from the people they had conquered.

Although there were almost constant intrigues around the court, most of the Asante elite—noblemen, army officers, chiefs, priests—lived very well indeed, and four noble families were so exalted that they were above the law.[82] But as the sight of a man being taken away for execution dramatically illustrated, not everyone in the empire prospered equally. Conquered people were ruled by Asante law and power, which offered them some protection, but Asante rule was always arrogant and could be harsh.[83] In addition to paying tribute in gold, ivory, and other valuables, conquered people were required to contribute a quota of slaves and free men as conscripts for military service. Because the Asante were in great need of slaves and soldiers, the numbers conscripted often grew so large that the conquered people rebelled, leading to brutal retribution by Asante troops.

Slaves were not usually treated as badly by the Asante as they were in the plantation economies of the New World, but they were forced to do most of the agricultural work because so many Asante men were in military service. Slaves were also made to do all of the work in the gold mines. A few became wealthy and even married free Asante, but their children always remained slaves, and a master always retained the right to send an offending slave away for human sacrifice, an act that took place often in the empire, as the human fat on the executioner's stool graphically illustrated.[84]

The Asante Empire was controlled by a small political, religious, and military elite, but the great majority of the population consisted of common people whose lives were only somewhat better than those of most slaves. Far from the splendor of the court, most lived modestly on small farms. They were often engaged in military service from which they profited very little and in which many died, often from epidemic diseases. Bowditch described the common people as "ungrateful, insolent and licentious," and the King did not disagree, calling them "the worst people existing" and declaring that he was only able to rule by the draconian use of force.[85] It is impossible to be specific about the level of discontent among the Asante commoners, the conquered peoples, or the slaves, who together made up the bulk of the Asante Empire; but there can be no doubt that the empire was ruled by a small elite that prospered brilliantly from the labor and military service of the many.

Although very different one from another, the Aztecs, Zulus, and Asante were successful in defeating and devastating neighboring societies. If it had not been for the intervention of European forces, all three would probably have maintained their power for many more years. However, smaller and weaker societies that threaten their neighbors are less likely to succeed. For example, the Tonkawa Indians of central Texas were cannibals who, like the Aztecs, raided neighboring societies for captives. Unlike most of the North American Indian societies that practiced cannibalism, the Tonkawa ate people without religious justification or ceremonial purpose.[86] The open gusto with which they consumed human flesh was offensive to neighboring tribes, and the frequent Tonkawa raids in search of more captives were so threatening that in 1862 a coalition of six disparate tribes, united only by their detestation of the Tonkawa, attacked them and killed half the people in the tribe.[87] There are other examples of small societies that have threatened their neighbors and suffered accordingly.

Even the most menacing of conquest states are seldom wholly destroyed, no matter how much they endanger other societies. European armies spread colonial rule over much of the world, and when subject people resisted, as they usually did, they were killed, frequently in very large numbers. Not until the men of Belgium's King Leopold killed an estimated six million people in the Belgian Congo did the world community seriously object, and even then Leopold's only punishment was the loss of control over the Congo as his personal chiefdom. Stalin killed untold millions in the Soviet Union and Eastern Europe, only to die a natural death at the age of 74, and the Stalinist state he created survived for almost four decades after his death. The genocidal murders of the Khmer Rouge in Cambodia killed perhaps two million people, but the Khmer Rouge are still a political force in that tormented land. The only remarkable thing about the fact that states with great military power may exercise genocidal tyranny with impunity is that it is so unremarkable.[88]

It is also unremarkable that societies routinely degrade their own environments and, increasingly, those of their neighbors and the world. The destruction of irreplaceable natural resources began long before the emergence of states. The Paleolithic hunters who drove thousands of large animals over cliffs to their deaths even though they were only able to consume a few of them not only destroyed a precious resource, they endangered their own survival. It is not only modern development that can threaten the destruction of a tropical rain forest, as has occurred in Brazil; even the Semang, a hunting and gathering people of Malaya, can have a significantly negative impact on their forest enviroment. By their heavy smoking of cigarettes and burning of domestic fires, the Semang create a level of atmospheric pollution surpassing that of downtown Los Angeles.[89] And the deforestation of virtually the entire Middle East was carried out by people who lived in small societies as well as by people in the nascent states of that region.[90]

Of course, states have destroyed forests for their own purpose and continue to do so; they have polluted and destroyed environments with the same impunity that they have conquered other peoples. The destruction of native environments brought about by colonial powers has been described so often that it does not bear repeating here, but it should be noted that it was often done in full knowledge that it was the subject people and not the colonial powers that would suffer. Even diseases were sometimes introduced with full awareness of the devastating effects they would have on people who lacked any immunity.[91] Today, great industrial societies spray pesticides, pollute rivers, lakes, and oceans, strew nuclear waste here and there, create smog and acid rain, destroy the ozone layer, and in many other ways endanger human well-being more or less unchecked.

Conclusion

What have these observations about the nature of state systems to do with human maladaptation? The observations themselves may be familiar to many, but their implications for an assessment of maladaptation are far-reaching. First, we have seen that some cultural beliefs and practices can be maladaptive for some or all members of a society, and we have also seen that some societies appear to serve the needs of their members better than others do. However, and this is the point that has been emphasized in this chapter, in all societies—not just class-stratified societies, as Marx believed—some people are better served than others, and in large, complex societies those best served tend to be a small elite whose well-being is achieved at the expense of a majority of the population. By criteria such as well-being, life satisfaction, good health, and longevity, elites are better "adapted" than the rest of the population.

If though the core criterion of adaptation is reproductive success, the equation may have to be turned around because elites today often do not reproduce as often as the majority of the population. Their children are more likely to survive, but there are likely to be fewer of them. The reproductive success of the poor not only sharpens the Malthusian sword that rises above the entire population, it threatens the power and hence the adaptive success of the elite. A population that grows too large to feed itself may meekly die off in starvation or disease, but it may also rebel, destroying the well-being and lives of the elite.[92] Human history is a testimonial to this paradoxical outcome of relative reproductive success, and the future is likely to continue the pattern. Kenya, for example, has quadrupled in population over the past three decades, and its current growth rate of over 4 percent per year is probably the highest in the world. This remarkable rate is evidence of greatly improved health care and food supply, but unless Kenya's very prosperous and powerful political elite can find ways to ameliorate conditions that even now threaten its rapidly growing population of urban and rural poor, Malthus's axiom may bring it to ruin. And so it is too in Bangladesh and many other countries.

The self-interest of elites may also, if only inadvertently, bring benefits to the majority. Irrigation projects are an obvious example. Built by peasant labor for the welfare of the state, they nevertheless tended to benefit the population as a whole. The industrial revolution is another example. The widespread use of machines that allowed one man to do the work of many did not come about in Europe because industrialists, political leaders, or the nobility wanted to improve the lives of working men and women. Workers understood the threat to their livelihood perfectly well, and throughout Europe they smashed machinery in violent protest. Although in England such destruction was punishable by death, the so-called Luddite textile workers began to smash machinery so sytematically that in 1811 the government was forced to deploy more troops to quell their rebellion than Wellington had with him at Waterloo four years later.[93] There can be no doubt that generations of British working men and women suffered appallingly in the mills, factories, and mines that machines made so profitable, but had British leaders chosen to reject industrialization because it was a form of cruel exploitation, Britain would soon have ceased to exist not only as an empire but as an independent nation, with unforeseeable but probably calamitous consequences for the British people, most of whose descendants eventually benefited from Britain's industrial strength. Many advances in health care and food production came about in similar fashion.

Unlike their British counterparts, the rulers of Tokugawa Japan chose to reject advances in military technology. Only twenty-five years after the Portuguese introduced firearms to Japan in the mid sixteenth century, Japanese feudal lords had manufactured so many improved versions of the crude Portuguese originals, and their armies had become so skilled in their use, that Japanese soldiers may have been the best-armed troops in the world at that time.[94] The use of these weapons led to great slaughter in warfare, but it also created the specter of an armed peasantry increasingly able to challenge the shogunate. Armed with a gun, the rudest peasant could kill the noblest lord. By the end of the sixteenth century, the feudal lords had already begun the process of removing firearms from the peasants and preventing their manufacture or import. The peasants were disarmed, and the Tokugawa samurai elite established a military dynasty that ruled for its own benefit until Commodore Perry arrived in Japan in 1853 to find a people with no firearms and indeed no remaining knowledge of how to manufacture them. As a result, the Japanese were defenseless against Western weapons, and to forestall a military occupation, the Tokugawa authorities were compelled to grant trading concessions to the United States and other Western countries. The Meiji restoration of imperial power soon ended Tokugawa rule and replaced it with a Western-oriented government that sought to develop self-sufficiency in European military technology. In the long term, the self-interest of the samurai elite proved to be its undoing.

Inequality in its many forms is universal. The presence of inequality creates the potential for the establishment of traditional beliefs and practices that serve the needs of some people at the expense of others. Because of the presence of inequality and of all the other potential causes of maladaptation, there are many reasons to believe that maladaptive practices would occur widely and have serious consequences. In the following chapters, I will review the evidence pointing to the frequent occurrence of seriously harmful beliefs and practices.

Chapter 5

Sickness, Suffering, and Premature Death

A prevailing assumption among anthropologists who study the medical practices of small, traditional societies is that these populations enjoy good health and nutrition.[1] Instead of finding fault with their medical beliefs and practices, many anthropologists have emphasized the ways in which traditional medical systems function positively to explain the causes of ill health, prescribe remedial action, and offer reassurance to those who are suffering from illness or are fearful of doing so. Indeed, we are often told that seemingly irrational health practices such as food taboos will, once fully understood, prove to be adaptive.[2] It cannot be denied that the traditional medical practices of some small non-Western societies are sometimes effective or that some small, preliterate societies have developed ingenious and effective drugs and therapies that even include some surgical procedures. For example, although admittedly they are atypical of folk societies, the Maasai of East Africa had some relatively skilled surgeons, and other populations, such as the Tungus of Siberia or the Aleut, had specialists who possessed extensive anatomical knowledge of the human body. Many small societies have utilized medically effective drugs: ephedrine, *Rauwolfia serpentina*, curare, coca, quinine, emetine, and many others. Nevertheless, many traditional medical practices were not only useless but could be downright dangerous.

People's faith in the skill of native practitioners, along with the use of confession, suggestion, catharsis, and group support, could lead to positive treatment outcomes, but for many infectious diseases and organic pathologies, available treatments could do more harm than good.

After studying Apache shamans, Morris Opler concluded that ". . . the less he does, the better for the patient."[3] The Yoruba of Nigeria treated convulsions in children with a "tonic" consisting of green tobacco leaves marinated in urine and sometimes topped off with gin. The decoction contained so much nicotine that children treated with it were "often deeply unconscious" when taken to a European hospital in Ibadan.[4] And medical specialists in many small societies, including the technologically ingenious Inuit, were inept surgeons. So were the Mae Enga of highland Papua New Guinea, who had great need of medical skill as their almost incessant warfare left many men wounded, some gravely so. Yet, according to Mervyn Meggitt, their medical knowledge and surgical skills were woefully inadequate.[5] Many arrow wounds were simply left untreated, or else the shaft was pulled out, sometimes by the agonizing practice of tying it to a rafter until the suppuration of the wound and a friend's twisting of the arrow eventually worked it loose. Some grievously wounded men were also subjected to a surgical procedure that was more likely to hasten their death than their recovery. Acting on the Mae Enga belief that the wounded man's blood was contaminated, a specialist used a bamboo knife to make an incision under the victim's armpit and then broke a rib with a wedge so that he could insert two fingers into the thorax, collapsing a lung in the process. He next poured water into the cavity and shook the patient vigorously to mix the blood and water. Finally, he rolled the patient over to drain out the mixture. Meggitt expressed surprise that some men actually survived both their wounds and this treatment.

The Sirionó of Bolivia's tropical forest (described in chapter 1) lived in a harsh and dangerous environment. Often cold and hungry, the Sirionó were frequently ill, suffering from malaria, skin diseases, hookworm, and dysentery, among other maladies. Anyone too ill to travel was abandoned to die alone. Not surprisingly, people lived in terror of falling ill, but despite their fear they did not develop effective medical treatments or medications. They had few herbal medications of any kind, and these few were of dubious value. They had no remedies for snakebite or the major illnesses that afflicted them, and they had no surgical skills, not even the ability to set broken bones. What is more, some of their beliefs about health were less than helpful. Children were allowed to play with their feces, and sick persons lay unattended in hammocks that were exposed to cold and rain. They also believed that the principal sign of sickness was a person's loss of appetite. In fact, they believed that if someone who was ill did not eat, the patient was certain to die in a few days. Terrified by this prophecy, a sick person was understandably determined to eat. Indeed, some Sirionó who became ill gorged themselves to death, a phenomenon Holmberg witnessed on a number of occasions.[6] He described an episode in which a man suffering from stomach pain and dysentery (ordinarily not fatal symptoms among the Sirionó) insisted on devouring huge amounts of a highly acidic fruit that was then ripe. Ignoring Holmberg's warnings, the man managed to eat a hundred of these plum-sized fruits each night, and, not surprisingly, his painful diarrhea grew worse. The night before the man died, he consumed an entire basket full of fruit. The Sirionó were surprised by the man's death because he had been eating so well.

That traditional medicine should be less than optimally adaptive as a means of preventing or curing illness should scarcely come as a surprise to anyone. Modern Western medicine is hardly without its ineffective or dangerous practices, and the recent history of our own medical reliance on bleeding, purging, septic surgery, and all manner of noxious (and ineffective) nostrums can turn the strongest stomach. To take but one example among many, in the late 1800s opium was traditionally used to soothe babies. Packaged in a variety of elixirs, opium-laced preparations were widely available (from grocers!) in countries that included Britain, Australia, and the United States. At the turn of the century, an Australian Royal Commission estimated that 15,000 babies a year were killed by overdoses of opium contained in these "soothing" preparations.[7]

Furthermore, effective medical practices were often rejected by Western medical practitioners. The dangers of septic surgery had been known for many years before doctors eventually adopted even perfunctory antiseptic procedures. In 1847 Hungarian physician Ignaz Semmelweis attempted to reduce the high mortality rates in the maternity ward of a prominent Viennese hospital by insisting that doctors wash their hands in strong chemicals before examining patients, delivering babies, or performing surgery. As a result of Semmelweis's reform, the mortality rate rapidly fell from 18 percent to

107

2 percent, but the doctors found Semmelweis's newfangled hygiene to be a nuisance, and they saw to it that he was fired. The mortality rate quickly returned to 18 percent.[8] Although the experience of Semmelweis and the research of British surgeon Joseph Lister on antisepsis was widely known by the 1870s, many surgeons continued to practice without the least concern for hygiene. When President Garfield was wounded by an assassin in 1881, his "expert" doctors probed the wound with unwashed fingers and unsterilized instruments. Garfield died of secondary infection. There is no need to continue this litany of iatrogenic practices.

Like those of Garfield's surgeons, the unhygienic practices of many folk populations contribute to their ill health. Lacking a knowledge of infectious agents, the Sirionó believed that all illness was caused by evil spirits or violations of food taboos. A population like the Sirionó that does not understand the dangers of infection from, say, fecal matter is more subject to illness and death than one that buries feces, keeps them away from toddlers, and makes certain that they do not contaminate the water supply. In this respect, then, the inhabitants of Duddie's Branch who defecated in the open and drank feces-contaminated water were engaging in a maladaptive practice, unless their goal was high infant mortality and debilitating adult illness. So two were the inhabitants of Paris who defecated in the open until well in the seventeenth century. And East African pastoral societies, like the Maasai, Pokot, or Samburu, that did nothing to remove flies from the eyes of their children (because flies were associated with cattle feces and cattle were the ultimate in wealth), were also engaged in a maladaptive practice, unless there was some benefit to be had by allowing their children to become blind as a result of fly-borne trachoma. The benefit to a society of blind children is not self-evident.

Ill Health and Suffering

Many folk societies are not blessed with good health or effective systems of medicine. Sickness, suffering, and premature death so plague every human population that for most people fear, grief, and mourning are as much a part of life as laughter, joy, and celebration. But some populations, far more than others, must watch their children die, live with recurring illness, and come to terms with the realization that few among them will live to be older than thirty. Among the

Yanomamo Indians, mentioned earlier with regard to their perennial engagement in warfare, 43 percent of all females who were born alive died during their first year (probably more than half due to female infanticide), and only 22 percent of the population lived beyond the age of 30. Among the Xavante of Brazil, only 15.4 percent of the population lived to be over 30.[9] And in Mexico, not the poorest of developing countries, it has been estimated that nutritional deficiencies directly account for 25 percent of the deaths of preschool children.[10]

Victims of an exploitive plantation economy, the sugarcane workers who lived in the impoverished shantytown of Alto do Cruzeiro that encircled the town of Bom Jesus da Mata in the northeast of Brazil endured what Nancy Scheper-Hughes has called "short, violent and hungry lives."[11] In some poor neighborhoods of the town, 40 percent of all live births ended in death before age 1, and almost all of those who survived suffered debilitating ill health throughout their brief lifetimes.[12]

Other forms of economic and political exploitation or neglect are so commonplace around the world that in 1982 UNICEF estimated that on each day during the previous year, more than 40,000 childlren died from malnutrition or preventable disease, a staggering total of over 14 million dead children during that single year. If 14 million needless childhood deaths each year were not sufficiently chilling, consider that in 1990 the mortality total remained the same, and this figure included only children, not adults who also needlessly starve and die of preventable disease, and it makes no mention of the six times as many children whose lives will be shortened by disease.[13]

The poor and powerless characteristically suffer ill health and early death even in the most affluent countries. For example, in the United States, the most disadvantaged groups have long had lower life expectancies, so much so in fact that black men in Harlem die more than twice as often before the age of 65 as the average for U.S. whites, and they are even less likely to reach the age of 65 than men in Bangladesh.[14] A similar pattern also exists in Canada, where the politically dominant English-speaking population has the longest life expectancy and disadvantaged Canadian Native peoples the shortest.[15] Although poor populations often maintain beliefs and practices that endanger their own health, their overall ill health and high mortality are consequences not primarily of their own maladaptive practices but of external socioeconomic forces that they are relatively powerless to change. Other populations, however, are more clearly responsible for developing and maintaining practices that adversely affect their own well-being.

To be sure, sometimes people's practices are clearly beneficial. For example, Mormons in California who have never smoked cigarettes, slept seven to eight hours daily, and regularly engaged in physical exercise have one of the lowest mortality rates from cancer and cardiovascular disease ever recorded.[16] And the robust good health and remarkable longevity of the Greeks living on Paros Island in the Aegean must also be attributed in large measure to their good nutrition, low-cholesterol diet, moderate smoking and consumption of alcohol, and regular exercise.[17] As we well know, however, the lifestyle that people prefer can also be harmful to their health. A telling case in point is the decision made by people throughout the world to abandon a foraging mode of subsistence in favor of agriculture, even though their health suffered as a result.

A well-documented example of the health hazards of living as sedentary agriculturalists has been provided by two prehistoric archeological sites in Kentucky. Before there was any contact with Europeans and their diseases, the people of Indian Knoll lived as seminomadic hunters and gatherers. The people of nearby Hardin Village, on the other hand, were agriculturalists who lived in a permanent village enclosed by a stockade. Based on analyses of skeletal remains, life expectancies for all ages and both sexes were determined to be lower for the agriculturalists than for the foragers. The agriculturalists also had higher infant mortality, greater iron-deficiency anemia, and more childhood infections, tooth decay, and diseases that caused arrested growth. According to Claire M. Cassidy, who has summarized this research, the agricultural people of Hardin Village were "clearly less healthy" than the hunter-gatherers of Indian Knoll.[18]

This was not an isolated occurrence. In his recent, carefully documented book *Health and the Rise of Civilization*, Mark Nathan Cohen has concluded that until quite recent times, particularly the twentieth century, agriculturalists throughout the world were always less healthy than hunters and gatherers. According to Cohen, the growth of agricultural populations was due to their increased fertility, not to improved health or longevity. In fact, Cohen believes that until the nineteenth century life expectancy among agricultural populations actually declined over time.[19] Indeed, in much of Europe until quite recent times, life expectancy at birth was only in the high twenties or low thirties, a pattern of longevity that was exceeded by some hunting and gathering populations. In India life expectancy at birth may have been lower still.[20] Urban populations were even less healthy. At its peak around A.D. 500, the Aztec city of Teotihuacan covered a larger area than imperial Rome and may have been the largest city in the world at that time. But its population was in dreadful health. Rates of malnutrition, stunted growth, deciduous tooth hypoplasia, and infant and child mortality were higher than in any known population of that time or earlier. Life expectancy at birth ranged betwen 14 and 17 years, infant mortality was about 40 percent, and only 38 percent of everyone born lived to be as old as 15. Life expectancy was almost as low in imperial Rome, while people lived twice as long in the provinces.[21] In Europe, urban populations probably did not match the longevity of hunter-gatherers until the mid nineteenth or even twentieth century.

It would be absurd to say that people knowingly chose to impair their health and shorten their life span by living on farms or in cities. Whatever the allure of agriculture or urban living may have been for those who initially took up farming or moved to towns—a more regular food supply, more excitement, or the depletion of resources for hunting or gathering, to suggest a few possibilities—once the process of intensive farming and urban growth was established, the people involved had no viable option of returning to a hunting or gathering mode of life, nor could they be expected to understand that by living so closely together in growing numbers they were allowing dangerous microorganisms to flourish as they could not do in smaller, more mobile groups of people.

It should also be pointed out that while the health and longevity of agriculturalists may have been less good than that of hunter-gathers, the lives of these latter people were hardly as idyllic as they have sometimes been portrayed. With the exuberant exaggeration that has now and then marked his distinguished career, Marshall Sahlins once referred to hunter-gatherers as members of the "original affluent society."[22] It is true that many such populations have managed to survive, reproduce, and maintain their numbers, but their lives are short (life expectancy at birth ranges between 20 and 40 years, depending on the particular society) and infant mortality is high. Most hunting and gathering peoples must live through regular periods of extreme hunger, and coping with death, especially of their children, is a dread-

111

fully inescapable necessity.[23] No one who has read Allan Holmberg's account of the Sirionó could ever consider them affluent. As we have seen, they are almost perpetually hungry and frequently starving. No one could think of them as being particularly happy, either.[24] The Australian aborigines also managed to survive, but if Joseph Birdsell is correct, they could only feed their population by aborting as many as half of all fetuses that were conceived.[25] And anyone who looks upon the San as affluent innocents who are content with their very high infant mortality and short life expectancy will be quickly disabused of that idea by reading Marjorie Shostak's biography of a San woman named Nisa.[26] With anger, pathos, and resentment, Nisa makes it abundantly obvious that the San are not inured to the pain that the deaths of their children and other loved ones bring, nor are they by any means completely satisfied with their lot. On the contrary, they are openly envious of populations (including other San) who appear to have more food, better health, or more comforts.

Maladaptive Health Beliefs and Practices

Although some scholars continue to insist that seemingly maladaptive, even bizarre, beliefs and practices involving nutrition and health care may some day be shown to be adaptive,[27] there is a small group who agree that before European contact the inadequate diets and poor health of most small, traditional populations resulted, at least in part, from their own maladaptive beliefs and practices. Societies that maintain such maladaptive practices have been reported from many parts of the world.[28] For example, K. R. Howe has contested European descriptions of the spectacular health and beauty of early Polynesians by observing that in many parts of Polynesia arthritis, dental decay, parasitic disease, and other infections were so widespread that infant mortality was extremely high and very few of those who survived lived beyond the age of 30.[29] He added that such short life expectancies made Pacific Islanders seem healthier to Europeans than they actually were because so few lived long enough to appear to be aged or to become ill.

Recently Glenn Dennett and John Connell have argued that many societies in the highlands of Papua New Guinea have maintained practices that contribute to their poor nutrition and consequent poor health.[30] Referring to large societies in the central highlands as well as smaller and economically more marginal groups in the surrounding fringe area, Dennett and Connell point to consistently high infant and child mortality rates (20 to 30 percent before the age of 5), low fertility, short life expectancy, and stunting of growth as evidence that by and large these were not well-nourished or healthy populations.

Many of these societies had manifestly inadequate diets based on the sweet potato, which though high in carbohydrates was very low in protein. Consequently, as Sillitoe reported for the Wola,[31] children were undernourished and vulnerable to disease. But it is not simply that these people lacked ready sources of protein; they did not make good use of the protein that was available to them. Many highland societies limited both the amount and variety of food that mothers could eat during pregnancy or while nursing, and small children were typically denied animal protein. People in some of these societies ate enormous amounts of pork during pig feasts but did not consume pork on a regular basis or during food shortages. Indeed, their complex of practices relating to the exchange and preservation of pigs, often in large ceremonies, led to periods of reduced food intake and child malnutrition.[32] Also, the general lack of concern for hygiene in the preparation and consumption of food must have substantially increased the risk of infection, as did the practice of allowing children to crawl on feces-littered ground and put contaminated objects in their mouths.[33] Dennett and Connell also believe that inefficient agricultural implements and practices along with endemic warfare combined to reduce food production and leave these societies "precariously adapted."[34]

An instructive confirmation of Dennett and Connell's thesis comes from Georgeda Buchbinder's research with the Maring of highland Papua New Guinea.[35] Many of the Maring—essentially vegetarians who rarely ate animal food—were severly protein-deprived, and in general these people were smaller and more susceptible to disease than other Maring who lived in areas where protein was more plentiful. Like many other undernourished people in marginal environments, the Maring suffered population decline from disease, and at least one of their customs exacerbated their plight. As might be expected, young adults who were able to work hard to produce food were relatively well-nourished, but the very young, old, and ill were severely undernourished, and many died. This was a tragic situation but one that Maring society could survive, at least over the short run.

However, Maring culture further required that the widowed spouse and close relatives of a deceased person mourn by reducing their food intake for an extended period and, moreover, that they not enter their gardens to produce or harvest food for several weeks after the death occurred. As more and more nutritionally marginal people died, increasing numbers of previously healthy adults were compelled to deny themselves food while mourning, and they too soon suffered from malnutrition and the consequent risk of infection. And as more people died, the Maring, who were already anxious about their dwindling population, began to accuse one another of causing these deaths by sorcery. In this anxious atmosphere, even close relatives stopped helping one another, young men left the area in search of wage work, and potential brides from areas where food was more abundant refused to marry Maring men. All of these apparently disruptive consequences may not have resulted solely from Maring mourning practices, but it is difficult to believe that a practice which endangered or drove away so many of the reproductive-age members of the society was adaptive.

As I mentioned earlier, the practice of abortion or infanticide may help individual mothers, families, or coresiding kin groups survive under severe environmental conditions, although evidence that such acts are altruistically undertaken to control the population growth of the entire society continues to be questionable at best.[36] But finding an adaptive advantage in the practice of restricting the nutrition of pregnant or lactating women is a good deal more problematic. Alexander Alland has hypothesized that food restriction during and after pregnancy would prove somehow to be "medically positive" in small-scale societies but would become medically ineffective in societies that were threatened by rapid population growth. Support for this adaptively optimistic idea has not been forthcoming.[37] In addition to the health hazards that such a restriction may impose on the mother, food restrictions lead to low-birth-weight infants that are at risk both for survival and for normal cognitive development. Such a practice ensures that *all* offspring, even coveted boys, will be endangered. Nevertheless, the practice of restricting the diet of pregnant and lactating women has been extremely widespread even in societies where both male and female offspring were desired and both abortion and infanticide were rare.[38]

With a handful of exceptions, women and children in all societies eat less food—and less-prized food—than men, and in many societies,

114

womens' diets are restricted even further in both calories and protein when they are pregnant.[39] Optimally, of course, pregnant and lactating women should eat an enriched diet, and this is precisely what happened among the Mae Enga of highland Papua New Guinea, who were attempting to increase their population after a devastating epidemic.[40] To what extent dietary restrictions in folk societies may affect the developing fetus or the nursing child is very difficult to determine, but in East Africa the severe anemia suffered by many pregnant women has been related to their dietary restrictions during pregnancy,[41] just as the infantile beriberi of Burmese children has been associated with the greatly restricted diets of Burmese mothers.[42] Restricting the food intake of pregnant or lactating women endangers the health of both mother and child without providing any compensatory benefits, unless one chooses to believe that reducing the size of the fetus significantly reduces the risks of childbirth.[43]

It may be adaptive for families in some societies, particularly those with limited food resources, to eliminate mentally or physically handicapped children. However, it is difficult to understand what adaptive advantage there might be for populations that want many children— as economic resources, hunters, warriors, or wives—to adopt practices that endanger normal children. Yet many societies maintain practices that leave children malnourished, even though there are food resources available that could permit these children to develop normally. For example, in Ethiopia and many parts of East Africa, the youngest child is fed whatever may be left over after his father, any guests, his mother, and older siblings have eaten. As a result, many small children are malnourished, some so severely that they develop kwashiorkor, marasmus, or rickets.

When children developed malnutritive disorders like kwashiorkor, some of these societies either denied these children available protein-rich food or took other measures that inadvertently caused their condition to worsen. Kwashiorkor is a West African term that refers to a child who is displaced from his mother's breast by a newborn sibling. When such a child is weaned to a protein-scarce diet, it suffers from edema, muscle wasting, the accumulation of fluid in the abdomen, and an enlarged liver. The child's hair turns a reddish blond, and it may lose its appetite, become withdrawn, and die, most often from gastroenteritis.[44]

In 1961 there were many severely malnourished children among the Kamba of Kenya. The area had suffered the effects of a severe drought followed by heavy rains that devastated any remaining crops. Although famine relief was provided by the government, thousands of children were severely malnourished, and many suffered from kwashiorkor. In earlier times, the Kamba, like many other societies in various parts of the world, refused to eat chickens or eggs, but by 1961 this food avoidance had broken down, at least for men. Nevertheless, malnourished children were still not permitted to eat eggs, which were in plentiful supply; instead, they were eaten by adults or sold to Europeans, while the malnourished children were weaned onto a low-protein, difficult-to-digest, high-fiber diet.

The Baganda of Uganda also responded to kwashiorkor in a manner that caused the condition to worsen. Confusing cause and effect, as was done in West Africa, the Baganda believed that children developed kwashiorkor not as a result of being weaned onto a low-protein diet, but because they were harmed by the jealousy of an unborn baby toward its suckling sibling. Therefore, the nursing child was taken from its mother and given to a relative—often a grandmother— who had no breast milk and lacked the means to provide a nutritious diet. The loss of protein in its diet exacerbated by the stress of sudden separation and weaning predictably enough made the child's condition worse, a result that was thought by the Baganda to be caused by the cold nights the child spent away from its mother.[45]

Another maladaptive practice is the denial of colostrum to infants. Colostrum is the yellowish or bluish fluid secreted by the breasts during the first few days after birth before it is replaced by milk. Colostrum transfers specific immunoglobins to the infant during the earliest days of life when its own immune system is poorly developed. Colostrum contains macrophages that can kill bacteria and fungi, protecting the child against deadly enterocolitis (childhood diarrhea). T lymphocytes also occur in large numbers, with their highest activity in synthesizing immunoglobins and antibodies occurring immediately after the onset of lactation. For this reason, many physicians believe that breast-feeding during the first week is crucial in providing the infant with a high concentration of antibodies and in regulating the bacteria in its intestines. Colostrum also appears to contain antibodies against infectious agents specific to local environments. For example, colostrum from women in India contains antibodies against cholera; this is not the case among women in societies where cholera is not prevalent.[46]

To delay breast-feeding for several days until the colostrum is replaced by "true" milk is clearly harmful to the infant, yet this practice occurs widely. In a study of fifty-seven societies, Dana L. Raphael found that the largest number (nineteen) began breast-feeding on the third day after birth, ten more began on the fourth day, three on the seventh day, and in one society mothers waited ten days to begin breast-feeding.[47] Mothers in only nine societies began to breast-feed immediately after birth, in seven others they began to breast-feed on the first day, and in seven more breast-feeding began on the second day. Because so many factors other than the denial of colostrum are related to infant illness or mortality, there is no precise evidence showing that the longer an infant is denied colostrum the greater its risk of death may be, but there is strong suggestive evidence that this is the case,[48] and there is compelling evidence from animal experiments showing that colostrum-deprived animals suffer far greater mortality than those that receive it.[49] As Jerome Barkow has noted in his review of this practice, the dangers of denying colostrum to infants are obvious, and if there are any benefits they are unknown.[50]

It is not only infants and young children who are endangered by some traditional health practices. As our own history documents all too darkly, what is done to older children in the interest of maintaining their health can have deadly consequences. It is no different in many other societies. Many Latin Americans, including Mexican Americans, believe in the existence of an illness called *empacho*, which is thought to cause a variety of gastrointestinal symptoms such as constipation, gastritis, indigestion, diarrhea, and nausea. Empacho is thought to be caused by eating improperly cooked food, swallowing chewing gum, or otherwise ingesting something that causes a bolus of food to adhere to the wall of the intestine. Infants are believed to suffer from empacho, and so are older children, teenagers, and women who have recently given birth.[51]

Many of the favored treatments for this disorder are presumably relatively benign—abdominal massage, herbal teas, and laxatives—but one fairly common treatment can have lethal consequences. In a survey of Mexican-American households in the American southwest, Robert F. Trotter found that 50 percent of these families had treated empacho, and many of these did so by giving the patient a drink containing lead compounds, mercury, or toxic laundry bluing.[52] The dangers of lead in even tiny amounts for young children are now well documented,[53] and Trotter reports that a number of cases of lead poisoning among older children and adults have been reported to authorities.[54] Presumably, many other cases were not reported, perhaps because the primary symptoms of lead-poisoning—diarrhea, vomiting, and lethargy—are the same as those of empacho itself. The use of heavy metals such as lead and mercury to treat childhood illness was also common in Ayurvedic and Islamic medicine, a practice that Carl Taylor has referred to as "extremely dangerous."[55]

Ayurvedic medicine contains other beliefs and practices that can be manifestly harmful. To take but one example, in Vellore, South India, a young child who developed classical symptoms of life-threatening severe dehydration (diarrhea, vomiting, sunken eyes and fontanelle) was thought to be polluted because of transgressions committed by its mother, such as feeding the child after seeing a woman who had a miscarriage, crossing a grave, or not bathing properly after seeing a bier. The treatment for the child consisted not of rehydration, which could have saved its life, but of arranging for various religious specialists to recite chants.[56] These traditional chants may have been comforting to the child's parents, but they could not have saved the severely dehydrated child.

Although we have been emphasizing maladaptive beliefs and practices that endanger children, it should be self-evident that adults become victims as well, sometimes as a result of what they eat and drink. Over fifty years ago, Robert Lowie wrote about the "capricious irrationality" of people's food preferences and avoidances around the world.[57] As Marvin Harris has pointed out, Lowie's evidence was often inadequate, but Harris himself admits that not all aspects of "foodways" (as he refers to people's beliefs and practices regarding food) "enhance human health and well-being."[58] In fact, while arguing that most foodways are beneficial, he grants that a significant number of them may be harmful. Nevertheless, Harris warns against "blanket condemnations of exotic foodways as useless or harmful."[59] This is a reasonable principle, but it does not follow that all or most foodways would prove to enhance human health or well-being if only we had a better understanding of neurochemistry.

A case in point is the continuing attempt to explain why large numbers of people in Europe, Africa, and Asia eat fava beans even though they are highly toxic to a substantial number of people. Fava beans are the large, flat "broad beans" with huge stalks on which the Jack and the Beanstalk story was based. Nutritious, tasty, and easy to grow, they have been consumed over large portions of the world since the Neolithic. Yet people who are deficient in a certain enzyme

118

(glucose-6-phosphate dehydrogenase, or G6PD) may suffer severe hemolytic anemia within hours after eating fava beans—the anemia is fatal in approximately one in twelve cases in modern times and was undoubtedly more often so in the past before effective medical treatment was developed. Between 5 and 30 percent of the affected populations carry the gene that puts them at risk for the fatal hemolytic shock. Why, then, have so many people persisted for so long in eating something that makes many of them ill and kills no small number? Several recent investigators have hypothesized that because the beans contain oxidant chemicals that may increase a person's resistance to malaria, the benefits of this protection for the population as a whole outweigh the risks of hemolytic shock for the minority.[60]

This hypothesis may someday be confirmed, but it is possible that people have continued to eat fava beans for reasons that are entirely unrelated to malaria. First, there would be no evident reason for people not to eat fava beans. The beans were eaten with other foods and vegetables, and sometimes the beans were processed or cooked in ways that reduced their toxicity. Most people ate beans without ill effects; those few who became ill would hardly have been likely to blame the beans for their misfortune. Indeed, although there are many ancient beliefs about fava beans in Greece, Rome, Egypt, India, and elsewhere that attribute unusual and even fearsome powers to the bean (it contains various potent compounds such as L-Dopa), the most consistent warning about these beans is that they produce flatulence, not that they might be deadly. But most significant for the adaptivist hypothesis about malaria, they are still considered to be edible and are widely consumed, for example, in the circum-Mediterranean region, where a significant proportion of the population is still G6PD deficient but where malaria is no longer the endemic problem it once was. Is it not possible, then, that people today, like those in the past, eat fava beans not because they confer some degree of protection against malaria but simply because they are tasty, nutritious, and easy to produce?

Whatever the truth about fava beans, the foodways of some peoples are clearly harmful. The Inuit practice of eating seal blubber raw rather than cooking it has caused an untold number of deaths from botulism, as has eating cattle that have died of anthrax, something that occurred in various parts of the world.[61] The widespread use of feces as fertilizer in the water farming of fish and plants has led to millions being infected by liver flukes. One such fluke, *Schistosoma*, has been the third leading cause of death (after malaria and tuber-culosis) in much of Asia and Africa.[62] Even allowing for a good measure of skepticism about the pronouncements of modern science concerning the benefits and hazards of our own foodways, it can hardly be denied that many of the contemporary American practices involving overconsumption of fats, sugars, alcohol, nicotine, caffeine, and the like are harmful to our health.

Beliefs about physical beauty can also have maladaptive health consequences. Some populations, most notably ones in Africa and Polynesia, believed that obesity was beautiful, and not surprisingly, most politically powerful people tended to be grossly overweight. The Zulu King Cetshwayo's legs were so stout that he could not walk without chafing them painfully, and some Polynesian chiefs and their wives were too obese to walk at all. It has been surmised that because obesity can be an efficient means of utilizing energy from carbohy-drates, it would confer an adaptive advantage during periods of fa-mine.[63] Thus, for example, it has been suggested that fat Polynesians would have been more likely to tolerate the famine and hypothermia that was presumably present during the long ocean voyages that led to the discovery and peopling of the Polynesian islands.[64] These very heavy early Polynesians avoided gross obesity by strenuous physical exercise, and in any event, they seldom lived long enough to develop the degenerative diseases associated with obesity. Today, however, some Polynesians such as the Samoans have dramatically reduced their activity levels while continuing their traditional high-caloric diet.[65] As a result, they now often suffer from hypertension, diabetes, and cardiovascular and renal disease.[66]

A cultural preference for obesity can be hazardous, but so can a be-lief system that fosters an intense fear of becoming overweight. In much of western Europe and the United States, this fear leads growing num-bers of people, particularly young women, to develop *anorexia ner-vosa*, defined as a weight loss in excess of 25 percent of previous body weight.[67] By every imaginable criterion, except the need for a society to reduce its population, weight loss that leads to *anorexia nervosa* is maladaptive. Young women with the condition are infertile, young men tend to be impotent, and the condition can be life threatening.

The total solar eclipse that affected various parts of the earth during the summer of 1991 reminded us that many populations have been greatly fearful of such "unnatural" phenomena. What they did to bring an eclipse to an end might seem comical (as when thousands of people

120

shouted in unison to bring back the sun) or tragic (when human victims were sometimes sacrificed), but whatever action people took invariably succeeded in bringing back the sun. Despite this success, an eclipse was widely thought to bring about all manner of misfortune. Blaming human misfortune on a solar eclipse was probably more benign than blaming other people for bringing about evil (a total eclipse was a rare event, after all, and there might be no necessity for human scapegoats), but the result can still be maladaptive. For example, when a cholera epidemic broke out in parts of Mexico shortly after the eclipse of 1991, some people chose to attribute the symptoms of cholera to the eclipse rather than to contaminated food or water, and the public health consequences were hazardous.[68]

Traditional medical treatment has included some effective drugs, physical manipulations, and even surgical procedures. The social support and reassurance given to patients probably often helped to speed recovery (as I once attempted to show by describing the therapeutic regimen of a Hehe curer in Tanzania). Folk beliefs can sometimes lead to invaluable medical developments. For example, the eighteenth-century British folk belief that milkmaids who were exposed to cowpox would not contract smallpox led Jenner to develop a vaccine that eradicated that once terrible disease. But despite the presence of cattle in North India, no folk belief about the protective properties of cowpox arose. Instead, smallpox was attributed to a goddess and many thousands died each year until Western inoculations became available. Indeed, most traditional medical practices were ineffective and some were deadly. When the Sebei of Uganda treated a person with a severe headache by pressing a red-hot spear blade against the sufferer's forehead, they may well have convinced that person not to complain about headaches again, but it seems unlikely that the treatment addressed the source of the pain. The Pokot of Kenya sometimes held a psychotic person down while he or she was pounded on the head with a sizable rock for a considerable time. Unless this treatment was intended to kill the patient, as sometimes happened, it would not appear to have great efficacy.[69]

Stress and Well-Being

Freud was hardly the first to decide that the demands of social living could be highly stressful, but his belief that the pressures of "civili-

121

zation" had made many societies "neurotic" is the best-known exposition of this point of view. The belief that certain societies—our own, for example—are more stressful than others is certainly commonplace today, as is the idea that some parts of our country are more stressful than others. Most Americans would probably not hesitate to say that New York City is a more stressful place to live than, say, Provo, Utah, or a small town in Oregon. Many New Yorkers apparently agree. In a survey conducted in 1990, 73 percent of the people polled said that the city was dangerous, 78 percent said that it was dirty, and 60 percent said that they worried about crime "all the time or often." Another 73 percent said that it was "getting tougher" for them to live in New York City, and when asked if they could choose where they lived, only 37 percent said that they would remain in the city.[70] The survey may have been flawed, but the point remains that the belief that some countries, cities, or social practices can be more stressful than others, or even too stressful to endure, is very much a part of our common sense view of the world. It has also appealed to a number of scholars and scientists from Erich Fromm, with his 1955 formulation of the "sane society," to the utopian experiments of the 1960s and 1970s, to many investigators in psychiatry, medicine, and public health who continue to explore ways of reducing the stress burden imposed by modern living.

Unfortunately for those who believe that some social setting or entire societies are more stressful than others (and here I include myself), the idea of a stressful or "sick" society has proven to be so complex that it threatens to overflow its conceptual dikes. Stress has shown itself to be not only an omnibus idea but one whose results in human populations have been difficult to measure with precision. Unlike animal research, where specific stressors can be related to specific physiological responses, the stressors in human sociocultural systems are often linked to one another in such a way that any one presumed stressor may be difficult to separate from others. Moreover, the people themselves may not be able to identify those aspects of their environments that impose the greatest strains on them. A fear of witchcraft, which anyone can identify as a major stressor, may indeed bring about a lessened resistance to infection via hormonal pathways, but chronic protein deprivation and protozoan infection may be even more damaging yet go unrecognized. What is more, it is difficult to work back from the appearance of a symptom to the stressor that induced it.

Nevertheless, illnesses that are generally considered to be largely psychosomatic vary greatly from society to society. Asthma, for example, is remarkably common in Libya and on Tristan de Cunha but rare in Senegal and Finland, and ulcerative colitis rarely occurs in developing countries. Coronary heart disease is many times more common in Finland than it is in Japan or Nigeria.[71] And the effects of stress can sometimes be measured. For example, some of the long-term consequences of stress early in life can be assessed by the study of dental enamel hypoplasia (i.e., deficiencies in the thickness of the enamel that resemble indented rings in the tooth) due to systemic disruptions in ameloblastic matrix formation. Because enamel is secreted in regular fashion, teeth provide a permanent chronological record of metabolic disturbances that took place during their development. Although several factors can lead to hypoplasias, those due to stress can be distinguished from those due to hereditary conditions, localized trauma, or other conditions. Alan H. Goodman and George J. Armelagos analyzed stress hypoplasias among 111 adults who were buried at Dickson Mounds, Illinois, between A.D. 1000 and 1350. Those with no evidence of hypoplasias-stress periods during childhood lived an average of 35.8 years, while those with two or more hypoplasias-stress periods (presumably resulting from severe illness or undernutrition) lived on average over 10 years less.[72]

Assessing the impact of stress on living populations can be more difficult. It is generally agreed that symptoms such as ulcers, eczema, phobic reactions, and asthma are in large part the product of psychosocial stress, but they may also be related to genetic predispositions, diet, and a host of experiential factors that either exacerbate the condition or protect an individual against it. Let us take the development of peptic ulcers as an example. While emotional stress reportedly is related to their development, so too are factors such as a person's genetic predisposition, the excessive use of cigarettes, alcohol, and aspirin, and the activity of a bacterial microorganism—*Helicobacter pylori*—that thrives in the mucus layer of the stomach.[73] What is more, the development of ulcers is said to be a result less of the stressful events in the lives of ulcer patients than of how they react to these events. That is so, apparently, because ulcer patients tend to be negative and depressed. However, as the authors of this research recognize, it is possible that developing a peptic ulcer may make a patient view the world in a more negative way, just as it is possible that various kinds of social support or personality features

123

may buffer a person against the development of ulcers. This research illustrates that although peptic ulcers are one of the best studied of the presumed-to-be psychosomatic disorders, it is still not certain to what extent emotional stress plays a part in their development. It seems clear, however, that several mediating factors may either predispose one toward this disorder or prevent its occurrence.[74]

With these complexities in mind, consider the finding of Shore and Stone that women in an unnamed Northwest Coast Indian tribe suffered from duodenal ulcers more often than men (although men smoked tobacco and drank alcohol much more often than women did) and, indeed, four times more often than non-Indian women in the United States.[75] Shore and Stone attribute this apparently quite significant difference to the stress that these Indian women endured because of their poverty and their changing social roles as the matrilineal structure of their traditional society broke down. This interpretation is plausible, but no data are presented that would rule out all of the other factors that may have led to this finding.

This cautionary note is important because research on the apparent effects of stress in human populations is rarely sufficiently comprehensive to allow a definitive conclusion. Nevertheless, the cumulative impact of this admittedly complex body of research has led most scholars to the same conclusion; namely, that social and cultural change, particularly when it is rapid, leads to decreased physical and mental health as a result of what, for want of a better concept, we can call stress.[76] And some recent research has been able to relate specific kinds of psychosocial stress to unwanted and dangerous health outcomes. Christine Dunkel-Schtetter, Marci Lobel, and Susan Scrimshaw have shown that both low-birth-weight babies and preterm delivery were associated with the relative stress of the mothers (as measured by their anxiety level, perceived stress level, and the occurrence of major life crises, such as job loss or the death of a loved one). However, high stress levels did not affect the relative difficulty of labor or the general physical health of the baby.[77] In another study, William W. Dressler was able to link stress to the occurrence of depression in a Southern black community.[78] Perhaps the most compelling evidence for the linkage between psychosocial stress and illness has been provided by Sheldon Cohen and his colleagues at Carnegie-Mellon University, who exposed volunteers to viruses known to cause the common cold. Those persons who developed cold symptoms were far more likely to have experienced recent stress (as a result of divorce, loss of a job, or death of a loved one, for example) than those who did not develop colds.[79]

No one seriously disputes the reports that recent immigrants, such as the Vietnamese boat people who came to the United States, were (and often still are) under great emotional stress and that they suffer both physical and mental disorders as a result. So it has always been whenever a population has had its traditional world torn apart or when it has been wrenched away from that world by events beyond its control. But the question we need to address is a different one. All societies change, that is axiomatic; but many traditional societies change very slowly. Do societies such as these, societies largely unaffected by the major disruptions of famine, epidemic disease, warfare, or political conquest, differ markedly in the amount or kind of stress they impose on their members? Do some stable societies, like rapidly changing ones, *make* their members sick?

It may as well be said at the outset that there is no sure answer to this question. The evidence is too controversial, and the issues are too complex for that. But the evidence that will be summarized in the pages to come suggests that the answer should be yes. Some small traditional societies appear to have been more stressful than others, and they still are.

As I said earlier, the occurrence of witchcraft or sorcery can produce such fear and suffering that it can clearly be maladaptive. You may recall that John Kennedy and Theodore Schwartz (among others) warned that the paranoia associated with witchcraft could make life in some societies terribly uncomfortable, if not altogether unlivable. Kennedy was referring primarily to Africa and Schwartz to Melanesia, but the tendency to suspect others and be fearful of them is not confined to those areas. It is widespread in Latin America[80] and, in fact, most other parts of the world.[81] This level of fear hardly seems adaptive, any more than the stress created by feuding and warfare seems to have been adaptive for the societies that were devastated by the unremitting killing that resulted. People in small, traditional societies may not have experienced the same degree of stress that invalided and incapacitated shell-shocked soldiers from World War I or left veterans of the Vietnam combat with posttraumatic stress syndrome, but there can be no doubt that the result of perpetual feuding and warfare can produce such high levels of fear that people are vastly relieved when the fighting comes to an end.

There are many kinds of taboos, and some of them no doubt enhanced the well-being of people who practiced them, as Marvin Harris has never tired of trying to demonstrate with regard to the Israelite's taboo on eating pork and the Hindu prohibition on the slaughter of cattle.[82] Beginning with Radcliffe-Brown's famous Frazer Lecture, functionalists have interpreted taboos positively, pointing to their role in making people aware of the values that give their society cohesion. But some kinds of taboos have also been a significant source of stress, one that has been as common as feuding or warfare and perhaps even more anxiety producing.

Let me provide an example from the Walbiri of Australia. Like other aboriginal Australians, the Walbiri had many sacred objects and ceremonies that were the exclusive province of older men. It was taboo for a woman to see these sacred objects, and should one do so, she would automatically suffer death as supernatural retribution. Mervin Meggitt described an occasion in which an old woman named Maisie inadvertently chanced upon some men who were preparing sacred shells for a ceremony. She withdrew in terror, and in a matter of days, she had wasted away to "skin and bone" and was psychotic.[83] She was declared dead by a Walbiri medicine man, but Meggitt's wife discovered that Maisie was, in fact, still alive and intervened to prevent her burial. Although she lived, Maisie remained psychotic. This dramatic episode no doubt reinforced the importance of sacred materials in Walbiri life, but it also created great fear, not only for Maisie but, we must presume, for other women as well. After Maisie's misfortune, all Walbiri women now knew, if they did not before, that an accidental glance in the wrong direction could cause them to die or become psychotic.

Adaptivists continue to interpret many kinds of taboos in terms of their positive social uses. Marvin Harris believes that when individuals have difficulty calculating the costs and benefits of their actions, taboos prevent them from taking unwise recourse to short-term satisfactions that might have long-range costs.[84] This formula, it should be obvious, allows anyone great latitude in interpreting the positive function of a taboo. Unlike adaptivists, the people in small-scale societies themselves can typically offer no explanation for the existence of their taboos beyond saying that they have always been that way.[85] Perhaps that is because some taboos are innocuous—such as the Mbuti belief that they must splash themselves with some water whenever they cross a stream[86]—and the reasons for taboos like these could understandably be forgotten. But others would appear to be

126

anything but harmless. The Netsilik Inuit believed that when a pregnant woman first felt labor pains, she had to be confined to a small snow house if it was winter or a tent during the summer. The woman herself was considered to be unclean, and a newborn child was thought to give off a particularly dangerous vapor at birth. Because the entire community was thought to be in great danger, no one was permitted to assist the woman in giving birth. If the birth proved to be difficult, a shaman might be summoned to drive away evil spirits, but no one was allowed to touch the woman.[87] This taboo might have served as a population control measure because it probably increased infant mortality, but it also endangered the mother, and there is no evidence that the Netsilik had any desire to reduce the number of fertile and sexually attractive women in their society.

Because taboos are often thought to be enforced by automatic supernatural punishments that cause sickness and death, they create fear—fear that can disable, distract, and demoralize. As recently as 1961 the Kamba of Kenya still lived in immobilizing fear of many of their taboos. Even people with substantial Western education were fearful of violating some of the numerous taboos that made their everyday lives seem perilous. One such taboo (not of Christian origin) required people to make a gesture roughly similar to the sign of the cross whenever they passed by a crossroads. My interpreter, a dignified, wealthy, and politically prominent man who spoke excellent English, never failed to make this gesture whenever we came to a crossroad until one day when he was distracted by a conversation with me. Later, when I regrettably reminded him of this omission, he immediately looked faint and said that he had to return home at once. The next day he was quite ill, and for several days he lingered, sometimes in delirium. Not until a complex and very expensive cleansing ceremony was performed did he begin to recover. I fail to see how this taboo was adaptive for him or for his society.

The Navaho Indians have been called "perhaps the most hypochondriacal people known to the anthropological literature" because of their obsessive concern with curing ceremonies.[88] Navaho men astonishingly spent between one quarter and one third of their time in "sings," as these ceremonies were called, and women spent only slightly less time.[89] The Navaho had many reasons to fear illness. Illness was caused by witches, and witches were thought to be numerous, as were similarly dangerous ghosts, and there were as well many serious taboos that caused people to sicken. As a result, the

127

Navaho lived with what Clyde Kluckhohn and Dorothea Leighton, longtime students of these people, referred to as "high anxiety," "worry," and "uneasiness."[90] But however fearful their beliefs made the Navaho, taboos were even more fear provoking among the Inuit.

The Inuit lived in an environment as demanding as any on earth, and it might be expected that their taboos and other supernatural beliefs would be helpful to them in avoiding danger or reducing anxiety about their precarious circumstances. Perhaps some did, but few would seem to qualify as helpful in either regard. Many had no imaginable utility, and on the whole the Inuit felt that their taboos were burdensome and fearsome.[91] Most Inuit groups lived in what Asen Balicki referred to as "dreadful" fear.[92] To be sure, taboos were not alone in creating fear—evil spirits and all manner of monsters were also a part of the Inuit world. Indeed, when Knud Rasmussen asked a "wise man" among the Iglulik Inuit about their beliefs, this was his answer: "What do we believe? We don't believe, we only fear."[93] We cannot assess the cumulative effects of high levels of fear among the Inuit, but it does not seem likely that these people were well served by their taboos. As John Kennedy once observed, ". . . taboos are among the most dispensable of man's social creations."[94] It is tempting to conclude that the Inuit would have been happier and better adapted without most of their taboos. So, it would seem, would most other populations.

Mental Illness

Few psychiatrists today would deny that social and cultural factors play a role in the etiology of mental illness. Scholars such as anthropologist Gregory Bateson and psychiatrist R. D. Laing located the cause of schizophrenia in family dynamics, and Thomas Szasz, a psychiatrist himself, asserted that to the extent that mental illness existed at all (something he personally doubted), it was entirely a product of societal labels and reactions.[95] French historian Michel Foucault achieved great prominence in the 1960s and 1970s by arguing that mental illness was an historical invention that came into being because all societies require categories of people who can be dominated or scapegoated. When D. L. Rosenhan demonstrated that psychiatrically normal "pseudo-patients" who were admitted to mental hospitals in the United States with a bogus diagnosis of schizophrenia were treated by the psychiatric staff as if they were in fact psychotic, the shock waves were felt throughout the psychiatric establishment.[96] Today such claims—that mental illness is entirely a product of social and cultural forces—are generally attributed to inadequate historiography and poor scientific research, but the less dramatic assertion that these forces influence the etiology and prognosis of mental illness is still viable.

The belief, for example, that people who live in certain kinds of social arrangements (cities, for instance) are more likely to develop mental illness than those who live in others (such as folk societies) has an ancient history.[97] The association of city living with "madness" grew more pronounced during the seventeenth and eighteenth centuries in Europe as well as in the United States, where Thomas Jefferson's views on the virtues of the agricultural life and the corruption of "manufacturing" had a powerful appeal.[98] "Insanity," it was often said, was part of the price we had to pay for civilization.[99] Indeed, as we have seen, the idea that people experienced less stress and consequently exhibited less individual pathology in small folk communities than in urban societies has been one of the most implicitly taken-for-granted assumptions of modern social science. For example, psychiatrist E. Fuller Torrey has concluded that schizophrenia is a product of urbanization; he believes that the disorder is rare in small, traditional societies and was even rare in the West before 1800.[100]

Others, however, have noted that schizophrenia is very common in some rural communities. Nancy Scheper-Hughes attempted to relate the allegedly high rates of schizophrenia in rural western Ireland to the prevalence of social stressors that she believed caused schizophrenia. She painted what she referred to as a "grim portrait" of social isolation, hostility between men and women, late marriage, childlessness and celibacy, contradictory role expectations, and family relations characterized by ridicule, scapegoating, and a fear of intimacy. Her contention that these factors combine to produce unusually high rates of schizophrenia has not been verified, but there can be little doubt that they contributed to the anomie, despair, heavy drinking, depression, and emigration that were common in rural western Ireland.[101]

Until quite recently, some anthropologists believed that there might well be folk societies that were so well adapted, so stress-free, that mental illness was entirely absent.[102] This belief is no longer commonly held, in part because the evidence strongly indicates that

129

mental illness, including schizophrenia and depression, occurs in all societies,[103] and also because it is now accepted even by the most zealous cultural determinists that genetic predisposition plays a major role in the development of many forms of mental illness.[104] Nevertheless, even biologically oriented psychiatrists usually agree that various kinds of psychosocial stress may increase the numbers of persons with vulnerable genotypes who actually develop mental illness.[105] In fact, the most recent psychiatric diagnostic manual used in the United States (DSM-III-R) declares that psychosocial stressors play a part in the etiology of all mental illness.[106]

Schizophrenia can hardly be considered adaptive; most persons who suffer from this disorder have severe difficulty coping with the demands of life, and they infrequently mate or marry. Their fertility is reduced as well. Yet the disorder appears to be unusually common in some parts of the world, such as northern Sweden, and Finland, southwest Croatia, and, perhaps, western Ireland, while it is infrequent in others, such as Papua New Guinea.[107] Rates of depression also vary from society to society,[108] as do phobias, anxiety, obsessive-compulsive disorders, hysteria, and similar disturbances.[109] Some of the evidence for this variation must be discounted because it is based on hospital admissions. Even the long-standing finding that schizophrenia is very common among the Irish has been challenged on these grounds,[110] but the weight of the evidence from every source still strongly suggests that populations do differ in their susceptibility to mental illness.

However, it is less clear whether, or how, these differences relate to stressors that derive from maladaptive practices or beliefs. An illustration of how this can occur is the phenomenon of postpartum depression. It has been estimated that 50 to 80 percent of American mothers suffer a transient period of dysphoria (often called the "maternity blues") after childbirth, and as many as 20 percent of these women experience a mild to moderate clinical depression.[111] The causes of postpartum depression are thought to include the stress of the event for the mother and family (including fears of being an inadequate mother), individual psychological characteristics of the woman, and changes in levels of estrogen and progesterone. Yet despite the frequency and seriousness of postpartum depression in the United States, the phenomenon appears to be quite rare in non-Western societies.[112] For example, when Sara Harkness asked Kipsigis women in Kenya about their emotions following child birth, they unanimously denied that they felt sad or cried during the early weeks after giving birth. In fact, they declared that such things *never* occurred.[113] For these Kipsigis women, despite hormonal changes, postpartum depression did not exist; giving birth was a happy event, one looked forward to by women who received positive social support throughout their pregnancies and after the birth of the child. The reasons why American culture (and the cultures of Western European countries) has made giving birth a depressing event presumably have to do with psychosocial stress. The Kipsigis and other societies have not made giving birth a stressful occurrence.

For another example, take the kingdom of Tonga. Tonga is an archipelago in the South Pacific inhabited by some 90,000 people who are relatively untouched by modernization. Few foreigners live in Tonga, few tourists visit there, and few Tongans go overseas for education or employment. There is no landless plantation labor force, and every family owns land sufficient to grow its own food, while pigs and fish are available for protein. According to H. B. M. Murphy and his Tongan collaborator, B. M. Taumoepeau, when they studied Tongan society in the late 1970s, it was stable, traditional, nonindustrial, and free from the complexities of modern life. After determining that mentally ill Tongans were not emigrating to New Zealand, as some other Pacific islanders did, Murphy and Taumoepeau studied a small, isolated Tongan island where they examined patients and asked villagers to identify any persons who behaved in ways indicative of mental illness. Because conditions on this island made it very unlikely that anyone exhibiting unusual behavior could escape notice or fail to be reported to the investigators, Murphy and Taumoepeau were reasonably confident that they were able to identify all, or almost all, mentally ill Tongans there. Comparing what they found on Tonga with data collected in rural Canada by identical methods, Murphy and Taumoepeau concluded that Tongans had low rates of psychosis (the schizophrenias, affective disorders, and chronic organic disorders) and that they may have had low rates of neurosis as well. Alcohol abuse was not a problem, and suicide was uncommon (unlike nearby Samoa and many other Pacific islands). Tongans were quite free of psychosomatic disorders as well. Although they were unable to demonstrate that the low rates of mental illness or social pathology on Tonga were due to an absence of stress, Murphy and Taumoepeau speculated that such conditions as the lack of competition and the presence of social support may buffer people against stress.[114]

131

There is also evidence that lower-social-class populations more often suffer from affective disorders, including depression, than their higher-class counterparts.[115] This appears to result from the greater onslaught of familial, social, and economic stress among lower-social-class groups. Compared to higher-social-class groups, these people are more likely to experience problems of physical abuse, eviction, loss of a job, arrest, recurring illness, and the death of loved ones. A persuasive illustration of this pattern comes from the research of British psychiatrists George W. Brown and Tirril Harris, who studied depression in Camberwell, a rundown, economically troubled, working-class area of London.[116] They found that severe depression was four times more common among working-class women (especially those with the burden of a child living at home) than it was among comparable middle-class women.

It is clear that some populations enjoy better health than others. Much that people in folk societies believe and practice is harmful to their health. But some societies buffer their members against the stresses of life by maintaining beliefs and practices that enhance well-being. Others, including small-scale societies, create stresses for no readily apparent adaptive reason, while holding to beliefs and practices that undermine health and endanger life.

Chapter *6*

From Discontent to Rebellion

Some populations have failed to survive or have lost their culture, language, or social institutions because they were not able to cope with the demands that their environments made on them. This failure to thrive is the most calamitous form of maladaptation, but it is not the only one. A few people in all societies, and many people in others, feel alienated, become depressed, or attempt suicide. Others withdraw from social life or emigrate, and it is not uncommon for people to protest or rebel. Some populations are deeply committed to the beliefs and practices that make up their cultural world, but others are less so, and some are profoundly dissatisfied with their lives. This is true not only in urbanized societies like our own but in small-scale, folk societies throughout the world. Beliefs or practices that leave a population seriously discontented or rebellious are, under most circumstances, maladaptive because they threaten the survival of that sociocultural system and endanger the physical and emotional well-being of the people in it.

How people feel about the established customs and institutions of their society can be a powerful indicator of how adequately that society and its culture serve their needs. But between blissful contentment and open rebellion lie many complexities and contradictions of human emotion and behavior. For example, women and men alike have gone to remarkable lengths to beautify themselves. They tattoo themselves over their entire bodies, cover themselves with scars, mutilate their

133

genitals, and blacken their teeth, file them into points, and knock some of them out, among other things. These are only a few examples of painful practices that have been, and in some quarters still are, eagerly pursued in the quest for beauty. As painful as these practices are, few things done in the quest for beauty were more extreme than the Chinese practice of binding the feet of women. Young girls, some still in infancy, suffered excruciating pain because their feet were bandaged so tightly that normal growth could not occur. So tightly, in fact, were the toes folded under the foot that the bones were often broken. Accounts of the anguish these children suffered during the process of replacing blood- and pus-soaked bandages with new and still tighter ones are truly harrowing.[1] The pain was so severe that the girls could not walk or even sleep, and they were too young to understand why they were being made to suffer. Eventually, the acute pain subsided, but for the rest of their lives these women were barely able to hobble, and some were carried everywhere in a sedan chair.

Chinese men have admired small feet in women since before Confucian times, but the practice of footbinding apparently did not begin until around 1100 A.D. It was at first confined to the Chinese elite, but it eventually spread throughout society, even including some peasants and the urban poor. The reasons for the origin and spread of footbinding were complex, but in addition to aesthetic considerations, Chinese men said that they saw the practice as an effective way to control the sexual liaisons of their increasingly bold wives. Once women's feet were bound, they could no longer "run around," so to speak, because they could not even leave their houses without assistance.[2] What is more, a woman with bound feet could not work; so her husband achieved prestige by demonstrating that he could afford to have a wife who did not need to work. Men also saw the practice as a clear and necessary expression of their dominance over women.[3] Before long, men also saw fit to praise the erotic advantages of footbinding, saying that the tottering style of walking it produced created more beautiful buttocks and tightened the vagina. The naked bound foot itself—"the golden lotus"—became as much a focus of erotic desire for Chinese men as women's breasts were for Westerners.

The Manchu conquerors outlawed footbinding, but to such little effect that some members of the Manchu court adopted a modified version of the practice themselves. Footbinding endured for over a thousand years without any widespread social protest by women. For one thing, Chinese women lacked political power, but at the same time they could appreciate the advantages of footbinding. It could give them beauty and sensuality, lead to a good marriage, and offer a life of leisure. Of at least equal importance, parents who imposed the practice on their young daughters were not thinking only of their daughters' futures. A daughter's marriage to a wealthy man was of obvious benefit to the entire family.[4]

With these benefits in mind, it is perhaps less surprising that footbinding lasted so long than that it ended as suddenly as it did. Opposed by Christian missionaries, the expansionist Japanese, and Westerners of all sorts, the reform-minded revolutionary governments of early twentieth-century China were able to eradicate footbinding in a decade or so among their urban population although it lasted until the 1930s in some traditional rural areas. That a practice so painful and disfiguring to women can nonetheless persist should not be surprising. In Victorian times, the same Western women (some of whom were the wives of missionaries in China) who deplored footbinding as a "barbaric" custom willingly had themselves cinched into steel- and whalebone-reinforced canvas corsets so tightly that they had difficulty breathing and their internal organs were sometimes damaged. Girls as young as 3 were corseted, and over time their corsets became progressively tighter. By adolescence many girls' back muscles had atrophied to such an extent that they could neither sit nor walk for more than a few minutes without someone's support.[5] The pursuit of beauty may be directed by men, even imposed by them, but women can find it to their advantage to acquiesce. With the controversy about silicone breast implants so freshly in mind, we need hardly be reminded that many American women (and some men) today endure painful and expensive cosmetic surgery in an effort to "beautify" their faces or bodies.

These cautionary examples alert us to the need to proceed judiciously in evaluating how dissatisfied people may be with their culture. For example, the practice of sending widows or household slaves to the grave with their deceased husbands or masters was known in many parts of the world, including China, Africa, ancient Greece, Scandinavia, and Russia. The reasons for putting a man's wives or slaves to death varied. Sometimes it was said that the deceased would need his wives or slaves to provide him with earthly comforts in the hereafter. Sometimes it was said (more cynically) that this practice would encourage wives or slaves to do everything in their power to keep their husbands or masters alive as long as possible. There were other reasons, too, ranging from jealousy about the sexual activities of surviving wives to elaborate religious justifications. Nowhere did the practice become as widespread or take on such profound metaphysical meaning as in Hindu India, where a widow could achieve virtual divinity by voluntarily immolating herself on her husband's funeral pyre.

Known as *sati* in Sanskrit and Anglicized as "suttee," this practice was observed as early as the fourth century B.C. when Alexander the Great recorded it, and despite heated controversy it has continued to occur now and then in contemporary India. Originally practiced by the wives of kings and great warriors, sati spread first to Brahmins, then to members of lower castes. Although Hindu scriptural justifications for the practice (or practices, since a widow could choose to be buried alive instead of being burned to death) were contradictory, many indicated that by choosing sati she could reduce the pollution that endangered her husband's surviving relatives, absolve herself of sin (wives were thought to bear responsibility for their husbands' death), and rejoin her husband in a cycle of future rebirths. As Richard Shweder has commented, sati can be a heroic act that represents and confirms the "deepest properties of Hinduism's moral world."[6]

Much like a wedding, the sati ceremony required elaborate ritual preparations. Priests, mourners, and an excited crowd followed the ornately dressed widow and her husband's corpse to the funeral pyre. After circling the fire, the widow distributed her jewels and money and looked into a mirror where she saw the past and the future; then a priest quoted scriptural passages that likened the pyre to a marriage bed. After the necessary ritual acts had been completed and the widow had joined her husband's corpse on the pyre, it was set alight by her son (who sometimes collapsed in grief after doing so). After the ceremony, the spot where the sati died became a shrine, and she was revered as a heroine and goddess.[7]

As improbable as the spectacle of a woman willingly, even eagerly, burning herself to death may seem, there are numerous eyewitness reports to the effect that sometimes, at least, that is exactly what took place.[8] William Carey witnessed a sati in 1798 in which the widow actually danced on the pyre to show her contempt for death before lying down next to the corpse of her husband and being consumed by flames.[9] In 1829 a British magistrate named Halliday attempted to convince a widow not to become a sati. "At length she showed

136

some impatience and asked to be allowed to proceed to the site."[10] Horrified, Halliday tried once again to dissuade her by asking if she understood how much pain she was about to suffer. The woman looked scornfully at the Englishman, then demanded that a lamp be brought to her and lighted. "Then steadfastly looking at me with an air of grave defiance she rested her right elbow on the ground and put her finger in the flame of the lamp. The finger scorched, blistered, and blackened and finally twisted up . . . this lasted for some time, during which she never moved her hand, uttered a sound or altered the expression of her countenance."[11] Halliday gave permission for the ceremony to proceed.

Over the centuries, many Hindu widows must have chosen sati deaths sublimely and reverently. But there was another reality to sati, one that falls well short of sublimity. First, it will not have escaped the reader's attention that sati was for women only; widowers had no duty to join their deceased wives in the divine devotion of a fiery death. Second, despite great pressure, very few widows actually chose sati. Even in Bengal where sati was most common, only a small minority of widows—less than 10 percent—chose sati although the prospect of widowhood was a dismal one at best.[12] Widows were not only forbidden to remarry but were compelled to live in socially isolated asceticism—praying, fasting, reading holy books, and avoiding any hint of worldly pleasure. Because widows were thought to endanger others and often were accused of being witches, they were also scorned and feared.[13] Despite the wretched conditions of widowhood, the promised rewards of sati, and the often relentless pressure exerted by the deceased husband's relatives on the widow to choose this supreme act of devotion, the great majority of widows preferred to live. Sometimes, however, they were given no choice. Because many women were married as infants, they became widows and "chose" sati while still children. One wife burned with the corpse of her adult husband was only four years old; others were scarcely older.[14]

Sometimes the pressures imposed on a widow to choose sati were anything but subtle; indeed, they amounted to murder. In 1827 a British observer witnessed a sati ceremony in which the fire had no sooner been lighted than the widow leapt off the pyre and tried to flee; several men seized her and flung her back into the blaze. Once again the widow fled, and although badly burned she managed to outdistance her pursuers and throw herself into a nearby stream where she lay "weeping bitterly."[15] She swore that she would not go through with the ceremony. Seeming to take pity on her, a man promised that if she would sit on a large cloth he had spread on the ground, he would carry her home. When she did so, she was once again seized, sewn into the cloth, and thrown back into the inferno. The cloth was immediately consumed by the flames, and the wretched victim once again tried to flee. This time she was beheaded with a sword, and her body was thrown back onto the pyre. Not exactly a serene act of wifely devotion.

It was not just tormented widows who frequently wanted no part of sati; some Hindu scriptures sharply criticized the custom. In *Mahamivantantra* (verses 79 and 80) it is said that a woman who accepts sati will go to hell.[16] And there was a vigorous anti-sati movement in India even before the British attempted to abolish the practice (the movement was not led by women but by a Brahmin man). It was also been observed that there were economic reasons for sati. It was most common in Bengal, and it was only in Bengal that a widow without a son had the same rights to the family property formerly possessed by her deceased husband. Surviving family members therefore attempted to protect family property by convincing the widow that it was her duty to join her husband in death (thereby conveniently leaving the property to her husband's family).[17]

In recent years opposition to sati in India has grown, but the ceremony has not been abandoned. In 1987 Roop Kanwar, a beautiful eighteen-year-old, college-educated woman, immolated herself with her dead husband's head on her lap while a crowd estimated at 300,000 watched in admiration. But many Indians were outraged at the death of this young woman, partly because it was reported that she had been injected with morphine before the ceremony, which raised questions about undue influence on the part of her husband's relatives.[18] Following Kanwar's death the government of Rajasthan, where the sati took place, made it a crime punishable by seven years in prison to "glorify" sati by collecting funds, building a temple, or performing a ceremony to preserve the memory of a person who committed sati; it also decreed that any attempt made to abet an act of sati was punishable by death.[19] Many Indians were indignant about this criminalization of the ritual, arguing that a widow's immolation was a courageous, inspirational tradition that reaffirmed marital devotion and belief in rebirth.[20]

The point of this example, perhaps overlong in the telling even

138

though greatly oversimplified, is that people in a society can take quite different views of their customs and institutions. It is not only we outsiders who have differing views of sati; so have Indians themselves. A similar disagreement has existed, and indeed still does, in many parts of Africa with regard to the practice of female genital mutilation, generally known as female infibulation, circumcision, or clitoral excision. As noted earlier, in parts of the Sudan, for example, the genitalia of young Nubian girls are still almost completely cut away, and the vaginal opening is sutured closed except for an opening the size of a matchstick for the passage of urine and menstrual blood. Done without anesthesia, the operation is excruciatingly painful, there can be dangerous complications, and some girls die.[21] Nubian men are sometimes squeamish about the practice,[22] but women have continued to support infibulation despite governmental efforts to abolish it.[23] Farther south, in East Africa, the operation does not involve closing the vaginal opening, but it does require excision of the clitoris and both sets of labia—as in Nubia, the pain is terrible. There the operation does not take place until the girls are adolescents, and not every girl is able to stand the pain. Some have to be excised while they are held down by men. For many years, educated East Africans have deplored the practice, and it has been illegal in Kenya for some years. It nevertheless still takes place both in Kenya and elsewhere in Africa.

When I did research among the remote and then quite unacculturated Pokot of northwest Kenya in 1961 and 1962, I could not find a single Pokot woman among the more than sixty I interviewed who would criticize the operation. Some had no idea why the operation was performed, saying only that it was a Pokot custom, but others said that it made childbirth easier and that it did not reduce their sexual satisfaction. (Pokot women at that time typically had sexual relations before being circumcised, but they did not bear children). Pokot men approved of the operation, too. But many Kamba women in central Kenya detested it. Although the Kamba operation, in 1962 at least, was somewhat less extreme than the one carried out by the Pokot, many Kamba women were bitter about the practice, and some refused to participate in it. Furthermore, although Kamba men tended to support the practice, some openly expressed ambivalence about it.

Though the Pokot and Kamba were quite emphatic in their views regarding female genital excision, how people feel about various aspects of their cultures can sometimes be difficult to determine. When a police post was established among the Dugum Dani of highland Irian Jaya in 1961, Karl Heider, who was then conducting field research among these people, predicted that pacification would only "rechannel" their violence. Heider was convinced that warfare was so central to Dani life that if it were abolished, the result would be an increase of within-group violence, including suicide, which he thought of as a form of hostility directed inward. Heider was wrong, as he later freely admitted. For two years following pacification, there were no suicides and no increase in within-group violence. What is more, the Dani never complained to him about the police-imposed prevention of their presumably all-important practice of warfare.[24] The Dani, it seems, were not as devoted to the practice of warfare as Heider had believed.

A useful index of how committed a population, like the Dani, may be to its traditional beliefs and practices is their reaction to colonial contact. Various ethnographers have observed that people in small, traditional societies may willingly give up one of their apparently important practices after only minimal contact with Christian missionaries or European administrators. Societies throughout highland Papua New Guinea (before Australian contact) required that boys go through initiation ceremonies in which they were forced to drink only partly slaked lime that blistered their mouths and throats, were beaten with stinging nettles, were denied water, had barbed grass pushed up their urethras to cause bleeding, were compelled to swallow bent lengths of cane until vomiting was induced, and were required to fellate older men, who also had anal intercourse with them. These ceremonies were generally thought by anthropologists to play a vital role in these societies; but soon after Australian contact took place, several of these societies gave up their violent initiation rituals without apparent reluctance.[25] Some men even volunteered the information that they did not regret giving up the more violent aspects of their initiations.[26]

Other societies gave up traditional practices just as willingly. Although the highlanders of Papua New Guinea were among the most warlike people ever known, like the Dani many of these populations gave up warfare as soon as Australian police patrols appeared, and sometimes they remained completely pacified as long as a single European was present.[27] Sterling Robbins has reported that Auyana men freely admitted that they had been terribly afraid when there

140

had been warfare and that their lives were better since the government prohibited it. Robbins wrote that one man told him that ". . . he could now eat without looking over his shoulder and could leave his house in the morning to urinate without fear of being shot."[28] Similarly, according to Van Baal, the Marind-anim quickly gave up their practice of anal intercourse after Dutch pressure because, according to Van Baal, the Marind-anim themselves found this behavior repugnant.[29]

Sometimes, however, evidence of people's dissatisfaction need not be inferred from their reactions to externally imposed change. Some people clearly, even passionately, say that they dislike their society's customs or feel guilty about taking part in them. Although men among the Cheyenne Indians of the North American Plains sometimes gang-raped an errant wife as custom dictated, many said that they disliked doing so. Some Yanomamo Indians, whose culture exalted ferocity and perpetuated warfare, frankly admitted that they disliked having to live in fear of violent death,[30] and Nisa, that outspoken !Kung San woman, found much to criticize about San culture. She even declared that the ways of the San god were "foul."[31]

Comparable examples can be drawn from the highlands of Papua New Guinea. Women among the Mae Enga said that they detested the frequent warfare that the men engaged in, no matter how just the cause of the violence might have been,[32] and according to Donald Tuzin, Ilahita Arapesh men openly admitted that they felt "deeply shamed" about their treatment of their sons during the physically painful and emotionally terrifying Tambaran initiation ritual.[33] Tuzin also quotes an Ilahita Arapesh man as follows: "It is true that sometimes men feel ashamed and guilty over eating good food while their wives go hungry."[34] And FitzJohn Porter Poole reports this about the Bimin-Kuskusmin practice of cannibalism: "Many Bimin-Kuskusmin men and women whom I interviewed and who admitted to socially proper cannibalistic practices acknowledged considerable ambivalence, horror, and disgust at their own acts. Many persons noted that they had been unable to engage in the act, had not completed it, had vomited or even fainted, or had hidden the prescribed morsel and had lied about consuming it."[35] What is more, Poole observed that on the eleven occasions that he actually witnessed cannibalism among the Bimin-Kuskusmin, they exhibited "extreme reticence and ambivalence" about the act.[36]

Examples like these could easily be multiplied from societies

141

around the world. People sometimes dislike certain of their traditional practices and give them up if the opportunity arises. In fact, some individuals so dislike a particular custom that they attempt to change it or eliminate it altogether. One of the best-known examples of this phenomenon occurred in 1819 when members of the Hawaiian aristocracy and priesthood intentionally violated some of their most central and sacred taboos. The Hawaiian taboo system imposed many proscriptions that regulated the conduct of the nobility and commoners alike. Many foods, such as bananas and coconuts, were forbidden to women, and the two sexes could not eat together. It was these food taboos that paramount chief Liholiho and his high priest Hewahewa chose to violate. Alfred Kroeber concluded that this act was due to what he called "culture fatigue"; he believed that the Hawaiians were simply tired of their burdensome system of taboos.[37] Subsequent analyses have indicated that although many Hawaiians did find their taboo system to be onerous, complex social, political, and economic factors, including Western contact, were also involved in the decision to abolish it.[38]

This Hawaiian illustration shows that a few individuals can eradicate an unwanted or troublesome aspect of their culture, but these individuals were not ordinary people but were chiefs, nobles, and priests, and people like these have often been able to bring about social change. For example, Leo Pospisil described how a wealthy man among the Kapauku of the highlands of Papua New Guinea was able to change his society's incest rules—rules that were enforced by a penalty of death—because he wanted to marry a comely woman who would otherwise have been denied to him.[39] Some African kings made and remade customs almost willy-nilly. Shaka Zulu is a particularly well known example, but there were many others.

However, sometimes customs are so tenaciously defended that even people of power and influence can do nothing to change them. The Skidi Pawnee Indians of Nebraska (a tribe of perhaps 5,000 people), like their Caddoan-speaking neighbors to the south, sacrificed human beings for religious purposes.[40] Whether in response to a priest's request that a sacrifice be conducted to prevent misfortune or simply because a warrior who had captured someome from another society chose to offer the captive for sacrifice to propitiate the sacred Morning Star, the unfortunate victims—men, women, children, and even infants—were tied to a scaffold and tortured before they were killed and dismembered.

142

Sometime in the early nineteenth century, Knife Chief, the political leader of the Skidi Pawnee and a greatly respected man, decided that human sacrifice was cruel and unnecessary. Whether he did so simply because he was a compassionate man or because he had been influenced by his occasional contacts with white Americans is not known. What is known is that he began to speak against the practice, and in 1817 he attempted to halt the sacrifice of a captive girl. Just before the torture of the young victim was about to begin, Knife Chief's son, by all accounts the most honored warrior among the Skidi Pawnee, stepped in front of the girl and declared that it was his father's wish that she be set free. As the Pawnee audience looked on in amazement, he freed the girl, threw her on his horse, and delivered her safely to her own people. A year later, father and son again prevented a sacrifice—this time of a ten-year-old Spanish boy—by ransoming the captive from a warrior who was determined to offer the child for sacrifice.

As courageous, determined, and influential as Knife Chief and his son were, their efforts to put an end to the practice of human sacrifice failed. Led by their priests, the Skidi Pawnee continued to propitiate the Morning Star by sacrificing human captives at least until 1834 and perhaps much longer. Knife Chief and his son had failed, but they stand as striking examples of individuals who did everything in their power to change a custom that they found abhorrent even though that custom was held sacred by the rest of the society.[41]

The preceding examples are meant to illustrate the fact that people in small, traditional societies object to some aspects of their culture, just as people do in complex, postindustrial societies like our own. If there were to be a worldwide opinion poll of people's satisfaction with their customs or their lives, it is very likely that people in various societies would express quite different levels of satisfaction. When Gallup's organization actually conducted such a poll in several western European countries, that is what they found,[42] and surveys in the United States have often reported substantial differences in verbal expressions of life satisfaction in different parts of the country as well as among various age and ethnic groups.[43] Determining how satisfied people from radically different cultures may be with their lives would be a difficult undertaking, but it might not be an impossible one, at least within relatively homogeneous culture areas. Even if such a survey were never carried out, the principle it rests upon is nonetheless important. People do evaluate various aspects of their lives, including specific practices that their cultures require of them, and a systematic appraisal of their evaluations would almost certainly show that people in some societies are far more satisfied with the various aspects of their cultures than are people in others. However, we need not rely on people's vocal expressions of displeasure about their lives because their actions sometimes offer more compelling evidence about how effective certain social systems are in meeting the needs of their members.

When people's needs are not met, they may feel alienated. Few concepts have generated more widespread interest in the West than alienation. Although the larger part of the thousands of published items relating to this concept focus on the West, a sufficient number relate to non-Western societies to leave no doubt that feelings of meaninglessness, powerlessness, normlessness, social isolation, and estrangement from one's culture have been experienced by people in many parts of the world.[44] Sometimes people's sense of alienation—or dysphoria, as it is also known—can lead to such apathy that essential tasks are left undone. Dysphoria has often been associated with the excessive use of alcohol or other drugs. Of course, heavy drinking is not always a product of dysphoria or alienation. Long before the Cheyenne Indians were defeated by U.S. military forces and while their warlike culture was still proudly intact, they sometimes drank to such excess that whole bands were too drunk to feed themselves, and warriors were occasionally so intoxicated that they had to be tied to their horses so that they could escape from attacks by the U.S. Cavalry.[45] Drinking can have positive social functions, as many scholars have shown, but this kind of drunkenness by the Cheyenne would be difficult to construe as adaptive.[46] When some American Indian societies were defeated and confined to reservations, many individuals became depressed and in their unhappiness drank to excess. It is possible to argue that a retreat into the gentle fog of inebriation might be adaptive for people undergoing severe culture loss, but for so many of these Indians, there was nothing gentle about their drunkenness.

The alcohol-related death rate among American Indians in the United States in 1982 was almost three times that of the nation as a whole, and in some tribes the rate was even higher. Among the Coast Salish of British Columbia ten years ago, 80 percent of all accidental and violent deaths were associated with alcohol, and 7 percent died of cirrhosis of the liver versus 1.3 percent for the general population.[47] In 1989 so many Indian women in the United States were drinking alcohol that their death rate from cirrhosis of the liver had almost matched that of Indian men, and it far exceeded the national average. In the United States as a whole, between 1 and 3 babies out of each 1,000 are born with fetal alcohol syndrome, but among some Plains Indian tribes the rate is 10 per 1,000.[48] It is difficult to imagine how it could possibly be adaptive for any population to have 1 percent of its children born with fetal alcohol syndrome. Reports of equally maladaptive uses of alcohol are readily available from many parts of the world.

Profoundly disaffected people may have recourse to all manner of socially disruptive actions, from theft or homocide to blasphemy or false accusations, but a common outcome is suicide, which has been reported to occur in all but a handful of societies. Some motives for suicide, such as altruism or revenge, may not represent cultural protest or estrangement, but suicide often results from and gives expression to alienation, a sense of the meaninglessness of one's life, or refusal to accept a culturally approved practice such as wife beating or the kind of arranged marriage in which the bride is forced to marry a man she does not like. Among the Lusi-Kaliai of West New Britain, wives who are badly beaten by their husbands often express anger or despair, and some run away, but their kinsmen are likely to force them to return out of fear that failure to do so would compel them to surrender the brideprice given them by the husbands' relatives. Confronted by such an impasse, the distraught wife may kill herself.[49] In parts of East Africa, a woman who was forced by her father and brothers to marry a man she found repellent—a common occurrence—might also run away, and as among the Lusi-Kaliai, her relatives would force her to return for fear of losing the bridewealth. These women, too, sometimes hanged themselves, leaving no doubt how they felt about the custom of arranged marriage.[50]

In most societies, suicide is an uncommon event, but it can sometimes occur with such frequency that social survival is imperiled. The rise in suicides among young black men in the United States during the past two decades has elicited widespread concern,[51] and suicides have occurred so frequently among young people in Samoa and Truk in recent years that the situation has been characterized as epidemic.[52] Frequent resort to suicide is not confined to societies that are

145

undergoing Westernization or the stresses of urban poverty and racism. People in some small, traditional societies also kill themselves frequently. The loss of a friend, relative, or spouse to suicide can be deeply troubling to survivors and may lead to social conflict of various kinds, but the occurrence of a few suicides should not threaten a society's viability.[53] However, it is not the case, as some anthropologists have declared, that suicide is always a rare event, nor one that offers no threat to a society's viability.[54] Among the Bimin-Kuskusmin of highland Papua New Guinea, suicide occurs so often that, according to Poole, "its genesis, prevention, and ultimate social costs are of paramount concern to the Bimin-Kuskusmin."[55] Ten percent of all deaths known to Poole during the six generations prior to his field research were due to suicide, and some suicides, such as those of children, may not have been reported. This is a dangerously high percentage and one that deeply troubled the Bimin-Kuskusmin. What is more remarkable, during the twenty-four months of Poole's field research in the early 1970s, thirty of the fifty-eight deaths that occurred—a startling 57 percent of the total—were suicides. In addition to these actual suicides, many people threatened suicide, and others attempted to kill themselves but failed. For example, while Poole was with these people, eleven women killed themselves, and another sixty-seven women made ninety-three serious threats to do so. In addition, two children between the ages of 5 and 7 attempted suicide. It is little wonder that the Bimin-Kuskusmin were concerned. Try to imagine a two-year period in any Western society during which 57 percent of all deaths were due to suicide.

Except for the rare "altruistic" suicide of a failed ritual leader or a heroic warrior, the Bimin-Kuskusmin strongly deplored suicide and did everything they could to prevent it by making the actual act or the failed attempt highly stigmatizing. In spite of these measures, Bimin-Kuskusmin killed themselves at an unprecedented rate. Most suicides were by men in the 23-to-34 age range who found the demands of their culture for manliness too great to bear. Strength, power, bravery, self-control, and influence over others were highly prized, and men who failed to meet these cultural standards for masculinity expressed "resentment" about the demands the culture put upon them.[56] Women, who killed themselves less often than men, did so primarily because they were dissatisfied with the conditions of married life. As was noted earlier, many Bimin-Kuskusmin found their practice of ritual cannibalism repugnant. It is evident that an

146

extraordinary number of these people found that life in Bimin-Kuskusmin society was not worth living.

Consider the despondent peasants who lived in the small county of T'an-ch'eng in northeastern China in 1670. As described so evocatively by Jonathan Spence, the suffering of these people was extreme even for rural China. Ravaged by bandits, droughts, floods, locusts, epidemics, killing frosts, and finally, a devastating earthquake, the population of the county decreased from 200,000 in 1620 to 60,000 in 1670. Over the same period the area of land under cultivation fell by two-thirds. Many peasants starved, and others survived only by becoming cannibals.[57] When Huang Liu-hung arrived in 1670 to take up his duties as magistrate, he found a population whose lives had lost all meaning. He wrote that "many people held their lives to be of no value," and he was horrified to hear "every day" that someone had committed suicide. He was so alarmed by these suicides that he tried to shame the survivors out of killing themselves by posting proclamations throught the county that accused the peasants of having no respect for their own lives. He threatened to leave the bodies of those who committed suicide where they died "as food for the flies and maggots."[58]

People who are truly despondent about the conditions of their lives often seek release from their despair in drunkenness or suicide, as the people of T'an-ch'eng did, but sometimes people take more constructive actions in an attempt to revitalize their culture. Revitalization movements, as anthropologists have called these attempts to renew or repair one's culture, have occurred throughout the world. For example, when the proud and powerful tribes of the Iroquois Confederation in New York and Canada were eventually defeated and confined to reservations, they began to drink heavily whenever they could, and their drinking was accompanied by murderous violence. When sober, they tended to be depressed and suicidal. Despondent and disunited, they believed that their misfortune was the work of witches among them. But instead of destroying themselves as others did, they adopted a new religion proposed by the prophet Handsome Lake. Handsome Lake and his followers designed a way of life that led to the renaissance of Iroquois society and culture.[59] Many other populations that have experienced a degradation in their way of life have taken similar steps to renew their old culture or design a new and more satisfying one. Many of the ethnic minorities of Eastern Europe and the former Soviet Union are currently attempting such a revitalization, and other populations, such as Islamic fundamentalists, are attempting to revitalize their religions as well as their societies.

We are likely to think of people in small, traditional societies as being emotionally and psychologically committed to their way of life, and in fact this is often the case. People in many societies refer to themselves as "the people" and regard all others as alien and repellent, if not downright subhuman. The Hopi Indians, for example, who have long believed that their way of life is superior to all others, continue to maintain cultural barriers that separate themselves from all other people. Not only the Hopi but many people believe that their way of life is the only one, and in many parts of the world today, commitment to one's ethnic group and religion is growing in intensity, surprising many who in post-Enlightenment optimism expected such devotions to diminish as rationalism grew.[60] Even the miserable Ik of Uganda, who were quite literally starving to death when Colin Turnbull visited them in the mid 1960s, preferred to stay together and die rather than move away from their sacred mountain in search of food and survival.

It is true that many societies—even the people of Duddie's Branch—not only command the emotional commitment of their members but are closed to outsiders.[61] An outsider cannot become a Hopi any more than a European can become a Japanese. But other societies are more open and have long attracted people to them from other cultures. For example, the tribal boundaries in Kenya that have seemed so pronounced to many observers (and that continue to generate social conflict) were in large measure the product of the administrative needs of the colonial government. Before the advent of colonial rule, ethnic affiliations were more fluid, with trade and intermarriage regularly taking place among many culturally and linguistically distinct populations.[62] A similar phenomenon occurred in South Africa.[63] Indeed, human history has been marked as much by population movement as by closed societies that zealously defend their homelands against outsiders. For one thing, trade has taken place almost everywhere in the world, and traders sometimes settle down in foreign societies, as French and American "mountain men" often did in various North American Indian societies.[64].

Population movement also occurs because individuals and small groups of kinsmen may hive off from the larger society to avoid conflict, improve their subsistence, or escape some unwanted activity such as feuding or taxation. The membership of bands among hunting and gathering societies such as the Dogrib, Inuit, Mbuti, Australian Aborigines, and San is quite fluid. Among the !Kung San described by Richard Lee, each year 13 percent of the population made a permanent residential shift from one camp to another, and another 35 percent of the people divided their time between two or more camps.[65] There are many reasons why people like these have chosen to change their band affiliation, but displeasure with the beliefs and behaviors of members of their previous band must number among them. Sometimes large groups such as Bantu-speakers throughout Africa or Polynesians in Oceania have migrated to escape from a tyrannical chief, but on other occasions only an individual or a small family will leave the remainder of the society behind to live separately. Men often lived alone for long periods among the Hadza hunting and gathering people of Tanzania,[66] and recently a woman and her two daughters were discovered living entirely on their own as nomadic gatherers in the vast Manu National Park of southeastern Peru.[67] Sometimes people such as these have been exiled, but others appear to have been so estranged that they preferred to live alone.

It cannot be estimated how many people who leave the society in which they were born and enculturated did so because that society was not meeting one or more of their needs, but the phenomenal growth of cities throughout the world suggests that this must often have been the case. It is common for people to migrate to cities, expecting to achieve wealth and then return home.[68] Some of these people, like those in the young city of Jos in northern Nigeria, remain there unwillingly, still hoping to return to their native villages,[69] but other people throughout the world have sought out cities to escape some unwanted aspect of village life and have remained in those cities because they preferred to. When a squatter in the squalid slums of Manila was asked whether he would not prefer to be back in his province where he could see coconut trees and rice fields and feel the sea breezes, the man replied, in words that must have been uttered the world over, "But life in the province is dull."[70] Whether to escape boredom or for some other reason, untold millions have migrated to cities in search of better lives.[71]

When people are dissatisfied with their cultures, they can express their distate by, among other things, a dysphoric retreat from it—an act of suicide—or they can emigrate. They can also remain active members of the society but engage in social protest or rebellion.

149

Children, needless to say, regularly protest against the newly experienced constraints of their culture, and sometimes they band together to lash out at adults, but in most small-scale or folk societies by the time children reach puberty, they are sufficiently in their culture's thrall that all but a few endure adolescence, including painful initiation, without major protest and eagerly look foward to taking on adult roles. Sometimes, however, the system goes awry, as it did among the Samburu of northern Kenya.[72]

The Samburu were warlike, Maasai-speaking cattleherders, whose young men had traditionally served as warriors protecting the rest of the tribe and its cattle against raids by neighboring tribesmen. Organized by age-grades, these young men lived in warrior encampments that served as military outposts on the Samburu borders. Life in these camps could be exciting, with the ever-present prospect of warfare and heroism. The British colonial government of Kenya prohibited cattle raiding, but their control was only partially effective, and raids sometimes still took place. What is more, encampments of unmarried women were established near the warriors' camps. The combination of romance and glory made this situation quite tolerable for a while, but the greatest goal for Samburu men was not to remain lifelong warriors but to marry, accumulate many wives and cattle, and live prosperous and respectable lives as married men. However, Samburu society was gerontocratic, and the elders who wielded power were in no hurry to allow the warriors to marry and settle down. For one thing, older married men coveted the same young women as wives that the warriors already had as lovers. For another, the more warriors who remained on active service, the safer the married men's herds were from enemy raids.

This system was viable only as long as the warriors and their lovers were content, and when the elders continued to deny an age-set of warriors the right to marry (sometimes until they were in their thirties), there were open protests and near rebellion. Warriors went on unauthorized cattle raids that provoked retaliation against the elders' herds and fines from the government, they seduced the young wives of married men, and these excitable young warriors even posed a continuing threat of violence against the elders themselves. A Samburu warrior was taught to respect elders and to aspire to become one, but the main thing that prevented outright revolution was a belief, shared by all Samburu, that elders possessed the supernatural power to place a deadly curse on any young person who offended.

hiv, a small horticultural population in the
lso rejected their leader because he behaved
ded privileges that were unacceptable to his
e who lived as foragers in small bands that
or positions of authority may protest against
their culture by refusing to behave as their
e them to do. For example, all hunting and
w a principle of generalized reciprocity by
sity of sharing food is inculcated very early
it life not only by praising those who do share
en threatening those who do not. Yet despite
are, it quite often happens that people do

consistenly exhorted one another to share,
do so,[88] and the Sirionó of eastern Bolivia,
ral emphasis on sharing, rarely actually did
lant. It was noted earlier that the Sirionó ate
ght or in the forest rather than share it and
their vaginas.[89] Among the Mbuti Pygmies,
aramount value, but in reality food was often
t Turnbull wrote, "It would be a rare Mbuti
ceal a portion of the catch in case she was
ers."[90] The refusal to share food in the face
do so would appear to be evidence of dis-
inent cultural value.

toward authority has frequently been rit-
popularized the term "rituals of rebellion"
which women behaved aggressively toward
hich subjects derided their king.[91] Edward
erm "rituals of apparent conflict," and this
more apt because these ceremonies involved
tual rebellion, and they also served other
g, the resolution of disputes, and rites of
in many African kingdoms participated in
which their king was ritually ridiculed and
ression of public discontent, but these cer-
f actual rebellion because they eventually
of royal rule. Other societies have delegated
ism toward authority to a jester, who, like
mong the Plateau Thonga of Mozambique,

The power of this curse held the Samburu society together, however precariously, but unmarried men and women made their dislike of the system plain. As anthropologist Paul Spencer, who studied the Samburu in the later 1950s, put it, the British-imposed ban on warfare as well as the frustrations the warriors endured at the hands of the elders had turned them into "angry young men."[73] Of course, because the Samburu had not been studied before British pacification, it is possible that their warriors had always chafed under the frustrations of prolonged bachelorhood.

Generational conflict has occurred in the smallest, most egalitarian societies as well as in the largest and most stratified ones, but as much as young people have been dissatisfied with their cultures, women have typically been even more discontented. The extent to which women accept and value their culturally prescribed roles varies from society to society, but in a good many of them, women have been quite unhappy and have (not without justification, I might add) blamed men for their plight. Women have launched spirited verbal and even physical assaults against their husbands in various parts of the world, but with rare exceptions men physically dominate women, and they are often far from gentle about it. As a result, when women protest, they usually do so indirectly. Sometimes women consciously adopt a sick role, as in *susto* (or fright sickness, common in Latin America), to escape, if only temporarily, from the burdens of their lives. Writing about the Zapotec of Oaxaca, Douglas Uzzell concluded that women who claimed to suffer from *susto* were able to withdraw from ordinary relationships—including beatings from their husbands—because the illness was thought to be fatal unless the patient was indulged.[74]

In many parts of Africa, women who objected to their husbands' dominance chose (often consciously, there is good reason to believe) to become possessed by spirits instead of adopting a sick role. Once possessed, these women (frequently speaking in tongues) demanded material goods from their husbands, and they sometimes dressed as men or ridiculed them as well.[75] In order to rid themselves of the spirits, whose continued presence could prove fatal (depriving husbands of the valuable resource and investment that a wife represented), men regularly acceded to their wives' demands. Spirit possession, which occurs in many parts of the world in addition to Africa, allows women to protest against the circumstances of their lives and to receive at least temporary benefits; like claiming a sick role, it can be an effective form of protest. Another form of indirect protest was practiced by women among the Awald 'Ali Bedouin in Egypt's western desert. Distressed by the cultural constraints of arranged marriage and enforced segregation, these women indulged in various kinds of irreverent discourse about men and masculinity, including oral lyric poetry that discreetly but pointedly ridiculed, chided, and sometimes excoriated men.[76]

Women have also taken aggressive action against what they have perceived as intolerable behavior on the part of men. From Ulithi Atoll in Micronesia to the Inuit of the far north, aggrieved women sometimes gathered together to direct obscene and abusive taunts and songs against men. Women among the Andean people who were first incorporated into the Inca Empire and later subjugated to Spanish colonial rule protested against the misery of their lives in a number of ways. Sometimes they became so desperate that they preferred suicide to a tormented life.[77] Other Andean women preferred killing their own children to allowing a new generation to suffer under the rule of colonial officials. Those who did so killed their sons rather than their daughters to protest the manifold ways in which men had betrayed them. Still other women fled with their children to inaccessible regions where they established an underground culture of resistance to colonial rule.[78]

Among the Samburu (whose warriors, as we have seen, were also discontented) bands of twenty or so women would sing ribaldly abusive and threatening songs outside the house of an elder who, for instance, was unusually harsh with his wives.[79] In other parts of Africa, women's protests could become particularly overt and even painful.[80] When women among the Igbo of Nigeria were offended by something a man did (such as mistreating his wife or infringing on women's economic rights), they would gather at his household where they danced and sang abusive songs that detailed his offenses (and not infrequently questioned his masculinity). They would also pound on the walls of his house, and if he came outside to object, they would even rough him up a bit. All this would continue until the man apologized and promised not to repeat his offenses.[81] Among the Bakweri of West Cameroon, if a woman was offended by a man, she might call out all the women of the village, who then descended on the culprit and demanded an apology and recompense.[82] A similar phenomenon occurred among the Kamba of Kenya, whose women were ordinarily quite subservient to their harshly domineering husbands.[83] However, when Kamba women felt that something had taken

152

was allowed to insult and accuse a chief with impunity.[93] The Society of Fools in medieval Europe played a similar role, as did clowns in Samoa, who were allowed to ridicule their political leaders without fear of retaliation.[94] So it was for the "fool dancers" of the Kwakiutl Indians of America's northwest coast, the *Koyemshi* society of clowns of the Zuni Indians, and many similar groups.[95]

The actions of these clowns, like those taken in collective rituals, represent a good measure of dissatisfaction with authority even though they do not involve overt rebellion. However, during some ceremonies people do become violent. King Henry IV of England was very nearly killed by masked Christmas mummers,[96] and violence was a common feature of the pre-Lenten carnival ceremonies of West Indian slaves. [97] The threat to authority posed by masked revelers during carnival in the French town of Romans in 1580 has been described in detail by French historian Emmanuel LeRoy Ladurie.[98] Every year the people of Romans staged two carnivals. The one engaged in by wealthy nobles involved rituals of reversal but was entirely peaceful. The carnival of the poor commoners was quite different. It involved serious social protest against such things as the heavy taxes imposed on commoners by the tax-exempt nobles and clergy. The nobles recognized the threat posed by the commoners' carnival protest. One of their leaders said, "The poor want to take all our earthly goods and our women, too; they want to kill us, perhaps even eat our flesh."[99] Such threats were not confined to late sixteenth-century France. The disrespect for authority and the threat of violence during Carnival or the Christmas season alarmed the wealthy and powerful members of many societies, including those in contemporary American cities who clamped down on mummers (Philadelphia) and who recently imposed many restrictions on Mardi Gras revelers (New Orleans).[100]

Social fission, secession, and disbandment have been commonplace occurrences in small-scale societies, as was the internal conflict that led to disharmony and social disruption.[101] It is not uncommon for people's dissatisfaction with some aspect of their lives to become so profound that they attempt to kill their political and religious leaders or other people who are thought to be the cause of their distress. Like many other people whose social and economic circumstances have become troubled, Mayan Indians in the township of Teklum in Mexico killed many suspected witches despite the efforts of Mexican police to prevent these homicides.[102] And, of course, the orgies of witch killing in Africa and Europe need no retelling here. But it is not only persons thought guilty of sorcery or witchcraft who become victims when a population is discontented. Many categories of objectionable people become likely targets: merchants, strangers, and people who profess a different religion, practice a suspicious trade (like smith or healer), or are racially different.

Religious and political leaders may be vulnerable, too. Among the southern Nilo-Hamitic pastoralists of East Africa, prophets had enormous influence because of their ability to divine and make rain. Prophets used their supernatural powers to plan cattle raids and to determine when it would be propitious to plant crops and conduct circumcision ceremonies. When their divinatory predictions were successful, prophets were treated with great respect and received many economic benefits. But prophets were also feared because of their mystic powers, which were often thought to include witchcraft.[103] If their prophecies failed, they could be killed. As recently as 1962, many Pokot said that they revered their prophet and would obey any command he gave, but a previous prophet was killed when his prophecies failed.

When people are discontented, political leaders from head men to kings have also frequently been killed despite—sometimes because of—their power. As we saw, in only a dozen years Shaka transformed the Zulu from a small, insignificant tribe to an empire with considerable wealth and great military power. Early in his reign Shaka was extremely popular. When he was wounded (by men from a conquered tribe), some 30,000 people assembled to grieve, but over the years his popularity waned as he killed his own people ever more capriciously and often. Eventually, his reign became one of unrelieved terror. He also began to mismanage his army. When his beloved mother died, Shaka became unhinged. After ordering ten of his mother's hand-maidens buried alive with her, he gave orders that led to the death of thousands of his subjects.[104] He then declared a period of mourning for his mother during which time no crops could be planted and no milk could be drunk; sexual relations were to cease as well, and any woman found to be pregnant was to be killed. The public outcry was so great that Shaka ended the mourning edicts after three months, but Zulu displeasure with their increasingly bizarre king emboldened his half-brothers to assassinate him. He was buried in an unmarked grave, and the Zulu people rejoiced.[105]

As so-called social bandits have done in many parts of the world, disaffected populations have often focused their indignation on the wealthy.[106] The fourteenth-century English peasants were so embittered by high taxes, corruption, and seemingly unending war that they formed lawless bands that ravaged the English countryside, and the legend of Robin Hood once again became popular with all save the rich. A similar pattern developed in nineteenth-century Ethiopia, other parts of Africa, and the Middle East.[107] The wealthy have been killed in violent uprisings in states the world over, and they were often not safe in small tribal societies, either. To take but one example the Kapauku of Papua New Guinea highly valued the accumulation of wealth, which brought with it respect and influence, but if wealthy men were not sufficiently generous, they could be killed, and they frequently were.[108]

As the chapters of world history so dolorously record, it was a rare year in our past when people somewhere on earth were not in overt rebellion against their government. When Pitirim Sorokin reviewed twenty-four centuries of European history, he found that there were only four peaceful years for every one of civil strife. Other parts of the world were even less stable.[109] Between 1961 and 1968, civil violence was reported in all but 7 of the world's 121 largest nations, and over the past two centuries, ten of the world's most bloody conflicts were civil wars or rebellions. During the first two decades after the end of World War II, there were more attempts to overthrow governments than there were national elections.[110]

Whether the reason for their rebellious rage was hunger, taxation, governmental venality, police brutality, or some other perceived injustice or inequity, slaves, peasants, and the urban poor have fought to change their societies. Often they have failed. Spartacus's slave rebellion resulted in the deaths of 30,000 slaves, 6,000 of whom were crucified, and it did not end slavery in the Roman Republic or Empire. The Maroons in Surinam, on the other hand, found their freedom, even though the institution of slavery remained, but Toussaint L'Ouverture's slave rebellion on Haiti led to the abolition of slavery, though not oppression, in that still unfortunate country.

Although most peasant uprisings failed to bring about lasting social or cultural change, some were more successful.[111] The anti-Manchu Taiping rebellion—led by a man who thought himself to be the son of God and younger brother of Jesus Christ—laid waste to twelve of China's provinces and cost between twenty and forty million lives, but after fourteen years of fighting, the Manchus had lost most of

157

their control over China. Other revolutions in Mexico, France, and the United States brought about significant political changes, as did communist revolutions in Russia, China, Cuba, and elsewhere. The dramatic anticommunist revolutions of 1990 and 1991 in Eastern Europe and the Soviet Union have also brought about fundamental social, economic, and political change. Whether rebellions succeed or fail and whether the changes they bring about are lasting or temporary, the fact remains that throughout history people have disliked some aspects of their society enough to risk their lives in an attempt to change them. Rebellion is a melancholy staple of human existence.

The point of this chapter is not that all people everywhere dislike the societies in which they live. Surely, all people are dissatisfied with something in their lives much of the time, but populations differ in the extent and intensity of their discontent. Norwegians and Swedes may not be the most satisfied people in Europe, as Naroll concluded, but despite their heavy consumption of alcohol, high rates of depression and suicide, and complaints about taxation, most of what they say and do suggests that most of them are indeed quite content with their lives, something that cannot be said of people in many contemporary societies, such as the former Soviet Union or, for that matter, Russian in Czarist times. When the Marquis de Custine traveled to Russia in 1839, he stopped over in a hotel in Lübeck, where the landlord tried to dissuade him from going to Russia, saying that it must be a "bad country." The German based this opinion on his observation that when Russian visitors arrived in Germany after leaving Russia, they had a gay and easy air, "like . . . birds let loose from their cages." But when it came time for these same Russians to return to Russia, they became gloomy and morose.[112] How Russians felt about their motherland in 1839 was more complex than this innkeeper knew, but there was discontent even then, and the passing years were to demonstrate how profoundly dissatisfied with their society many Russians were and, it seems safe to say, still are.

To recapitulate, people everywhere express varying degrees of dissatisfaction with certain dimensions of their lives. Sometimes their discontent involves no more than ambivalence about a particular custom, but some discontent leads to self-destruction or violent rebellion. What matters most for our concern with the feasibility of evaluating social and cultural systems is that through their words and deeds people make their own evaluations, and by so doing, they

158

provide evidence of the extent to which those social and cultural systems are failing to meet the needs of their members.

A society whose members are perpetually intoxicated, capriciously murderous, or frequently suicidal must change, or both the system and its population will cease to exist. When discontented people take steps to transform some of their institutions to end internecine destructiveness, the result can be a more effective social and cultural system; but it is not legitimate—indeed it is tautologous—to conclude that all discontent is therefore adaptive. Not all systems require major changes (at least not in the short run), and discontent so extreme that it leads to rebellion is not an indication of a well-adapted society. There are no perfectly adapted societies, all fail to some degree to meet all of the needs of their members, and all could crumble under sufficient competitive pressure, but those whose members are reasonably content are more likely to survive than those whose members are not, just as those that can make necessary changes without violent rebellion are better adapted than those that cannot.

Chapter 7

The Death of Populations, Societies, and Cultures

The story of Ishi, the last surviving Yahi Indian, poignantly illustrates the annihilation of a small society. When Ishi walked out of the hills of northern California in 1911, his unforgettable dignity and humanity impressed all who came to know him. At first exhausted, emaciated, and terrified, he was dressed in tatters. He later dressed in a shirt and tie but kept his feet bare. Eventually he wore shoes as well and was on his way, albeit very slowly, to enjoying his life among white Americans when he died of tuberculosis in 1916. His death to a foreign disease was a suitable reminder of the devastation that Euro-American guns and diseases had visited on his people.

The Yahi Indians apparently lived in northern California for over 2,000 years before the arrival of more numerous people, such as the Wintu, forced them to abandon their game-rich valleys and move into the more isolated foothills of Mt. Lassen. Always a small tribe, there were probably only 400 Yahi left when white settlers arrived in the nineteenth century. The Yahi were unique among North American Indians in that they alone released arrows from their bows as the Mongols did, with the bow almost parallel to the ground and the palm of the hand that drew the bowstring facing up. They were hunters and foragers who also caught fish, usually salmon, in the fast, cold streams that fed into the Sacramento River and from there into

160

the sea. As far as it is possible to tell, they led a rewarding life. Despite the complexities of having two separate dialects, one for men and another for women—a phenomenon known from only two or three other parts of the world—there was apparently little antagonism among the Yahi, who were sufficiently committed to their way of life to hold out against armed white men longer than any other North American Indian society.[1]

The Yahi were a peaceful people who were neither organized nor equipped for war. Their only weapons were the bows and arrows and spears they used for hunting and fishing. When the first whites encountered the Yahi, their reception was friendly, but when more settlers arrived in the mid 1850s, followed by the unruly men who trekked west during the Gold Rush, the Yahi were hunted and shot down like animals. They fought back with remarkable courage, but the guns, numbers, and ferocity of the white men were too much. By the 1880s only fifteen or sixteen Yahi were left alive, and after 1894 there were only five, including Ishi and his invalid mother. By 1911 all except Ishi were dead, dying one by one by drowning in the rushing streams or falling victim to a bear or mountain lion. Their isolation in remote mountains, where stronger tribes had forced them to live, had given them a chance to prolong their independence; but their decision to fight for their way of life instead of surrendering to the whites, as most other California Indian peoples did, meant that their culture might die with them. If the Yahi way of life had a flaw, it lay in their courage and cultural commitment. Instead of agreeing to live under white rule, they resisted, and their bravery led to some military successes that only increased the genocidal rage of the whites. A complex and rewarding way of life came to an end not, as far as one can tell, because it contained pathological beliefs or inadequate institutions but because it stood in the way of an immensely larger number of people with superior weapons who believed that all Indians who opposed them should be killed.[2]

All but a very few humans have found it necessary to live in groups, and these groups have invariably developed their own cultures and languages. For many humans, perhaps the majority, the institutions, beliefs, and practices that constitute their society, culture, and language give their lives such meaning and coherence that to live without them would be terribly difficult and, for some, perhaps not possible at all. It is not uncommon for a population to think of itself as the best people on earth, even the only people on earth, and what defines its superiority is its customs, customs that bind people together, that give them joy and strength and purpose, customs so right that they need never change. There are such populations, known to us by such names as the Hopi, Maasai, Maori, and Yahi.

This is so obviously a truism that we express no surprise when people retain their cultures and languages over hundreds of years despite rapid environmental changes, conquest, or prolonged oppression. In spite of centuries of military occupation and foreign domination, Koreans have retained their culture and language. So did the Han Chinese, Gypsies, Poles, Armenians, Jews, and many others. The Kikuyu resisted British colonialism longer than any other people in Kenya and suffered great loss of life as a result, but the Kikuyu retained their social institutions, their culture, and their vitality with such success that they have been the most powerful ethnic group in that country for at least four decades. The Cham of Southeast Asia have a long history of struggling to maintain their Islamic religion and culture. When the Champa Kingdom in South Vietnam was defeated in 1471, most of the Cham people fled to Cambodia, where they again faced persecution culminating in genocide under the Khmer Rouge rule of 1975 to 1979 (approximately 90,000 of the 250,000 Cham in Cambodia were killed). A few thousand of the survivors migrated to the United States, where they are so determined to retain their strict Islamic culture that they would rather lose some of the children to inherited genetic diseases (mainly Thalassemia) than prohibit their preferred form of first-cousin marriage and risk, as they see it, the loss of an essential component of their way of life.[3]

Many other societies of all sizes and levels of social complexity have managed to thrive despite extreme stresses of all kinds. Yet there are populations whose customs have left them discontented, depressed, apathetic, angry, or rebellious, and not all of these societies have thrived. In fact, not all have survived. Sociocultural systems and populations that fail to perpetuate themselves provide the most extreme evidence of maladaptation. In the wake of the European contact that brought disease, economic change, military defeat, and political domination to most of the tribal world, so many small societies have undergone shattering social and cultural transformations that it is uncommon to find one that has successfully retained its tribal integrity. For every example like the Manus in Melanesia, whose persisting cultural vitality once so pleased Margaret Mead (recounted in *New Lives for Old*[4], there are hundreds of small societies that have seen

162

their systems of governance derogated, their arts and technology degraded, their social organization disintegrate, and their world of meaning become irrelevant, fall into disuse, or be forgotten. Whether they are prohibited by colonial powers or merely replaced, languages, too, have been lost.[5] Many small societies now live on the margins of survival,[6] and many others have lost so much of their culture that they have had to rely on the written accounts of anthropologists to preserve their religion, kinship systems, or history.[7]

That small tribal societies have been unable to retain their social or cultural viability in the face of European-led "modernization" is an unfortunate but unremarkable fact of history. A small society can hardly be considered to have been poorly adapted to its environment because it was destroyed by European weapons and diseases. However, some societies lost much of their culture and population before European expansion took place. Like the Tasmanians, various other societies have lost seemingly important aspects of their technology. For example, well before there was contact with technologically advanced people from Asia or Europe, canoes disappeared in various parts of Melanesia to be replaced by less seaworthy rafts. Pottery disappeared as well. In Polynesia, bows and arrows, once important in warfare, became toys for children, and an isolated group of 200 Inuit in northern Greenland lost the ability to make kayaks, the skin-covered boats so important in fishing.[8]

It is not only items of technology that have been lost. Many of the foraging societies that today occupy economically marginal environments once occupied larger territories and may have had greater social and cultural complexity as well. Sometimes this process of "deculturation," as it has come to be called, has been documented. The Sirionó Indians of Bolivia had no religious or medical specialists, little myth or ritual, no domesticated animals (not even dogs), and only the most rudimentary of shelters. They could not make fire and were frequently on the edge of starvation. Many anthropologists have believed that the Sirionó represented a relic "stone age" population, but Barry Isaac has more recently argued that the Sirionó were once a more numerous people who lost a more complex culture and technology.[9] The neighboring Yuqui Indians, who, like the Sirionó, are a small group of forest nomads whose technology is so simple that they too cannot make fire, nevertheless have among their number some people who are "slaves" and others who are "masters," strongly suggesting that these Indians also once had a more complex form of social

163

organization. Whatever the events were that led to the apparent deculturation of the Sirionó and Yuqui, they antedated European contact with the New World.[10]

Some small societies have lost not only their social or cultural complexitiy but their populations as well. The Yuqui are very close to extinction, as are many other Indian populations in Brazil.[11] These tribal societies and others like them have been subjected to such devastation by new diseases, military defeat, economic exploitation, and environmental changes that they appear to be the hapless victims of circumstances that have nothing to do with their own psychological, social, or cultural inadequacy. But it would be a mistake to conclude that populations undergoing culture contact have never contributed to their own demise. The rapid population decline before World War II on Ontong Java, a Polynesian atoll in Melanesia, was initiated by acculturation and disease, among other things, but according to Ian Hogbin, these people "acquiesced" in their own extinction by their extreme apathy and fatalism.[12] The disinterest, to gloss a complex psychological condition, of many peoples in their survival as a culture or a society has been noted many times.

The Batak Negritos of Pulawan Island in the Philippines are another example of a people who have contributed to their own decline. According to R. F. Eder, the Batak are on the road to "tribal extinction." At the end of the nineteenth century, the Batak numbered some 600 people who lived by hunting, gathering, and rice farming.[13] For some time, their culture served them well, or at least well enough, because their population was apparently stable. But in recent years, they have been hedged in by other populations, their quality of life has suffered, and their numbers have decreased. The Batak did not suffer from venereal disease, but their fertility was low, for men and women both, and their mortality rates were increasingly high as well. They were not reproducing themselves, and as a result, many Batak married Filipinos. Like their Filipino mothers, the children of these mixed marriages did not speak Batak and knew little about Batak culture. In 1980 there were 424 Batak in all, of whom only 254 were "pure" Batak. If Eder's account is correct, they were indeed on the road to extinction as a culture and perhaps as a people.

Yet the reasons for their decline are not obvious. They had not been displaced from most of their land, forced to change their way of life dramatically, or subjected to political oppression. Unlike many people under acculturative pressure, the Batak did not drink alcohol

164

excessively and were remarkably nonviolent, yet according to Eder, Batak society was "malfunctioning." It did not motivate its people to want to survive as Batak. Moreover, the Batak had little interest in working efficiently, they provided poor child care, and they chose to eat a nutritionally poor diet even though more nutritious foods were available. Eder concluded that the Batak could "do better" but did not make the effort. For Eder, the Batak were not so much victims of progress as responsible for their own decline and possible extinction. It is certainly true that many societies have faced far more extreme pressures and survived. The acculturative pressures on the Mbuti Pygmies of the Ituri forest in Zaire were in many respects more intense than those faced by the Batak, but the Mbuti consciously chose to retain the integrity of their culture, and for a long period they have very largely succeeded in doing so.[14]

The idea of societies competing with one another for resources or even survival may sometimes seem like a parody of Social Darwinism because some contiguous societies do not compete with each other in any way that involves social or cultural survival. Other societies may have quite permeable boundaries, and people may move to and fro, taking aspects of culture with them. But benign coexistence is not always, or even usually, the rule. The great majority of societies known to the ethnographic record practiced warfare.[15] A number of scholars have observed that to be "well adapted" a society must possess sufficient military technology and organization to defend itself against militarily aggressive enemies.[16] Bronze weapons in the hands of an organized political elite led to great military victories in the Near East, just as iron weapons did in Europe and stone ones did in Mexico. Lacking these weapons or the political will to cooperate in their own defense, many societies did not survive as political units. As Quincy Wright observed, "Out of the warlike peoples arose civilization, while the peaceful collectors and hunters were driven to the ends of the earth, where they are gradually being exterminated or absorbed."[17] Wright also noted that militaristic societies may eventually destroy themselves, but that can be little consolation to the survivors of those societies that lost their political autonomy, their culture, and their many friends and kinsmen to military conquest. Some societies, like Han China, Greece, and Anglo-Saxon England, have succeeded in absorbing their conquerors without losing their culture or language—some have even regained their political autonomy—but they are unusual.

Because so-called primitive warfare was relatively inefficient, it was uncommon for one small society to annihilate another's population, destroy its culture, or even permanently dislodge its people from more than a portion of their territory. Even militarily advanced states are much less likely to annihilate their enemies than they are to absorb them, sometimes allowing much of their culture and language to survive. In the nineteenth century the militarily superior Nuer of the southern Sudan absorbed some 100,000 Dinka and displaced at least as many more.[18] Nevertheless, the Dinka have survived as a culture and a people. Sometimes, however, warfare involving small-scale societies has had far more devastating effects. Tribal societies in Africa, New Guinea, Polynesia, the Americas, and elsewhere now and then drove their enemies off their lands, and others fought desperate battles that involved appalling loss of life.[19] To take a single example from many, in 1857 a large force of Quechan Indian warriors and their allies marched 160 miles over the southern Arizona desert, intending to destroy a Maricopa Indian village. Neither side used firearms—the battle was fought with clubs, staves, spears, and bows and arrows—yet, as a white eyewitness was able to determine, the Maricopa and their Pima allies virtually annihilated the Quechan raiders. So intense was the traditional warfare along the Colorado River that three small societies were decimated, their survivors forced to seek survival elsewhere.[20]

There is little to be learned about maladaptation by pointing out that small and technologically simple societies cannot easily resist military assault by larger, better-armed, and more disciplined armies. No amount of concern with military preparedness or technological innovation could have allowed many of the world's small, nonindustrial societies to compete against armies equipped with machine guns and artillery. Given their technological achievements, the Chinese might be faulted for their failure to develop weapons that could have allowed them to fend off European armies—but not the Sea Dyaks, the Papago, or the Maori. Yet there have been societies that had the technological and organizational capacity to compete with militarily superior neighbors but failed to do so and, as a result, were destroyed or absorbed. The Sebei of Uganda were able to resist the numerically superior Gisu by changing some of their political institutions; the Nomlaki of Northern California, on the other hand, were too anarchic to have defended themselves against any aggressive neighbors.[21] Fortunately for them, there was no attack. The failure of the United States and Britain to rearm prior to World War II until it was almost too late provides another cautionary tale. For some smaller, non-Western societies, the failure to keep pace militarily led to more catastrophic results.

In some areas of the world, like the North American Plains, the New Guinea highlands, and Polynesia, warlike societies developed such parity in weapons and military tactics that the annihilation of one society by another was improbable. Lives, property, and territory were lost, but neither political autonomy nor cultural integrity was often threatened, at least not until the introduction of European weaponry that allowed, for example, King Kamehameha I to conquer the Hawaiian Islands.

In some parts of the world, great military conquests took place without either radical technological changes or the introduction of foreign weapons. Until shortly after 1800, the Zulu were a small South African society no different from their Nguni-speaking neighbors in their rather diffident practices of warfare. At this time, few men were killed in warfare; indeed, sometimes the insults that were shouted back and forth were more painful than the spears that were ineffectually thrown from long distances. Nevertheless, soon after 1800 one of these tribes, the Mthethwa, became militarily more efficient, conquered the Zulu, and incorporated them into their army. One of the conquered Zulu was a young man named Shaka who replaced the traditional throwing spear with a stabbing spear (which required close rather than long-range combat) and trained his men to use their shields better to fend off spears. He forced his men to abandon their sandals and toughen their feet so that they could run faster. He also replaced the traditional battle formation —two lines confronting one another at a distance—with a crescent formation that consisted of a main body of men preceded on each flank by two "horns" that attempted to encircle the enemy. He rewarded bravery and attempted to eliminate cowardice. There was nothing about any of these innovations that could not have been matched by the neighboring and often more populous Nguni-speaking tribes. But because these societies did not change, or at least not rapidly enough (although the new Zulu tactics were know for years), many were defeated and absorbed into the expanding Zulu empire. Others were forced to flee, leaving their land and cattle to the Zulu; some were virtually annihilated. Eventually, some of the displaced tribes did adopt the Zulu tactics and weapons, and they too conquered many societies, some as far as 1,000 miles away from Zululand. [22]

In one respect, an even more remarkable history of military conquest took place in West Africa. As we saw in chapter 4, by the end of the eighteenth century, the Asante Kingdom was the strongest military power in West Africa and probably the strongest in all of Africa. The Asante empire was built by military conquest. Sometimes the Asante incorporated defeated kingdoms into their empire as tributary states; sometimes they simply decimated their enemies. Asante rule was anything but benign; most of the people whom the Asante defeated were enslaved to work in gold mines, to till Asante fields, or to serve in the Asante armies. Rather than risk enslavement and the loss of their wealth, neighboring kingdoms usually fought desperately against Asante invaders, but the Asante won most of these battles, as the growth of their empire so conclusively demonstrates. Those who refused to accept Asante rule were killed, usually in appallingly large numbers. Yet, and this is what is most remarkable about the Asante, they had no advantage over their neighbors in weapons. Prior to the introduction of firearms, all these societies had similar bows and arrows, spears, swords, and shields. Later, all acquired similar types and quantities of firearms; indeed, some coastal societies that were closer to European trading posts acquired these weapons before the inland Asante did. Asante military success appears to have resulted not from superior weapons, tactics, or numbers but from better organization, leadership, and discipline, all qualities that neighboring societies could conceivably have developed. The failure of these societies to develop competitive military organization and skill not only cost many of them untold numbers of dead and widespread suffering but also led to their destruction as independent polities. In time, many of the enslaved survivors lost their cultural identity as well. [23]

Militarily powerful societies have an obvious competitive advantage, but without the exercise of political prudence, even immensely powerful military establishments may destroy themselves, as happened to Nazi Germany and Japan in World War II and Iraq in 1991. Nevertheless, although some societies, small as well as large, have suffered from excessive militarism, it is likely that many more have ceased to exist as sociopolitical entities because they were militarily

invaders as a lesser evil.[29] The Eastern Empire eventually fell as well, but unlike the West, which disintegrated, Byzantium went down fighting against a vastly superior Turkish army.

Some of the tribes that tormented the empire went the same way. For example, almost a century after they sacked Rome, the Vandals were conquered by an army sent from Constantinople. The Vandals' women and children were sold into slavery, and the men were forced to serve in the conquering army; as a culture, the Vandals ceased to exist.[30] So it was too, Tainter writes, for the lowland Maya and the Chacoans of the American Southwest. When people saw more to be gained by leaving the existing polity than by staying in it, social dissolution rapidly took place.[31] Of course, a population or its disaffected segments may choose to rebel against its government rather than passively allow it to collapse, or it may renew its loyalty to that polity rather than see it fall under the dominion of a detested foreign power, as happened in France after it lost the war of 1870 to Germany.

But details such as these are less important than acknowledging the reality that some societies are more successful than others at meeting the needs of their people, and that when people are disaffected, they can respond in a variety of ways, which may include seeking a new and better way of life even if that means doing without much that was once of value to them. In considering how people come to be dissatisfied and how they decide to take some form of action (or, in some cases, inaction), it is important to recognize that such decisions, if they can be called that at all, may not be as rational as Tainter believes. It may be that people in some societies, including some now dead states, have reckoned their costs and benefits as rationally as Tainter suggests, but it seems more likely that even the recent political convulsions that have transformed the Soviet Union, Eastern Europe, and very nearly China were brought about by discontented people who could probably not readily calculate the costs or benefits of their actions. Only time will tell whether the economic, social, and political changes they set in motion will bring about the benefits they envisioned. People today, as in the past, can bring about monumental changes for reasons that cannot be reduced to a cost-benefit analysis.

Social collapse can be brought about by belief systems and related behaviors that involve scarcely rational assessments of the balance between investments and returns. Witchcraft is an excellent example of a belief system that can be socially destructive. Beliefs in witchcraft

171

and sorcery have led to the slaughter of innocent animals in many parts of the world, including Europe, where cats were commonly victimized because of their presumed association with witches and female sexuality.[32] Countless humans have also been victimized; most of them, like the cats, were no doubt innocent of the presumed malevolence that led others to take their lives. Beliefs in witchcraft, accusations against specific witches, and consequent homicidal reprisals have often been explained and even justified as socially useful means of explaining misfortune, giving victims a socially prescribed target for protective or remedial action, increasing group cohesion or individual catharsis by projecting hostile or sexual impulses onto outsiders, maintaining civility in everyday life (because failure to be polite could be interpreted as malevolence), and providing social control by ridding a community of deviant persons.[33] Beliefs in witchcraft may well have these and other adaptive social functions, but they can also create a maladaptive climate of fear and killing.

The Gebusi of Papua New Guinea are one of many small-scale societies whose fear of witches has been maladaptive. A very small society of about 450 people in a lowland rain forest area of south-central New Guinea, the Gebusi were still beyond the influence of missions or government officials when Bruce Knauft studied them between 1980 and 1982.[34] They were a remarkably noncompetitive, self-effacing, mutually deferential people who actively encouraged nonviolence. Yet they believed that all illness was caused by witchcraft, and their resulting attacks against presumed witches were so violent that their homicide rate was one of the highest ever recorded. Nearly one-third of all deaths among them were homicides, and almost all of the victims were suspected witches. Keith Otterbein has suggested that their practice of executing people thought to be witches was an adaptive "group survival" strategy because it controlled the malevolence of witches; but Knauft points out that their killing can hardly be considered adaptive because the population, small to begin with, was "dying out at an exceedingly rapid rate," and their extremely high homicide rate continues to be an important cause of their population decline.[35]

Like witchcraft, supernatural beliefs can aid a population in its quest for understanding, explanation, or reassurance, but such beliefs can also contribute to a society's demise. Religious wars provide a particularly sanguinary example, as the killing throughout much of the contemporary world so sadly attests. When the leader of a chief-

172

dom or state holds to strong supernatural beliefs, the potential for social disaster can be heightened. Idi Amin's often bizarre supernatural convictions led him to adopt policies that ravaged Uganda, and if C.A. Burland is correct, Emperor Montezuma's religious beliefs played a vital role in the destruction of the Aztec Empire.[36] According to Burland, Montezuma believed that Cortes was the reincarnation of the Aztec god Quetzalcoatl. Disregarding the repeated advice of his council, Montezuma made no effort to stop the Spaniards' march on his capital. Instead, he showered them with gifts and welcomed them to his palace. His immense and well-armed army waited in vain for orders to destroy the white men who soon proved even to Montezuma that they were anything but godlike.

The pages of history are also replete with examples of prophets who led their followers to their deaths. Here I want to describe an episode in which a people's belief in witchcraft and prophecy led to such widespread death and destruction that a society of over 100,000 people was devastated. This tragic example of the disastrous consequences of such beliefs took place among the Xhosa of southern Africa in the mid nineteenth century. In 1850 the Gcaleka Xhosa were an independent chiefdom led by King Sarhili. They lived mostly east of the Kei River beyond the direct authority of British colonial officials in Cape Town, but in previous years they had clashed with the British, who forced them to the north. Like many other African societies of that time, the Xhosa believed in the existence of witches, whom they blamed for all misfortune and evil. They also believed, although with less certainty and unanimity, in the powers of prophets.

As described by historian J.B. Peires, an eighteen-year-old prophet named Mlajeni emerged from a period of fasting and solitude in 1850 to declare that the great drought of that year was the work of witches.[37] Mlajeni's influence spread rapidly, and he soon called for the Xhosa to end the drought by killing all their dun- and yellow-colored cattle. How many cattle were actually killed is not known, but Mlajeni used his growing reputation for supernatural power to prepare the Xhosa for another war against the land-hungry British by devising ritual means of protection for Xhosa warriors. The war came later that year. The Xhosa won some victories and frequently held off troops of the regular British army as well as white-settler volunteers, but eventually the superior weapons and the brutal scorched-earth policy of the white men forced King Sarhili to sue for peace. Three years of bitter, bloody fighting left over 16,000 Xhosa dead; the British dead numbered

173

1,400, an enormous toll for colonial warfare in Africa at that time.[38] When a Xhosa warrior was killed, or when he killed an enemy, many ritual procedures had to be undertaken to prevent a pervasive evil from polluting and endangering the living. Because of the savagery of the war, there had often been no time for performing the necessary cleansing rituals. As a result, Xhosaland was pervaded by a sense not only of loss but of danger.

Shortly after the war ended, Mlajeni died, but despite the great defeat, his prophetic powers had not been discredited among many Xhosa. His last prophecy was that all those killed during the war would return to life. He also warned against the evil of witches. While Mlajeni's words were being considered by the war-dispirited Xhosa, the next stage in the tragedy that was soon to envelop them began when a Dutch ship brought cattle diseased with pleuropneumonia to a South African port in September, 1853. This fatal and highly contagious disease, often called "lung sickness," had already killed thousands of cattle in Europe, and it quickly began to ravage herds in South Africa. The Xhosa were soon aware of the spread of this terrible disease, and they did their best to avoid possibly infected cattle and move their herds to isolated areas. Nevertheless, because the disease was virulent and could be spread by asymptomatic cattle, 5,000 Xhosa cattle were soon dying each month, and in some areas entire herds were wiped out. At the same time, maize, the main crop of the Xhosa, was devastated by an infestation of grubs and then further ravaged by torrential rain.

For the Xhosa the result was economic disaster. Coming so soon after the war against the British—which had led to the destruction of fields and the capture of cattle, in addition to so many deaths— these calamities left the Xhosa distraught. They were certain that nothing so terrible as this had happened before in history, and they believed that they knew the reason why. The witches they all feared, the witches whom Mlajeni had warned them against, were spreading death and destruction. King Sarhili promptly and righteously had twenty accused witches put to death, but cattle continued to die, and the maize crop failed. In this troubled time, rumors of all sorts spread rapidly, and prophecies came from all quarters of the land. One prophet claimed that he was in contact with a vast African army, somewhere across the sea, that was on its way to aid the Xhosa. And when Sir George Cathcart, who had led the British in their savage war against the Xhosa, was killed by Russian troops in the Crimean

War in 1854, word of his death quickly reached the Xhosa. They had never heard of Russians, but when they were told that the Russians were white men like the British, they rejected this information, deciding instead that Russians must be the ghostly spirits of slain Xhosa warriors. For months Xhosa lookouts on high hills watched and waited for the arrival of the British-slaying Russians.

While the Xhosa continued to kill people who were said to be witches, lung sickness continued to kill their cattle. During 1855 several prophets declared that the only way to remove the evil from Xhosaland was for the people to kill their cattle and refuse to cultivate their fields. These urgings had no appreciable effect until the next year, when a new prophet, a teenaged girl named Nongqawuse, repeated this same prophecy. Claiming that her revelation came to her from mysterious strangers, Nongqawuse insisted only the slaughter of *all* Xhosa cattle and the *total* abandonment of cultivation could remove pollution from the land and destroy the evil power of the witches. She promised that if this were done and the Xhosa abjured witchcraft, new people would arrive in Xhosaland, bringing with them healthy new cattle and crops. At the same time, the Xhosa dead would rise, and there would be eternal youth and happiness for all.

In preparation for this millennium, Nongqawuse instructed the people to build huge enclosures for the healthy new cattle and dig deep grain pits for the new corn that would also appear. On the day when these life-saving miracles would take place, a blood-red sun would rise with such incredible heat that people would have to shelter themselves in specially shaded houses. Once the earth was scorched black by the sun, thunderstorms and terrible winds would destroy the impure cattle, crops, witches, and incidentally, all those Xhosa who did not believe in her prophecy and behave as she directed them to. After the storm, the dead would rise, the new cattle and corn would appear, and other food, clothing, and goods would emerge from the ground. The deaf, blind, and handicapped would all be cured of their afflictions, and the old would once again be young. Joy and plenty would reign in Xhosaland.[39]

Many Xhosa actually built new corrals, grain pits, and heat-proofed houses; they also slaughtered some of their cattle. But killing *all* their cattle was another matter altogether. For many Xhosa, like other African cattleherders, Nongqawuse's orders were unthinkably severe. Cattle were the basis of the Xhosa economy, not only because of the food, milk, and hides they provided but because they were also the major medium of exchange in marriages and important ceremonies. Their possession meant prestige as well as wealth, they were thought to be beautiful, and men sang to their favorites, composed poetry about them, and spent much of their time scheming about ways to increase their numbers. To kill all their cattle, then, was as close to being impossible as anything could be for the Xhosa. Nevertheless, King Sarhili killed his favorite ox as an example to others, and some other chiefs who believed in the prophecy did the same. Many commoners killed a few of their cattle as well. Still, no one killed *all* their cattle. In fact, some Xhosa rejected the prophecy altogether. The son of a prominent chief who believed in the prophecy said bitterly that he would rather kill his father than his cattle. Others openly called the prophet an imposter and did what they could to stop the cattle-killing movement. Neighboring tribes and British settlers, who were also urged to kill their cattle, scoffed at the idea.

But Xhosa women, apparently weary of their onerous agricultural duties, eagerly accepted the prophet's instructions to stop preparing the soil for planting. Many women also urged men to carry out cattle killing. In the areas hardest hit by lung sickness, killing did take place, but the Xhosa still held back from killing all their cattle. Nevertheless, the lung sickness grew worse, and the prophet's credibility rose when various people reported seeing the horns of the promised new cattle poking out of remote swamps or said that they heard them bellowing in the distance. The day on which the millennium was promised passed uneventfully, but Nongqawuse was able to point out, logically enough, that until all cattle were killed, the events she had prophesied could not take place. The Xhosa continued to hesitate, even though their cattle continued to fall victim to lung sickness. Finally making the painful decision to embrace the prophecy, King Sarhili ordered that his own vast herds be slaughtered. Others followed his example, and soon many Xhosa had killed all their cattle. While the cattle were being slaughtered, the Xhosa sang, drank beer, and danced as they gorged themselves on beef. There was so much that it was impossible to eat more than a small portion of it. The rest was left to rot. This was a time of almost hysterical ambivalence as the Xhosa committed unimaginable acts of cattle killing in the hope of escaping from the evil that plagued them.

In December 1856, those who had complied with the demands of the prophecy began to die of starvation. For months these people

176

had eaten nothing but roots, berries, bark, and even grass. Beginning with young children and elderly people, the Xhosa died of starvation or disease. Dogs ate the dead bodies that lay everywhere. Those people who still had the strength dragged themselves to nearby missions or the homesteads of disbelievers who had food. Usually they were driven away hungry, but a few managed to steal some food. Some even killed and ate children, but most cannibals were hunted down and killed. Others went to King Williams Town, the nearest British settlement, where they were denied food by the settlers, who objected to the idea of charity for what they called "idle natives."[40] In their desperation, the Xhosa stole what food they could, including some of the settlers' dogs.

In 1855, before the starvation began, there were approximately 105,000 Xhosa in King Sarhili's domain. By 1858 there were only 25,916. Some Xhosa moved to other areas, but it is estimated that between 40,000 and 50,000 people died. In addition to the cattle that died of lung sickness, at least 400,000 others were slaughtered. What is more, British colonial officials took advantage of the Xhosa's plight by permanently appropriating some 600,000 acres of their land, over two-thirds of Sarhili's entire kingdom. Xhosa political independence ended too, as they fell under British rule; their cultural and economic integrity would soon be lost as well. Most Xhosa men now had to rely on wage work for the British to survive. The expansion of white colonialism was inexorable, and Sarhili's people would have succumbed to British dominion eventually, even without the consequences of the cattle-killing prophecy. But without the prophecy's terrible consequences, Xhosa independence would have lasted longer, and many thousands of lives would have been saved.

There can be no easy explanation for the disastrous success of the cattle-killing prophecy. The epidemic of pleuropneumonia was probably a necessary factor, but it was certainly not a sufficient one. Lung sickness spread all over southern Africa, and no other society, including the neighboring Mfengu, who lost 90 percent of their cattle to it, adopted the cattle-killing prophecy. Neither can it be said that beliefs in witchcraft, pollution, and prophecy were sufficient causes because neighboring societies had these beliefs, too. Nor was the influence of Christianity with its ideas of salvation and resurrection in any way unique to the Xhosa. Perhaps the effects of their heavy war losses somehow made the Xhosa more vulnerable to millenarianism, but other southern African societies also lost heavily to the British in wars both before and after Sarhili's people did, and none sought their salvation in cattle killing.

Whatever led the Xhosa to behave as they did, and whether one chooses to think of their behavior as irrational or pathological, it was indisputably maladaptive. At the time, neighboring peoples regarded the cattle killing as irrational, and so did the minority of the Xhosa themselves who refused to comply with the prophecy's mandate. Today, all Xhosa are said to regard what happened as an inexplicably horrible mass delusion.[41] Inspired by a teenaged prophet and led by their King, Sarhili's people destroyed themselves.

The Gcaleka Xhosa were not the only people to suffer as a result of a belief in prophecy. Prophets in many parts of the world have urged their young warriors into battle against troops equipped with firearms by assuring them that the white men's bullets would be harmless because they would turn to water. One of the most catastrophic examples of this prophecy took place in Tanzania in 1905. In what was called the *Maji-Maji* rebellion (meaning "water, water" in Swahili), a prophet declared that the bullets from the German soldiers rifles and machine guns would turn to water. Suitably inspired, much of southern Tanzania rose against their oppressive German rulers only to die by the thousands, as young men sacrificed themselves against machine-gun fire. It is not known how many Africans lost their lives to "harmless" bullets, but before resistance ended in 1908, approximately 300,000 Africans were dead, many to disease and starvation but many others to German gunfire.[42]

A desire for revenge can also destroy a society. Belief that aggression against a member of one's kin or residential group must be avenged is extremely widespread. Some anthropologists have argued that blood feuding that limits the response of an aggrieved individual or kin group to an equitable killing—an eye for an eye—is adaptive because in the absence of strong central policy authority, it controls what might otherwise escalate into wholesale retaliation.[43] However, feuding very often spirals out of control even when societies try to control it, and the result can be a cycle of feuding that can create socially maladaptive conditions, as once-united hunting bands or horticultural villages fail to cooperate, break apart, or attempt to annihilate one another. City-states did the same, as the nearly thirty-year war of retaliation between Athens and Sparta illustrates.

A belief in the necessity of blood vengeance may have adaptive

178

value, however. As Herbert Spencer long ago recognized, if a group that has been attacked takes prompt and effective retaliation, future aggression may be deterred. Napoleon Chagnon has shown that the Yanomamo Indians of the tropical forest of northern Brazil and southern Venezuela share this belief in the deterrent effect of retaliation, saying that kinship groups that gain a reputation for ferocious and swift retaliation deter their neighbors from attempting violence.[44] Very often, however, the result of retaliation is not peace but an escalation of violence, like that which took place in Lebanon during the 1980s or among the Yanomamo themselves. Some societies, such as the Bedouin, have partially succeeded in preventing feuds from perpetuating themselves by instituting means for assuring that prompt and fair compensation will be paid for any injury, but even so, their feuds resulted in fear of vengeance so extreme that Sulayman Khalaf— himself of Bedouin origin—wrote that it could reach "obsessive proportions"[45] Many other societies have been unable to bring their feuds under control. In some the result, as we shall see, can be levels of violence so high that people are obsessed by terror; in others, it can be what Ruth Benedict referred to as a "cultural suicide."

Benedict was referring to the Kaingáng Indians, whose incessant feuds had reduced their population by perhaps 75 percent. The Kaingáng of Brazil's tropical forest were described by anthropologist Jules Henry in 1941 as nomadic hunters who lived in bands of related kin. Within these bands, relatives were usually kind and peaceable, and if conflict occurred, the group would split up without resorting to violence. But any conflict with Kaingáng from other bands led inexorably to violence, followed by more deadly retaliatory raids. The resulting cycle of raids and counterraids was so unbreakable that the Kaingáng population was drastically reduced, something the Indians themselves recognized. Henry asserts firmly that the Kaingáng were well on their way to "cultural suicide," a process that he believed must have led to the disappearance of many other small feuding societies.[46]

Henry does not provide the kind of demographic data that would conclusively support his argument that feuding was the primary cause of Kaingáng depopulation. Disease, among other factors, may also have played a role, and the Kaingáng population continued to drop even after pacification. However, there is enough evidence about the lethal outcome of feuding in small societies around the world to support Henry's contention that a society like the Kaingáng might indeed

179

feud itself into extinction. If actual extinction did not occur, then such numerical weakness and internal divisiveness could result that the depleted population would no longer be able to defend its hunting territory against aggressive neighboring tribes. This happened to the neighbors of the Mundurucu, a militarily aggressive society not far from the homeland of the Kaingáng.[47]

To turn to another part of the world, many small societies in Australia and Tasmania failed to survive the impact of European contact. Others very likely became extinct before contact. The Kaiadilt are an example of an Australian society that was destroying itself before European intervention took place. The Kaiadilt were a small society on remote Bentinck Island in the Gulf of Carpentaria on Australia's north coast. They were isolated from significant European contact until 1942 when anthropologist Norman Tindale studied them, and they also had virtually no contact with other Australian aborigines.[48]

Although Bentinck Island offered relatively few food resources to this small foraging and fishing tribe, their population rose slowly over a thirty-year period prior to Tindale's arrival, reaching a peak of 123 people in 1942. Five years later, only forty-seven Kaiadilt were still alive, and when a tidal wave salinated their only pools of fresh water, it appeared that they faced rapid extinction. But thanks to the efforts of Gully Peters (an Australian elder from a mainland tribe), who had learned to speak Kaiadilt, the forty-seven survivors were evacuated to a mission station on nearby Morningside Island.[49]

The dramatic decline of the Kaiadilt population coincided with a period of severe drought that apparently contributed to malnutrition and disease.[50] Although the Kaiadilt hunted lizards, frogs, and wild birds and gathered some wild vegetables and honey, almost all of their food came from the sea, where they speared and trapped fish, collected shellfish, and caught large turtles and dugong. Therefore, it is not immediately evident why drought should have reduced their numbers so rapidly. They also suffered from dysentery and pulmonary disorders, not because of European contact but rather because of undernutrition and exposure to periods of intense wind and cold (the Kaiadilt had neither clothing nor adequate means of shelter).[51]

According to Gully Peters, there was another, more fundamental reason for the demise of the Kaiadilt. They were killing one another. "Gully reported that a man who came back at night from fishing on a reef might be killed for his catch. The band that killed him would then take his wife and eat his children."[52] How frequently such killings might have taken place and whether children were in fact eaten are not known. But at least one aspect of Gully Peters's account is apparently true. Kaiadilt men killed other Kaiadilt men in order to take their women.

When asked about it, the Kaiadilt themselves rejected the idea that disease or hunger were responsible for their depopulation. As they saw it, the cause was fighting over women. What is more, they made it abundantly clear that they did not covet women for their ability to gather food or bear children; they wanted women as sexual partners. Now it is quite possible that Kaiadilt men did not understand all the reasons why they fought over women—a desire for prestige, revenge, offspring, or economic advantage, perhaps—but they adamantly insisted that their depopulation was due to fighting and not drought.[53] It is also possible that the stress of a prolonged drought could have triggered a wave of killing to possess women, but there are eyewitness accounts of Kaiadilt fighting over women as early as 1929, a time well before the drought conditions began.[54] What seems clear is that Kaiadilt men killed one another in pursuit of women, and these deaths, perhaps including those of children at times, contributed significantly to their population loss and their increasing fragmentation as a society.

The Kaiadilt were literally trapped on Bentinck Island. Their flimsy rafts could not take them to any safe landfall, and they could not easily avoid one another on their small island. Their subsistence activities did not require extensive interfamily or band cooperation, but they did require peace. Constant feuding not only cost lives, it disrupted subsistence activities. Although it might be possible to imagine some extraordinarily successful Kaiadilt warrior enhancing his reproductive fitness by capturing many women while killing all his rivals, social extinction was a far more likely outcome. When Kaiadilt men turned against one another in a relentless pursuit of women, the uncontrollable killing that followed could not have served any adaptive purpose.

The Kaingáng and Kaiadilt were not the only societies that may have been saved from self-destruction by the intervention of colonial administrators. While the guns and diseases of the Europeans undeniably decimated and even annihilated some non-Western societies (the Carib and Arawak Indian populations of the Caribbean Island being well-known examples), the colonial presence may, even inadvertently, have saved some societies as well. A case in point is the

Marind-anim, a horticultural people living on the southwest coast of New Guinea in Irian Jaya. Some analysts believe that the Marind-anim would not have been a viable society much longer had it not been for Dutch intervention because despite the fact that the Marind-anim were known as ferocious headhunters who raided enemies as far away as 100 miles, their population was dwindling.[55] Indeed, their own recognition of population loss was apparently what drove the Marind-anim to carry out their raids because in addition to taking the heads of the men whom they killed, they captured small children whom they took home to be raised as Marind-anim.[56] Marind-anim were not able to maintain their numbers because their women, it seems, were largely infertile. It was first thought that their infertility was a result of newly introduced veneral disease, but research demonstrated that many infertile women had never contracted veneral disease and, indeed that their inability to bear children began well before venereal disease was introduced to them. Van Baal, the principal source on this society, believes that the women's infertility was the result of an unusual sexual practice.

Marind-anim men, like men in many other societies in that part of Melanesia, practiced ritual male homosexuality, based on their belief that semen was essential to human growth and development. They also married quite young, and to assure the bride's fertility, she too had to be filled with semen. On her wedding night, therefore, as many as ten members of the husband's lineage had sexual intercourse with the bride, and if there were more men than this in the lineage, they had intercourse with her during the following night. That this intercourse was not merely a symbolic act is indicated by the fact that when the night ended, the bride was so sore that she could not walk.[57] Nevertheless, a similar ritual was repeated at various intervals throughout a woman's life. Instead of enhancing a woman's fertility as intended, this practice apparently led to severe pelvic inflammatory disease that produced infertility.[58] If this interpretation is correct, then the Marind-anim practice of repeated ritual intercourse achieved precisely the opposite of the effect intended and may have led to such a decline in their population that neither their long-range raids to capture children nor their purchases of children from neighboring societies, could replenish their numbers. Government intervention ended the practice of repeated intercourse.

Unfortunately, it cannot be said that the interventions of colonial officials have commonly had beneficial outcomes. More often, even their best-intended actions have led to disaster by creating conditions that produce new, or exaggerate preexisting, cultural stresses. A particularly graphic illustration of this process comes from the Ojibwa Indian Reserve of Grassy Narrows in northern Ontario. Before 1963 these Indians lived a relatively traditional life by hunting, trapping, and fishing. They lived in widely scattered cabins but came together for important ritual and ceremonial occasions, and they appear to have been tolerably adapted to the conditions of their life. In that year the Canadian Department of Indian Affairs relocated the more than 500 Ojibwa to a new reserve some five miles away in order that they could be provided with some of the amenities of modern Western life. Instead of the crude log cabins they had been accustomed to, they were provided with modern houses complete with electricity and running water. There was a school and a medical clinic, too, and jobs for those Ojibwa chosen to govern the rest.

These Indians, who previously lacked any significant social stratification, were quickly divided between their newly appointed and speedily well-to-do leaders and all the rest who remained poor. Instead of living far from one another as they had before, they now lived crowded together. As a result, conflicts were more common and more difficult to ignore or escape. And now, too, there was more cash as a result of welfare payments as well as some wage work. For reasons graphically described in Anastasia Shkilnyk's book *A Poison Stronger Than Love*, the Ojibwa quickly became demoralized by their new living arrangements, and in their depression and anger they used their cash to buy alcohol, which they drank very heavily.[59] Some two-thirds of the population over the age of 16—women as well as men—became "heavy" or "very heavy" drinkers. Although some people often went two or three weeks without alcohol, when they drank they embarked on a two- or three-day orgy of drunkenness that included the neglect and physical abuse of their children, brutal wife beating, gang rape of young women, incest, homicide, and suicide.

After sociologist Kai Erikson, a specialist in community responses to disaster, visited Grassy Narrows, he left with the conviction that it ". . . was more deeply damaged than any community I had ever seen or heard about or even imagined."[60] He characterized these Ojibwa as "a truly broken people," who neglected themselves and abused their children. "Grassy Narrows is a place of rape and murder and incest and thoughtless vandalism. It is a place of tremendous rage and frustration. It is, as one of the older men said to us, 'a diseased place to live' ".[61] Shkilnyk characterized these Indians as "drab, lifeless and demoralized," but they were also destructive. In 1977–1978, 20 percent of everyone in the age group 11–16 attempted suicide, and three succeeded. If that pattern were to continue, 75 percent of all people living in Grassy Narrows would die a self-inflicted death. In the five-year period 1974–1979, eight infants died of suffocation, usually because their drunken mothers lay on top of them, and four were abandoned. About 22 percent of all deaths in Grassy Narrows are infant deaths, compared with 4 percent in a nearby town of white residents. There was also a marked increase in birth defects, including fetal alcohol syndrome.

What happened to these Ojibwa Indians is not unique. Many North American Indians, like people throughout the world, have reacted to European-imposed changes in their way of life in similar fashion, but few have done so over such a brief period and with such terrible self-destructiveness. In a little over ten years, Ojibwa culture was lost, the people's sense of community was destroyed, and depopulation threatened their survival. It is difficult to believe that these horrendous events could have occurred in less than a decade if there were not some underlying features of Ojibwa culture or social organization that had a pathogenic potential.

In addition to the economic changes and loss of traditional roles that have already been noted, the Ojibwa have long been a highly individualistic, suspicious, and witchcraft-ridden people, whose scattered settlement pattern helped to prevent conflict by minimizing the opportunities for conflict and separating antagonists after conflict took place.[62] It is difficult to find evidence in recent Ojibwa history for a strong sense of community that might buffer the stresses of change. Most damaging, it would seem, was their belief, shared with many Indians and others around the world, that acts committed while drunk were not intended and hence should be forgiven. Like many other Indian peoples, the Ojibwa of times past used this belief to excuse deadly mayhem against friends and close kin[63] (eyewitness accounts of deadly drunken violence and sexual debauchery among the Ojibwa are recorded throughout the eighteenth century).[64] But in the past, drinking was less common, and fewer people were involved.

A belief like this is not the only reason why the residents of Grassy Narrows drank alcohol. Their need to escape from pain, rage, and feelings of inadequacy surely contributed to their drunken excesses.

But by excusing drunken acts such as murder, rape, incest, and child abuse, the Ojibwa can only have encouraged such acts to take place. Everyone knew what kind of behavior typically took place when people went on a drinking spree, yet people continued to go on these sprees. As one Ojibwa man put it, their attraction to the "poison" of alcohol was greater than their love for their children. When a society adopts a belief that feelings of worthlessness or anger can be obliterated by a drunken binge and that no one is to be blamed for anything done while drunk, it has adopted a fully-warranted prescription for self-destruction.

Populations large and small have lost their cultures, social institutions, languages, and lives. In many instances these losses have been the result of forces so ineluctable that no change in people's traditional beliefs or behaviors could have enabled the doomed societies to survive. Sometimes, however, people's beliefs and practices have contributed to their demise. From an historical perspective then, the ethnographic record is plain—some people have had more success than others in maintaining their sociocultural systems and their population size. But as a grace note to this point, we should consider further the role of reproduction and survival—of individuals, populations, social systems, or cultures—in social evolution.

There can be no doubt that principled individuals may choose not to live or not to reproduce and their decisions can inspire others to socially useful ends or contribute to their own reproductive success. Examples of both are commonplace. It has also been common for groups of people rationally to choose not to reproduce or not to survive. For religious principles, the Shakers chose not to reproduce, and when recruitment failed to keep pace with mortality, they failed to survive. Other religious groups assured that they would not reproduce by voluntarily undergoing castration. The Russian *Skoptsi* are an example of such a group that grew in numbers and influence in the eighteenth and nineteenth centuries.[65] The Skoptsi (or *Khlisti*, as they were also known) were millenarians who believed that when their numbers reached 144,000, utopia would arrive on earth. But in a dazzling display of illogic, especially considering that the sect included many educated people, they made castration their signal act of religious devotion. Despite purchasing children from peasant families to increase their numbers, the Skoptsi never came close to realizing their population goal. Other groups of men in various armies have chosen death over surrender in order to maintain their honor or better serve their gods. The Mahdist soldiers, or "dervishes," as the British called them, faced death from British guns in the later nineteenth century with an equanimity that awed their enemies. More recently, young Iranians volunteered to seek death in battle—and thereby enter paradise—during the war between Iran and Iraq.

From the rebellion led by Spartacus against Roman slavery to thousands of similarly desperate uprisings by African slaves in the New World, people have chosen to die in a quest for freedom rather than live in bondage. So it was also among several North American Indian tribes such as the Southern Cheyenne and the Nez Percé, many of whom lost their lives in their attempts to escape confinement on reservations. The Yahi died because they chose not to submit in the first place. And Jewish epic history records the decision to die made by nearly 1,000 men, women, and children who defended the rocky plateau fortress known as Masada against a Roman army in the first century A.D. Although the besieged Jews, who were known as "Zealots," had ample supplies of food and water, when it became obvious that they could not much longer hold their position against the Roman forces, they chose to die rather than surrender and face the future as slaves. After tearfully killing their wives and children, the men killed themselves. In all, 960 people are said to have died. The only survivors were two women and five children who hid in a water conduit.[66] Recent scholarship has questioned the number of suicides that took place, but whether they died fighting or by their own hands, surviving Jews have continued to honor the martyrs of Masada, and their deaths have contributed in some measure to the persistence and solidarity of Jewish culture and religion, suggesting that their actions were altruistically adaptive. But suppose that all Jews had died on Masada, leaving none to cherish their sacrifice. Would we then construe their mass suicide as maladaptive? Would physical survival in slavery, even though Jewish culture and religion might have been lost as a result, have been the better adaptive strategy?

Deranged political leaders have sometimes sought to destroy their own societies. Jonestown is a ghastly example, and if Hitler had possessed the means to carry out his will at the end of World War II, Germany would have suffered similar extinction. But the doomed residents of Jonestown did not want to die for any principle, and neither did most Germans, including, quite obviously, highly placed Nazi Party members. The Japanese present a more troubling example. The samurai Code of Bushido imbued its warrior class, and many other Japanese as well, with the belief that like wild cherry blossoms, which are so briefly radiant in the sun only to be blown away by the wind, life too is evanescent. This belief, coupled with fierce military discipline and the conviction that the beauties of Japanese culture were worth dying for, led generations of Japanese warriors to give up their lives with a serenity that astonished Westerners. In World War II, Japanese soldiers repeatedly charged to certain death rather than surrender.[67] Late in the war, thousands of young men gave up their lives in Kamikaze attacks against U.S. and British warships, and many more would have been willing, even eager, to die if the war had continued. Many prominent Japanese knew that the war was lost as early as 1942, and the Japanese government was negotiating for peace before the United States dropped nuclear bombs on two Japanese cities.[68] However, if the Japanese military had managed to continue the war, as many of its leaders wanted to do, the Code of Bushido could conceivably have led to the annihilation of the Japanese people.[69]

This example, although seemingly ludicrous in the light of Japan's postwar history, is instructive nonetheless. When Japan's leaders agreed to accept unconditional surrender, they could not have anticipated a conquest so benign that most aspects of Japanese culture would remain intact and Japan's economy would be encouraged to develop. The decision to surrender was made to preserve Japan's population at the risk of its political independence, cultural integrity, and economic viability. Even the life of their revered emperor was put at risk. Yet hundreds of thousands of Japanese gave their lives rather than risk conquest, and many millions more were prepared to continue that sacrifice no matter what the ultimate cost. They put cultural values above physical survival.

Because humans can transcend their biologically given urge to live in favor of culturally given choices that may include death, the task of evaluating maladaptation must take great care to distinguish between, on the one hand, people who choose not to reproduce, like the Shakers, or choose to die, like the Jews on Masada, and, on the other, those like the Xhosa, Gebusi, or the Kaiadilt, who want desperately to live yet adopt practices that threaten their survival.

187

Chapter 8

Adaptation Reconsidered

In the preceding chapters, we examined examples of maladaptive beliefs and practices that threatened population survival, led to the loss of culture or language, left people discontented or rebellious, and endangered their mental or physical well-being. While the amount and kind of maladaption varies, some ineffective or harmful beliefs and practices must occur in all societies because of the presence of inequality, conflicts of interest, environmental change, biological predispositions, and other factors. Populations like the Kaiadilt, Ojibwa of Grassy Narrows, Gebusi, Bimin-Kuskusmin, nineteenth-century Xhosa, and others mentioned earlier were dangerously mal-adapted. Populations as seriously disordered as these represent a minority of the world's known societies, perhaps a small minority at that, but all societies maintain some beliefs and practices that are maladaptive for at least some of their members, and it is likely that some of these social arrangements and cultural understandings will be maladaptive for everyone in that society.

There are many reports indicating that a number of small-scale societies throughout the world have become extinct, usually as a result of protracted warfare. Although some are anecdotal, there is reason to believe that a good many of them are true. However, they seldom tell us whether the destruction of these societies was in any respect due to some social or cultural inadequacy on the part of the extinct population—a lack of cultural commitment, a failure to develop a cohesive political organization, a reliance on inefficient weapons or strategies, internal divisiveness, or the like. In the absence of better documentation of the natural history of cultural extinction, we are left to speculate about how often populations have brought about their own demise. However, there is far better evidence that a substantial percentage of those populations that survived long enough to become a part of the ethnographic record nevertheless maintained some traditional beliefs or practices that endangered, dispirited, or killed certain of their members. I have argued that, by and large, these practices not only harm individuals but threaten the social system itself.

My insistence that maladaptive beliefs and practices are commonplace must not be construed to mean that humans *never* make effective adaptations to their environments. At the genetic level, for example, there can be no doubt that considerable natural selection took place during the Pleistocene and that most, if not all, of this must have led to improved adaptation. Likewise, physiological adaptation of various sorts takes place during the lifetime of most individuals. People may develop greater resistance to disease, tolerance of stress, facility in processing information, or any number of other adaptive responses to the particular circumstances in which they find themselves.[1] And it is patently obvious that many traditional beliefs and practices serve people's needs well and help to maintain their social systems. As Julian Steward and many other cultural ecologists have shown, there can also be no doubt that people can, and often have, altered their behaviors, including their systems of meanings that constitute culture, so that they better conform to the constraints imposed by the environments in which they find themselves. An example can be drawn from the "Culture and Ecology Project" in East Africa, in which I participated over thirty years ago.[2] Some people in each of the four societies studied utilized a dry lowland sector where they subsisted largely or solely by cattle pastoralism, while other members of the same society lived in a well-watered highland sector where agriculture was the principal mode of subsistence. Despite these similarities, the ecological circumstances of the four societies were not identical, and the societies differed culturally as well. Two of the tribes were Bantu-speaking, while two spoke Kalenjin languages, and the length of time these peoples had engaged in pastoralism varied, as did the intensity of their commitment to this mode of life. Moreover, in each tribe there was some population movement between

189

the two sectors. Given these circumstances, the environmental constraints that people faced were neither uniform nor compelling, and
given the presence of a well-established cultural core in each society,
it was assumed that each population would retain distinctive cultural
traits that would, so to speak, resist ecological pressures for adaptive
change. Indeed, this proved to be the case. Pokot pastoralists were
more like Pokot farmers in their cultural beliefs and values than they
were like pastoralists in any of the other societies.

Nevertheless, there were significant differences in values, atti-
tudes, and even psychological attributes between farmers and pastoralists in all four societies. Compared with the farmers, the
pastoralists in all of these societies were more open and direct in
their expression of emotion and in their interpersonal relations. Farmers tended to avoid conflict, presumably because their ties to the land
made it impossible for them to move away should they make an enemy,
while pastoralists could and did move their families and herds if they
had a serious quarrel. Many of the differences found between farmers
and pastoralists seemed to be adaptive responses to the differing
ecologies of pastoralism and agriculture, as was predicted before the
research began.[3]

To illustrate the adaptive success that a long-established pastoralist
society can achieve, we might point to the Turkana, who occupy a
large arid area just to the north of the Pokot cattleherders. Long
established as pastoralists in this environment, the Turkana employ
livestock management techniques that do not degrade their pasture-
lands in that the numbers of livestock they maintain do not exceed
the carrying capacity of the land. What is more, their social institutions
have been successful in coping with the essential task of safeguarding
their herds against disease, enemy cattle raiders, and carnivores.[4]

There are many other examples of what appear to be efficient economic adaptations to ecological diversity. One of most dramatic is the
development of North American Plains Indian culture. Before the
introduction of horses from Spanish settlements in what is now New
Mexico in the early part of the seventeenth century, the true grassy
plains of North America were largely unoccupied except for small
bands of Indians who occasionally entered the area on foot to hunt
buffalo before returning to their settlements beyond this treeless, arid
region where horticulture was seldom practicable. But as wild horses
spread north, Indians who acquired them were able to hunt buffalo
much more efficiently and thereby remain in the plains area through-

190

out the year. Lured by horses and buffalo, horticultural tribes moved into the area from the east, while foraging peoples came from the north, west, and south. In one hundred years or so, a distinctive culture had arisen, one based on almost total dependence on horse and buffalo. Buffalo provided for all the needs of these Indians, and there were no other resources in the environment that could substitute for them. Everything, then, depended on finding and killing buffalo and maintaining sufficient numbers of horses to make this possible. During the late summer, when buffalo came together in vast herds, large encampments of Indians were able to find and slaughter them with ease. For the rest of the year, the buffalo scattered in small groups, and to find them the Indians had to disperse as well, breaking up into small bands. To survive, all Plains tribes had to become expert in finding and hunting buffalo, in riding and caring for horses, and in fighting to protect their horse herds and replenish them by raiding other tribes. In addition to hunting skills, equestrian prowess, and militarism, Plains culture was characterized by the social powers given to warrior societies, the individual initiative of warriors, the importance of the vision quest, the war bundle, and annual ceremonies, particularly the Sun Dance.

The demands imposed by this life of equestrian buffalo hunting were compelling, and all the tribes who entered the true plains were forced to hunt buffalo, protect their horses, and live in small, dispersed bands for most of the year. But much of Plains culture—militarism, war bundles, warrior societies, and the vision quest—did not arise *de novo* in response to the demands of Plains life but already existed among the Indians who came to the Plains area from the Eastern woodlands.[5] It is true that the foraging societies that entered the Plains typically lacked these cultural traits and tended to adopt them after entering, but they did not all do so. For example, the foraging Comanche of the southern Plains might be considered the most successful of all Plains tribes because they possessed the largest number of horses, yet they did not adopt warrior societies or develop the Sun Dance (at least not until 1874, when their culture was badly disorganized by white American settlements and military action). Similarly, many of the formerly horticultural tribes that had clans before entering the Plains allowed these kinship units to decline in importance, perhaps because they were not an efficient organizational mechanism for people who lived most of the time in small, mobile bands.[6] But two prominent Plains tribes, the Crow and Gros Ventre,

191

retained clans after some two hundred years of Plains life. In a similar anomaly, only five of the more than twenty Plains Indian societies ranked men (and sometimes women) into groups that passed through a series of named age-grades that had various ritual, political, and military duties and privileges.[7] For these five societies, age-graded groups seemed to play an essential role in their lives, but all the other Plains societies managed to do without such forms. Despite the strong constraints imposed by Plains ecology, the tribes of the Plains were not as alike as peas in a pod. They were very much alike in their material culture, economy, and even many of their values and religions, but otherwise their social institutions and cultures remained distinctive. The importance that some of these people attached to age-grades, clans, or the Sun Dance was not matched by others. These social and cultural arrangements were not necessarily maladaptive, but they were clearly not essential for survival in the Great Plains. They were neutral.

As modern human ecologists are quick to point out, not all environments offer as few options as the American Plains did for mounted buffalo hunters. Many environments in which foraging societies live offer a surprisingly wide array of options for hunting and gathering. As a result, the foraging strategies of hunter-gatherer societies have been difficult to characterize as optimally adaptive.[8] Efforts to develop models capable of predicting the types and proportions of food foraging people should consume, where and what they should hunt or gather, and how long they should do so continue to produce equivocal results.[9] For example, the nomadic movements of foraging populations have long been thought to be finely attuned to the availability of food resources in their physical environment. However, as J. C. Woodburn has shown for the nomadic Hadza of Tanzania, the availability of game or wild plant foods is only one reason why these foragers move their camp. They also move because of social conflict, the occurrence of an illness or death, the accumulation of excreta and debris, plagues of insects, and, perhaps least related to the environment of all, nightmares.[10] And as Kristen Hawkes found in her study of the Aché foragers of eastern Paraguay, instead of maximizing the yield from their hunting to provide as much meat as possible for their families, men chose high-risk forms of hunting as if gambling to win a lottery. According to Hawkes, who refers to this stragegy as "showing off," men chose risky forms of hunting because by winning they could claim favors from other people that would not otherwise be available.[11]

192

These favors did not necessarily optimize the hunters' survival nor that of their close kin or the population as a whole.

It is also apparent that some ecological circumstances exercise remarkably slight influence over either social organization or culture. Morris Freilich studied the small farming village of Anamat in eastern Trinidad because the two English-speaking ethnic groups that lived there—Afro-Trinidadians and Indian-Trinidiadians—had similar-sized land holdings, grew the same cash and subsistence crops, spent the same amount of time working their fields, used the same farming technology (including market and transportation facilities), and had the same crop yields and income.[12] For all practical purposes, their economic activities were identical. However, their social organizations were quite dissimilar, and their cultures were dramatically different. The Afro-Trinidadians did just as well economically as their Indian counterparts although they are present-time oriented and reveled in their sociable get-togethers (called "fêtes"), while the Indians put their emphasis on the future well-being of their family.

For another example, we return to the Ituri Forest of Zaire. All the Pygmies of the Ituri Forest hunt, but the Efe are archers, the Tswa use nets, and the Mbuti are both archers and net hunters. Colin Turnbull assumed that the Ituri was so rich in resources that either mode of hunting could be successful, a presumption that subsequent research has shown to be quite improbable. Except for Turnbull, most investigators have assumed that there had to be some differences in the forest ecology that made archery more effective in some areas and net hunting more efficient in others. However, as the research of Robert C. Bailey and Robert Aunger, Jr., has indicated, there are no significant differences in the composition or diversity of the forests exploited by net hunters or archers.[13] Bailey and Aunger suggest that the Efe archers are reluctant to adopt net hunting, even though they know it would lead to larger catches of game, not because their environment was unsuitable for net hunting but because the initial effort required to make nets would be too great. That is, what determines how the Efe choose to hunt appears to have more to do with their psychological attributes and cultural values than the demands of their physical environment.[14]

Adaptation, then, may sometimes take place rapidly in response to environmental demands, but it need not, and often does not, lead to predictable changes in economic practices and is even less likely to do so in social organization or culture. Once again, it must be reiterated that beliefs and practices that developed in response to earlier, and presumably different, environmental pressures tend to persist, and the result may come to be far less than efficient utilization of an environment. A population may embrace some social and cultural features that are not optimally fitted to its particular environment; it may also maintain beliefs and practices that lack adaptive value altogether. It may also be the case that any of several kinds of social and cultural arrangements will serve a population tolerably well.

To come to this last realization should not require taking a trip on the road to Damascus. If one reflects for a moment on how most human populations solve their problems, it should be apparent that they will not always do so perfectly nor even very well. As preceding examples have shown, there are populations whose belief and behavior systems have gone awry, often very badly so. But others have done much better. Decision making is a complex process that has been inadequately studied in traditional societies. Therefore, why some populations have made better decisions affecting their ecological adaptation than others is not well understood. At one extreme, some studies of decision making in small, traditional societies have stressed the rationality and efficiency of the decisions made.[15] In fact, Christopher Boehm was so impressed by people's ability to anticipate selective forces and rationally cope with them that he declared that we ". . . should view natives as applied scientists."[16] Others believe that even when people do not consciously solve their problems through rational or "scientific" decision making, they nevertheless act rationally in a teleonomic sense, as Ernst Mayr put it. That is, they unconsciously act adaptively because evolution equipped them to do so. Napoleon Chagnon, for example, has used this argument to explain Yanomamo warfare as an adaptive system.[17] And French structuralism, to take another example, has championed the view that a rational structure always lies beneath the surface of any belief system.

As an example of how some scholars have imputed unconscious problem-solving abilities to populations—immanent omniscience, if you will—that allow people to achieve optimal adaptations to their environments without conscious awareness of what they are doing, Roy Rappaport has written that the Tsembaga Maring of highland Papua New Guinea controlled the size of their pig and human populations through the indirect symbolic communication provided in their ritual cycle. Like a homeostatic mechanism, this ritual supposedly helped to maintain their physical environment, control warfare,

194

facilitate trade, and assure people access to animal protein when they most needed it.[18] All this took place without conscious awareness on the part of the people of what their ritual cycle was doing for them.

For such remarkable adaptations to exist without human awareness of the mechanisms involved or even of the problems that needed to be solved, it might be proposed that the solution (the ritual cycle) was originally chosen rationally and over the years functioned so well that people eventually forgot why it was created. It might also be proposed that the positive regulatory functions of the ritual were simply fortuitous and therefore never understood by the Tsembaga Maring. It is possible that phenomena such as these have occurred in various populations—food taboos would be one example—but for a population to be unaware of why or how a practice such as ritual cycle contributes to its well-being is hardly ideal because environmental change could quickly make ritual control maladaptive without the population's becoming aware of the need for change. A better solution for the Tsembaga, or any other population for that matter, would be to bring ecosystem regulation under rational control so that changes could be made when necessary.[19] Of course it is also possible that Rappaport was wrong in maintaining that the Tsembaga pig ritual had the beneficial consequences he claimed for it. And indeed, several recent restudies of his data have insisted that he was wrong.[20] Still, Rappaport was not alone in believing that people are capable of developing unconscious mechanisms for keeping themselves in tune with their ecosystems. Betty Meggers seriously concluded that because unrestricted use of increasingly efficient hunting techniques by small societies in the Amazon basin would rapidly exhaust the available game, these people ingeniously developed supernatural beliefs that would limit the effectiveness of their hunting. One such belief involved the idea that animal spirits were able to control human behavior, including where and when they should hunt. These animal spirits led hunters away from the actual location of game.[21]

Referring to Meggers among others, historian Robert Harms noted that "Much of the writing about peoples in small-scale, pre-industrial societies has emphasized their almost unconscious, ecological wisdom. They are pictured as natural conservationists, desiring above all to live in harmony with nature."[22] According to Harms, who did ecological research among the Nunu of Zaire, these people were not natural conservationists, nor did they maximize their economic productivity. Instead, they competed with one another for economic advantage, and some of their economic practices seriously degraded their environment. If people in small-scale societies possess unconscious ecological wisdom, one wonders why the Sirionó, Kaiaidilt, Gebusi, and others did not use their natural wisdom to live more comfortable lives.

Unconscious problem solving aside, people in small-scale societies often consciously try to find answers to their problems, but under what circumstances and to what extent they make rational decisions about the problems that confront them is a vexed question. The evidence is fragmentary and contradictory, but it would appear that people in folk societies sometimes do act very much like applied scientists as they classify plants and animals, modify the hulls of their ocean-worthy canoes, experiment with new crops, or refine their tools and weapons. It may even be the case that they sometimes act teleonomically as, for example, in craving certain foods that serve to correct a nutritional deficit or practicing rituals that promote a sense of well-being or social solidarity. Some folk populations have decision makers, such as prophets, war leaders, chiefs, big men, councils of elders, and the like, who deliberate about problems their societies face and try to make calculated decisions intended to enhance their well-being.

Decisions about foraging among hunting and gathering people like the San of the Kalahari are made only after intense discussion that allows the band members to reach a consensus.[23] Leaders among the Sebei and Cheyenne intentionally changed aspects of their law, war leaders in some small societies have carefully calculated the costs and benefits of attacking a neighboring society,[24] and people in various folk societies have sometimes chosen to reject innovations for good ecological reasons.[25] What is more, once understood, seemingly wasteful practices have sometimes been shown to be quite adaptive, as Harold Conklin demonstrated in his classic study of the swidden agriculture practiced by the Hanunoo of the Philippines.[26] The bulk of available evidence suggests that people in all societies tend to be relatively rational when it comes to the beliefs and practices that directly involve their subsistence, yet as we have repeatedly seen, nonrational beliefs sometimes reduce the efficiency of economic practices in many small societies. Recall the Inuit, and their beliefs in man-killing monsters. The more remote these beliefs and practices are from subsistence activities, the more likely they are to involve nonrational characteristics.

There is ample evidence, for example, that people in many societies

196

can provide no rational reason for clinging to certain beliefs or practices, and some of their most important decisions—when to raid an
enemy, where to fish, whom to fear—are based on prophecies,
dreams, divination, and other supernatural phenomena. And even
when people attempt to make rational decisions, they often fail. For
one thing, no population, especially no folk population, can ever
possess all the relevant knowledge it needs to make fully formal
decisions about its environment, its neighbors, or even itself.[27] What
is more, there is a large body of research involving human decision-
making both under experimental conditions and in naturally occurring
situations showing that individuals frequently make quite poor decisions, especially when it comes to solving novel problems or ones
requiring the calculation of the probability of outcomes, and these
are precisely the kinds of problems that pose the greatest challenges
for human adaptation.[28] In general, humans are not greatly skilled in
assessing risk, especially when the threat is a novel one, and they
tend to underestimate the future effects of warfare and technological
or economic change. Even when disasters such as droughts, floods,
windstorms, or volcanic eruptions recur periodically, people consistently misjudge their consequences.[29] They also do not readily develop
new technology, even when environmental stress makes technological
change imperative.[30] Western economists use the concept of bounded
rationality to refer to people's limited ability to receive, store, re-
trieve, and process information, and economic decision theory takes
these limitations into account. Because of these cognitive limitations,
along with imperfect knowledge of their environment, people inevitably make imperfect decisions.[31]

Richard Shweder has reminded us that "there is more to thinking
than reason and evidence," but he does not deny that humans are
sometimes non- or irrational,[32] a point vividly made by Dan Sperber,
who wrote that "apparently irrational cultural beliefs are quite remarkable: they do not appear irrational by slightly departing from
common sense, or timidly going beyond what the evidence allows.
They appear, rather, like down-right provocations against common
sense rationality."[33] As Sperber and others have pointed out, people
in many folk societies are convinced that humans or animals can be
in two places at the same time, can transform themselves into other
kinds of creatures or become invisible, and can alter the physical
world in various ways through their own beliefs. They also think
magically at least some of the time; indeed, it is very likely that the

principles of sympathetic magic are universally present because the human mind has evolved to think in these ways.[34] Moreover, all available evidence indicates that humans, especially those who live in folk societies, base their decisions on heuristics that permit and even encourage them to develop fixed opinions despite the fact that these opinions are based on inadequate or false information. These same heuristics also encourage people to cling to their opinions even when considerable evidence to the contrary becomes available. As Shweder has concluded, human thought is ". . . limited to its scientific procedures, unsophisticated in abstract reasoning, and somewhat impervious to the evidence of experience."[35]

None of this should be surprising, really, for no less rational a thinker than Aristotle was convinced that male babies were conceived at times when a strong north wind blew, and despite many generations of secular education, contemporary Americans continue to be less than fully rational. Various surveys have reported that 80 percent of contemporary Americans still believe that God works miracles, 50 percent believe in angels, and more than a third believe in a personal devil.[36] As I mentioned before, our ability to identify the risks in our environment is far from perfect. Mary Douglas and Aaron Wildavsky noted in their study of risk assessment, that all populations concentrate on only a few of the dangers that confront them and ignore the remainder, including some that are manifestly dangerous. The Lele of Zaire, for example, faced many serious dangers, including a large array of potentially life-threatening diseases, yet they concentrated on only three hazards—bronchitis (which is less serious than the pneumonia from which they also suffer), infertility, and being struck by lightning (a hazard that is a good deal less common than the tuberculosis from which they frequently suffer yet which they largely ignore).[37] According to the Science Advisory Board of the Environmental Protection Agency, Americans do the same, worrying most about relatively unimportant environmental problems like pesticide residue on foods and radiation from X-rays while largely ignoring potentially much more dangerous risks like global warming, habitat destruction, and air pollution.[38]

Recently, Thomas Gilovich has described the cognitive and social processes that continue to lead even highly educated Americans to hold fervently to demonstrably false beliefs.[39] Taking note of surveys of American college students indicating that as many as 58 percent believe that astrological predictions are valid and that 50 percent think that the Egyptian pyramids were built with extraterrestrial assistance, Gilovich describes the many ways in which contemporary Americans distort reality by their tendency to impute meaning and order to random phenomena and to remember only those instances that confirm their established beliefs while forgetting those that are at variance with them.

If modern Americans are less than rational calculators—and these examples hardly exhaust the catalog of folly contributed to by those among us who are thought to be most rational, such as our engineers, physicians, scientists and educators—then it is unreasonable to expect people whose cultures are even less secular than ours to be more efficient problem solvers than we are. It is important to emphasize that I am not arguing that people in folk societies make less-than-rational decisions or hold maladaptive beliefs because they are cognitively less competent than people in literate, industrialized societies. C. R. Hallpike, among others, has concluded that the thought processes of people in small-scale societies are incapable of comprehending causality, time, realism, space, introspection, and abstraction as these are utilized in Western science.[40] But whether so-called primitive thought is less abstract, more magical, or less able to assess marginal probabilities is an issue that continues to be debated, and in any event its resolution is largely irrelevant to the point I am attempting to make. I am asserting that most people in all societies, including those most familiar with Western science, sometimes make potentially harmful mistakes and tend to maintain them. It is possible that people in small-scale societies make more mistakes of this kind, but maladaptive decisions are made in all societies.

For people to optimize the adaptiveness of their beliefs and practices, they must not only think rationally, they must first be able to identify the problems that need to be solved. This is often difficult. Some problems, like changes in climate or soil erosion, develop so gradually that by the time they can be identified, no human response will be effective. Others, like the encroachment of diseases or the hazards of dietary change, may not be perceived as problems at all. Humans lived with the deadly hazard of malaria for millennia before it was finally understood very late in the nineteenth century that it was transmitted by mosquitoes. Many populations still do not understand the causes of malaria, schistosomiasis, and other deadly diseases. And still other phenomena may be perceived as problems but prove to be insoluble because the society is torn by conflicting values or interest groups. How much energy are people willing to expend to increase their food supply? Will pepole give up a tasty but unhealthy diet for one that is more nutritious but less flavorful? Will leaders willingly give up some of their privileges to benefit the society as a whole?

This is not to say that people in various societies do not worry about what they perceive to be problems, and in societies with recognized leaders, councils, or bureaucracies they often make decisions that are intended to be solutions. Earlier, we saw how members of the Hawaiian priesthood and aristocracy abolished their system of food taboos in an effort to resolve what they perceived as a problem and how a Pawnee chief tried to abolish human sacrifice. Because he wished to put an end to the gratuitous killing of men whose clans were small and weak by men who belonged to large and powerful ones, a prophet named Matui among the Sebei of Uganda instituted a new ritual, translated as "passing the law," in which all men of a parish gathered together and swore not to commit a number of acts.[41] Matui's innovation was probably adaptive for the Sebei because it reduced inter-clan violence, but such farsighted leadership must have been uncommon in human history. The wisdom of various leaders' decisions over the entire course of human evolution is unknown, but if the written record of history is any guide, few of them led to optimally beneficial outcomes. On the contrary, as Barbara Tuchman pointed out in *The March of Folly*, a great many were horrifically counter-productive.[42] Marvin Harris, long a leading proponent of the view that virtually all traditional beliefs and practices are adaptive, recently reached the surprising conclusion that ". . . all the major steps in cultural evolution took place in the absence of anyone's conscious understanding of what was happening." And, Harris adds, "the twentieth century seems a veritable cornucopia of unintended, undesirable, and unanticipated changes."[43]

Rational, calculated decisions intended to resolve a people's problems seldom occur in small socieites. Most of the time, how people hunt, fish, farm, conduct rituals, control their children, and enjoy their leisure are not matters for discussion at all, or at least not discussion about how to make these activities more efficient or pleasurable. People complain incessantly about various things in their lives; sometimes they may try something new, but only rarely do they attempt any fundamental change in their beliefs or social institutions. Large changes, if they occur at all, are typically imposed by some external event or circumstance—invasion, epidemic, drought. In the absence of such events, people tend to muddle through by relying on traditional solutions; that is to say, solutions that arose in response to previous circumstances. Most populations manage to survive without being rational calculators in search of optimal solutions. It appears, for example, that folk populations typically adopt strategies that assure a life-sustaining but well below maximal yield of food and resist changes that entail what they perceive to be risks even though these new food-providing practices would produce more food.

The reluctance of people to change—such as that of the Efe to adopt net hunting—has led some anthropologists to refer to their economic strategies in terms of "minimal risk" and "least effort." Traditional solutions and long-standing beliefs and practices tend to persist not because they are optimally beneficial but because they generally work just well enough that changes in them are not self-evidently needed. Given all that we know about the sometimes astoundingly bad judgment of "rational" planners in modern nations, it seems unlikely that people in smaller and simpler societies that lack our scientific and technological sophistication would always make optimally adaptive decisions even should they try to do so. What is more, even if a population somehow managed to devise a near-perfect adaptation to its environment, it is unlikely that it could maintain it for any length of time.

The message of this book is not that traditional beliefs and practices are never adaptive and that they never contribute to a population's well-being; and I am not claiming that people never think rationally enough to make effective decisions about meeting the challenges posed by their environments. To do so would be absurd. I am not arguing either that human behavior is driven solely by the socially disruptive aspects of biological predispositions; people are also predisposed to cooperate, be kind to one another, and sometimes even sacrifice their interests for the well-being of others.

Much of what we have learned about human history and human nature suggests a picture of human accomplishment, not discord, failure, or pathology. Throughout the world, people have developed effective techniques of hunting, gathering, herding, and gardening, domesticated plants and animals, built houses, developed trade, established meaningful religions, and learned to govern themselves. They have also created moving forms of music and dance and dazzling works of art. Visitors to the world's great museums still gaze in rapture

201

at fabulous gold jewelry, masks, sculptures, baskets, pottery, and clothing that have been so intricately and tastefully moulded, woven, carved, sewn, incised, or painted that they endure as works of great art. They have also made formidable weapons and ingenious tools, devised majestic canoes and great pyramids, dug remarkable irrigation canals, and built great cities. It is not just the so-called high civilizations of China, Mesopotamia, Egypt, India, Mexico and Peru that have filled museums with their works; small-scale societies from all over the world have left us evidence of their ingenuity and artistic ability—Inuit stonecarving, Asante gold sculptures, Fijian tapa cloth, Tibetan weaving, Kirghiz saddles, Pomo feather baskets. And no one who has ever opened an anthropology textbook could fail to be impressed by humankind's ability to devise customs so incredibly diverse, so limitlessly inventive, that it is difficult to believe that these human creations would not make people's lives safe, satisfying, and meaningful.

Counterintuitive though it may seem after an exposure to this compelling record of human ingenuity, it must nevertheless be acknowledged that populations have not always gotten things right. Inefficiency, folly, venality, cruelty, and misery were and are also a part of human history. Human suffering is one result. To mention but one chilling example among a great many, the Chernobyl nuclear plant released more radioactivity than ten Hiroshima-sized bombs because, according to an engineer who helped construct the plant, there was almost incomprehensible inefficiency in design, construction, maintenance, and management of the facility. However, in an attempt to contain the disaster, Soviet fire fighters, electricians, engineers, doctors, nurses, helicopter pilots, scuba divers, and other workers rushed to Chernobyl without protective clothing, knowing full well that the radioactivity could kill them.[44] Incredible folly followed by incredible heroism is not a rare occurrence in human history.

Conclusion

As I observed in chapter 2, the belief that folk societies, "primitives" in an earlier, more judgmental parlance, were more harmonious and hence better adapted than larger, more urbanized societies is so ancient and deeply entrenched in Western thought that it has taken on the quality of a myth, a sacred story not to be challenged. In this story, folk community was said to consist of emotional sharing, personal intimacy, moral commitment, social cohesion, and continuity over time.[45] This sense of community, this harmony, was said to make possible the stable, positive adaptations that small-scale populations made to their environments. Due largely to the size and heterogeneity of urban centers, this sense of community—of common purpose—that had directed and united small-scale societies was lost. As a result, cities were said to be torn by dissention and conflict.

Although there was widespread acceptance of the thesis that it was the loss of community that led to urban pathology, some sociologists have pointed out that most large cities did not lack communities (in the plural). Cities are composed of many communities or neighborhoods based on ethnicity or race, as well as subcultures based on occupation (such as steelworker in some Eastern cities) or lifestyle (such as "artists' colonies") or sexual preference (gay and lesbian neighborhoods). These critics acknowledged that social and personal pathology did exist in cities but refused to attribute it to the loss of community. This is an important point, but an even more important one is seldom recognized. The sense of community said to typify small-scale societies is neither as common or as intense in these societies as proponents of the folk-urban distinction have thought.

There are many kinds of small-scale, "primitive" societies that can be termed "folk"—a "small communty," as one prominent scholar came to call such a society—by virtue of being small in population, homogeneous, self-sufficient, and aware of the social boundaries that separate them from other people.[46] As we have seen, some small societies such as the Chumash and Kwakiutl have had powerful chiefs, social classes, and even slaves; their sense of community was sharply divided. Throughout the world, people who live in small agrarian villages of horticulturalists or "peasants" are supposed to be equal members of the community. In reality, however, these people are notorious for being pitted against one another in perpetual envy, fear, and hostility. Like the Italian villagers of Montegrano, often their only community is the family.

Even the smallest of societies, roving bands that number but a few score who live by hunting and gathering, can have strongly opposing interests. Children and adults do not always share the same sense of community; neither do men and women, older and younger siblings, cowives, or various families and kin groups. Their competing interests sometimes provoke anger, quarrels, and even violence that can lead to the breakup of the local group. Even members of a Mbuti band, people who do have a sense of themselves as a community, nevertheless have competing interests and conflicts that are sometimes so severe that some may leave the band to join another or create a new one. The members of a Sirionó band had virtually no sense of community at all.

Urban dwellers suffer from various forms of personal and social distress partly because their own communities are less than idyllic but also because of the great diversity of cultures, religions, occupations, and classes. Small-scale societies are spared the disharmony that may result from such diversity, but they are not free from conflict. Some are cohesive communities, but most are divided in troublesome ways. In addition, all small populations maintain some beliefs and practices that do not serve their needs well, leaving them hungry, unwell, and fearful, and many of them have difficulty controlling internecine violence. Recall that 35 percent of all adult male deaths among the Gebusi of Papua New Guinea were due to homicide and that even higher rates occurred in the Amazon basin. Even the !Kung San, the "harmless" people of the Kalahari, had a homicide rate that matched that of a violent American urban ghetto. The Tasmanians, Kaingáng, Kaiadilt, and others were probably even more homicidal. Modern urban societies have done a better job of controlling homicide, as Martin Daly and Margo Wilson recently concluded in their review of homicide in the world's societies.[47] Modern urban societies may also have done better at feeding their populations and maintaining their health. The average life expectancy in the United States, Japan, and Western Europe today is more than twice that ever attained by any folk society and indeed is three times that of many. The desire to live a long and healthy life is surely universal, and some modern societies may have gone even further in giving at least their more affluent members greater life satisfaction than folk societies have ever done. One thing is certain: modern societies have survived and grown in numbers while many small-scale populations have dwindled or vanished.

It is not my purpose here to argue that modern urban societies are necessarily better adapted than folk societies, although in respects such as health, longevity, and the control of homicide I believe they are. What I hope to have shown, instead, is that folk societies are not necessarily well adapted. What I am calling for is a moratorium on the uncritical assumption that the traditional beliefs and practices of folk populations are adaptive while those of modern societies are not and a commitment to examining the relative adaptiveness of the beliefs and practices of *all* societies. The goal is a better understanding of human adaptation not just in particular societies but over the course of human history.

If that goal is to be met, there will have to be some changes in the way we think about social and cultural evolution. There is order and predictability in the social and cultural world, but there is also disorder and randomness. As Sir Edmund Leach reminded us long ago, there is no more a state of equilibrium in a human society than there is in other natural systems.[48] Just as physicists have had to come to terms with fractals—chaos and randomness—in the physical world, social scientists must learn to live with the reality of redundancy, meaninglessness, inefficiency, and malfunction in the evolution of human social and cultural systems. In doing so it might be useful for them to use an analogy from biological evolution. Traditional Darwinian theory has held that because of forces of natural selection, existing genetic variation must have a positive function, but Motoo Kimura's "neutral theory" argues that much of the genetic variation in any species, including humans, is adaptively neutral. Under certain circumstances, such as mutation and genetic drift, these neutral genes can become either more adaptive or maladaptive.[49]

So it is with social and cultural traits. No matter how long people may have lived in a particular environment, much that they believe and do may play no positive or negative role in their adaptation—it is neutral. As time goes on, these neutral beliefs and practices can become either more adaptive or more maladaptive, joining others that are already positively or negatively influencing a population's well-being. Stephen Jay Gould showed in his analysis of the Burgess Shale that evolution could have taken a very different course than it did—the world could have been peopled by vertebrates with five eyes, not two, for example.[50] The biological forms that survived and prospered did not necessarily have superior anatomies; they did so because biological evolution, like a lottery, can be indeterminate. So can the evolution of society and culture. Practices like head-hunting or penile mutilation can become such focal points for a population that people find it unthinkable to live without them, but that does not mean that these practices came into being as a result of some

205

ineluctable evolutionary force or human need nor that people who once practiced them could not learn to live without them. Many populations have done so.

If maladaptive beliefs and practices are as common as they appear to be, their existence—like that of neutral traits—poses a challenge to the prevailing adaptivist paradigm. Subsistence activities must be reasonably efficient for a population to survive, but they need not be optimal (in the sense of providing the best possible nutrition for the least expenditure of time and energy). It is highly unlikely that any population has achieved an optimal economic adaptation; indeed, it is not at all clear that any population has even attempted to do so. Social organization and culture will be affected by the technology available to a population and by its economic activities, but neither social institutions nor cultural belief systems commonly led to anything that could be considered maximally adaptive utilization of the environment. Neither will they unfailingly enhance the well-being of all members of that population.

Just as no population has yet devised an optimal means for exploiting its environment, so it is most unlikely that all members of a population have agreed about what an optimal environmental exploitation should be. Moreover, no population yet reported has met the needs of all its members to their own satisfaction. All, including those whose members are healthiest, happiest, and longest-lived, could do better. All could improve health and safety, all could enhance life satisfaction. There has been no perfect society, no ideal adaptation, only degrees of imperfection. Knowingly and not, populations adjust their ways of living in an effort to better their lives, but none has yet created the Garden of Eden. Not only are humans capable of errors, of misjudging the ecological circumstances that they must learn to cope with, they are given to pursuing their own interests at the expense of others' and to preferring the retention of old customs to the development of new ones. Culture, then, tends to be adaptive but is never perfectly so.

It should thus not be assumed, as it so commonly is, that any persistent, traditional beliefs or practices in a surviving society must be adaptive. It should be assumed instead that any belief or practice could fall anywhere along a continuum of adaptive value. No belief or practice in question should escape careful scrutiny before being deemed beneficial or harmful. It may simply be neutral or tolerable, or it may benefit some members of a society while harming others.

206

If we are to understand the processes of cultural adaptation and maladaptation, relativism must be replaced by a form of evaluative analysis. One cannot study the relative success of adaptation without making evaluative judgments. We would never countenance a relativistic prohibition against attempting to evaluate the conditions of life in our inner cities. We know that drug use, gang violence, child abuse, deteriorated housing, poor prenatal health care, rage, and hopelessness are not good for the impoverished and embattled people who live there, and these people know it far better than we do. Why then should the principle of cultural relativism prevent us from evaluating the feuding, wife battering, inadequate diets, and inefficient medical knowledge that exist in many small, traditional societies?

I have no doubt that the traditional, religious Pawnee practice of torturing children before sacrificing them to propitiate the Morning Star would be considered a moral outrage by anyone reading this book. We would all wish for a world in which no people felt obligated to torture or sacrifice others, especially children. But the Pawnee did so, year after year. The point is not whether this practice was abhorrent to us but adaptive for them. It could have helped to reduce their anxiety about life's potential dangers; people in various parts of the world have long sacrificed human victims to appease supernatural forces. But if so, we then must ask why the other societies in the same Plains area did not feel the need to do the same. Perhaps instead of lessening Pawnee anxiety, human sacrifice was a practice that created fear because failure to perform the ceremony could bring about supernatural displeasure. (Of course, there is also the possibility that the practice was insisted upon by Pawnee priests in order to maintain their religious authority and social privileges. If so, it would not be the only time that religious leaders have promoted ceremonies for their own benefit.) Without more information about the Pawnee than has survived, these questions cannot be answered; but if the practices of contemporary societies about which detailed information could be obtained were explored in this way, questions about the adaptiveness of human sacrifice and other practices might be answered.

Much of the burden of evaluating human adaptation must fall to anthropologists. Anthropology was once designated the study of man. We now know that it is the study of men, women, children, and the environments in which they live, but we do not yet agree about what anthropology is supposed to do. There are many reasons why a field of study like anthropology may come into being and many others why it may grow or decline into insignificance, but one central reason is the usefulness of the knowledge that the field generates. It hardly need be said that there is no consensus about what kind of knowledge will prove most useful, now or in the future, but the ability to distinguish what is harmful for human beings from what is beneficial to them should qualify as useful knowledge. To generate this kind of knowledge, it will be necessary to learn more about the needs and predispositions that men, women, and children bring with them to life in any society, and it will also be necessary to learn how to determine whether certain aspects of their culture may be harmful to a particular population in a particular context.

Maladaptation is a useful concept, embedded as it is in the more general concept of adaptation, but it may sound too sanitary, too lifeless to rally many people to its banner. The consequences of maladaptation, however, are anything but removed from life: they include alienation, despair, deprivation, fear, hunger, sickness, and death. A scholarly discipline that can illuminate the sources of these kinds of human misery should command a large following, and with better understanding of the sources of maladaptation may come means of reducing human suffering. We have no mandate to change other cultures because we find that some of their beliefs or practices are harmful to them, but we do have an obligation to understand and, when possible, to teach. By teaching—by teaching *well*—we may be able to make our understandings about human maladaptation available to people, people who can then help themselves to suffer less.

There are some, including Stephen Jay Gould, who believe that the prime mover of evolution has not been competition among species but environmental change that creates opportunities for some species more than others to proliferate. Whatever the truth of this idea for evolution in general, human evolution has involved competition that at times has been so violent that some human groups have failed to survive. Environmental change has played a determinative role as well: populations that have not been flexible enough to adjust to changing circumstances have not fared well.

These two evolutionary phenomena are sure to continue into the future, when the already great interconnectedness of peoples and their societies will no doubt increase still further. As world economic systems penetrate ever deeper into remote parts of the world and telecommunication brings people everywhere ever closer together, many small-scale societies will be transformed as they amalgamate into federations, become occupational specialists, clients, recipients of aid programs, or victims of government repression. Yet, paradoxically, if recent experience is any guide, neither these developments nor the increased power of regional or worldwide forms of governance will put an end to ethnic and religious factionalism, xenophobia, and strife. Instead, one form of irredentism or another can be expected to flourish virtually everywhere on earth. These ethnic and religious revivalisms, these passionate strivings for lost autonomy and misplaced meaning, will likely bring about ever more intense valorization of traditional beliefs, rituals, and customs. In a retribalized world, we can hope that people will choose wisely as they rehabilitate once-discarded values and ceremonies, but the factors that led to maladaptation in the past will continue to threaten future well-being. This is all the more reason why those who will take part in fashioning new cultures and societies should be aware that some beliefs and behaviors serve human needs and social requisites better than others. If they are, then perhaps the newly retribalized world will find a greater share of the harmony and well-being that have eluded so many peoples of the past and the present day.

Notes

CHAPTER 1.   Paradise Lost: *The Myth of Primitive Harmony*

1. Fox (1990:3).
2. Cf. Mills (1950); Nisbet (1973); Goldschmidt (1990:228); Shaw (1985).
3. Redfield (1947).
4. Sale (1991); see also Mills (1950); Wirth (1938).
5. Wokler (1978).
6. Belo (1935:141).
7. Lewis (1951).
8. Thomas (1958); Lee (1979); Schapera (1930).
9. Turnbull (1961).
10. Turnbull (1972).
11. For a discussion of these two books, see *Current Anthropology*, vol. 15, March 1974, and vol. 16, September 1975.
12. Turnbull (1978).
13. Heine (1985:3). In partial defense of Turnbull, he clearly reported that the Ik he knew before the full effects of the drought took place were kind, fun loving, and sociable. It is also possible that conditions during Heine's visit were better than they were during the drought Turnbull witnessed. See also Harako (1976).
14. E.g., see Cawte, Djagamara, and Barrett (1966). For discussions of these practices as pathological, see Favazza (1987). For infibulation, see Hayes (1975).
15. Goldschmidt (1976b:353).
16. Koch (1974:159).
17. Ellen (1982:195).
18. Kluckhohn and Leighton (1962:240).
19. Ibid., pp. 246–47.

20. Evans-Pritchard (1940).
21. Ibid., p. 83.
22. Ibid., p. 74.
23. Gregor (1977).
24. See Edgerton (1971a). For a more general discussion, see Hallpike (1986).
25. Harris (1960:601).
26. Holmberg (1969:259).
27. Ibid., p. 160.
28. Stearman (1987).
29. Banfield (1958).

CHAPTER 2.   From Relativism to Evaluation

1. Carden (1969).
2. Noyes (1937); Carden (1969).
3. Kephart (1976).
4. Gazaway (1969:53).
5. Ibid., p. 107.
6. Ibid., p. 230.
7. Leach (1982:52).
8. Brown (1991).
9. Levinson and Malone (1980); Naroll (1983); Brown (1991).
10. Harris (1968).
11. Ragin (1984). See also Goldschmidt (1966).
12. Rorty (1980).
13. Needham (1972:245).
14. Ibid., p. 246.
15. Sumner (1906).
16. Kluckhohn (1939:342).
17. Hollis and Lukes (1982:1). For a discussion of ethical relativism, see Renteln (1988). See also Marcus and Fischer (1986).
18. Bloom (1987).
19. Hatch (1983).
20. Maquet (1964).
21. Rosaldo (1984b:188).
22. Geertz (1984).
23. Schneider (1984).
24. Cf. Rosaldo (1984b) and Scholte (1984).
25. Nissam-Sabat (1987:935).
26. Malotki (1983).
27. Haugen (1977).
28. Spiro (1990).
29. E.g., see Spiro (1984) and Cohen (1989); for a historian's view of interpretivism and Clifford Geertz, see Biersack (1989). For another criticism, see Crapanzano (1986); and for a particularly frontal attack, see Appell (1989).
30. Geertz (1984); Marcus and Fischer (1986).
31. Tyler (1984:335).

32. Tyler (1986:123). For a discussion of this point of view, see Strathern (1987a). It may be of interest to note that twenty years ago, Tyler was a well-respected cognitive anthropologist who appeared to find no fault with scientific method.
33. Spiro (1990).
34. Sperber (1982).
35. Gellner (1982).
36. See Cole and Scribner (1974); D'Andrade (1990); Brown (1991).
37. Geertz (1973).
38. Wallace (1960).
39. Gellner (1982) and Spiro (1984).
40. Quine (1960).
41. For doubts on this score, cf. Needham (1972).
42. Berlin and Kay (1969).
43. E.g., see Bruner (1990), O'Meara (1989), and Washburn (1987).
44. Shweder (1990).
45. Sahlins (1976; 1985).
46. Evans-Pritchard (1962) and Leach (1982).
47. Cf. Shweder and LeVine (1984), Rosaldo (1984b), Lutz (1988), and Clifford and Marcus (1986).
48. Harris (1971:448).
49. Hallpike (1986).
50. Harris (1985:17). For another example of this presupposition, see Alland (1970).
51. Campbell (1975:1104).
52. Ibid.
53. Ross (1985).
54. Tylor (1871).
55. Malinowski (1936:132).
56. Hatch (1973).
57. Radcliffe-Brown (1949:322).
58. Sztompka (1974); Martindale (1965). For a discussion of neofunctionalism, see Eisenstadt (1990) and Alexander (1985).
59. Harris (1960:60–61).
60. Wynne-Edwards (1962); (1986).
61. Lack (1966).
62. Rappaport (1968).
63. Lopreato (1984:253).
64. Bernstein (1984:297); Boyd and Richerson (1985); Alexander (1990:249). Many other evolutionary biologists, including disciples of Alexander, are more willing to acknowledge the presence of maladaptive traits (Turke 1990), and some, like John Tooby and Leda Cosmides, believe there is "no reason to assume that any modern practice is adaptive" (1989:313).
65. Alexander (1990:249). See also Borgerhoff Mulder (1987b).
66. Lowie (1920).
67. Oswalt (1973).
68. There are exceptions, of course. Ross (1987:16) points out that sometimes a blowgun using curare-tipped darts paralyzes a monkey in a tree so that it falls to the earth. When shot with a bullet, the monkey's hands reflexively clutch

a branch, and repeated shots only riddle the animal without bringing it down.

69. Goldenweiser (1942).
70. Gladwin (1970).
71. Herskovits (1972).
72. Geertz (1988).
73. Benedict (1934:31).
74. Ibid., p. 31.
75. Geertz (1973:44).
76. LaBarre (1945:326).
77. Freud (1930).
78. Kroeber (1948:300).
79. Linton (1952).
80. Kluckhohn (1955).
81. Redfield (1953:163).
82. Murdock (1965:146). When the American Anthropological Association was called upon to draft its own statement on human rights following the one promulgated by the United Nations, its author, Melville Herskovits, included some ethnocentric language that Robert Redfield challenged by saying that it was necessary to include *all* values (Renteln 1988:67).
83. Ibid., p. 149.
84. Ibid.
85. Norbeck (1961).
86. Spiro (1968).
87. Schwartz (1974).
88. Ibid., p. 169.
89. Ibid., p. 168.
90. Ibid., p. 167.
91. Kennedy (1969:177).
92. Ibid., p. 167.
93. Hippler (1981:394).
94. Hatch (1983).
95. Herskovits (1951:23).
96. Harris (1981).
97. Washburn (1987:939).
98. Hippler (1981:402).
99. Ibid., p. 394.
100. Ibid.
101. Reser (1981).
102. Hallpike (1977:230).
103. Hallpike (1986:vi).
104. Hallpike (1972).
105. Ibid., p. 372.
106. Naroll (1983).
107. Ibid., p. 73.
108. Colby (1987).
109. See Boyd and Richerson (1985).
110. For example, see Alexander (1987).

111. Lopreato (1984); Tooby and Cosmides (1989); Scott (1989).
112. Boyd and Richerson (1985), Rogers (1988), Barkow (1989a,b).
113. Boyd and Richerson (1985:279).
114. Rogers (1988).
115. Barkow (1989a).
116. Lewontin, Rose, and Kamin (1984).
117. Ibid.
118. Symons (in press).
119. Barkow (1989a:322).
120. Barkow and Burley (1980); Symons (1989).
121. Lumsden (1989:25).
122. Tooby and Cosmides (1989); Symons (1989).
123. Barkow (1973).
124. See Barkow, Cosmides, and Tooby (1992).
125. Turke (1990).
126. Borgerhoff Mulder (1987a); White (1989) has challenged her interpretation of these findings.
127. Vining (1990).
128. Rogers (1990).
129. Symons (1989:142).
130. Harris (1989).
131. Miller (1981).
132. Aberle et al. (1950).
133. Goldschmidt (1959).
134. Hallpike (1986:88). For other approaches, see Levy (1952) and Parsons (1964).
135. Campbell (1975).
136. Malinowski (1944).
137. See, e.g., Lopreato (1984).
138. Boehm (1989).
139. Rogers (1988).
140. E.g., Hatch (1983); Bock (1980); Brooks and Wiley (1986).
141. Sapir (1924).
142. Naroll (1983); Colby (1987).
143. Rotberg and Rabb (1985).
144. Alland (1970).

CHAPTER 3.   Maladaptation

1. Jerome H. Barkow (1989a) has provided a helpful discussion of some of these sources of maladaptation, as has Hallpike (1986).
2. Cf. Cardoe (1991).
3. Jones (1977).
4. Jones (1978:21).
5. Roth (1899:103).
6. Jones (1978:12).
7. Roth (1899:113–14).
8. Plomley (1966:135).

9. Roth (1899:114).
10. Roth (1899); Jones (1977). Horton (1979) believes that there may have been more ritual activity than this, but even granting his point, there was nothing like the elaboration of ritual among the Tasmanians that took place in Australia.
11. Jones (1978).
12. Ibid., p. 47.
13. Ibid., p. 44.
14. Ibid.
15. Ibid., p. 41.
16. Plomley (1966:1967).
17. Jones (1977:203). Horton (1979) accuses Jones of overstatement, but I find his evidence unconvincing.
18. Ryan (1982:176).
19. Jones (1974:324).
20. Ryan (1982:13–14); Plomley (1966:150).
21. Kummer (1971:99).
22. Hallpike (1986). For an extended discussion of the difficulties that defining adaptation entails, see Alland (1970) and Ellen (1982).
23. LaBarre (1984:x–xi).
24. Ibid., p. 10.
25. Ibid., p. 131.
26. Sperber (1985).
27. For a more extended discussion of divination, see Hallpike (1986).
28. Moore (1957).
29. Vollweiler and Sanchez (1983).
30. Ibid., p. 200.
31. For another criticism of Moore's analysis, see Hallpike (1986). And for a discussion of the decline of belief in magic, especially in Greece, because it was seen to be ineffective, see Tambiah (1990).
32. Ferguson (1989:258).
33. Lewontin et al. (1984:264). See also Daly and Wilson (1988) and Barkow (1989a).
34. Ellen (1982:251).
35. Langness, personal communication.
36. Spiro (1984). For a discussion of rationality in thought, see Shweder (1984).
37. Johnson and Covello (1987).
38. Betzig (1986).
39. Schapera (1930:77).
40. Ibid., p. 151.
41. Ibid., p. 107.
42. Ellen (1982).
43. Campbell (1975).
44. Lopreato (1984:177).
45. Rogers and Shoemaker (1971).
46. Cf. Hallpike (1986:96).
47. Leis (1965:102).
48. Gellner (1958).
49. See Boehm (1978) for his discussion of "rational preselection."

50. Wagley (1951).
51. For a parallel discussion, see Barkow (1989a).
52. McGovern, Bigelow, Amorasi, and Russell (1988).
53. Abrams and Rue (1988).
54. *Los Angeles Times*, May 15, 1991.
55. Burch (1971).
56. Barkow (1989a). See also Boyd and Richerson (1985).
57. For a summary of these points of view, see Rogers (1988).
58. Geertz (1973:49).
59. Ibid., p. 49.
60. Ibid., p. 49.
61. Boyd and Richerson (1985:281).
62. McGregor (1946).
63. Childe (1942:16).
64. Lopreato (1984).
65. Bellah et al. (1985).
66. For a discussion of these and other approaches, see Boehm (1989).
67. Harris (1979:63). In fairness to Harris, he lists other characteristics that might have a genetic basis, but he rests his cultural materialism on this list of four factors.
68. Barkow (1989a).
69. Alexander (1987), Barkow (1989a), Bailey (1987), Campbell (1975), Count (1958), Konner (1982), Lopreato (1984), Symons (1979), and Wilson (1978).
70. Fox (1971).
71. Bailey (1987).
72. Konner (1982).
73. Pospisil (1958:834).
74. Lockard and Paulhus (1988).
75. Trivers (1985).
76. See, e.g., Lumsden and Wilson (1981), Symons (1979), Tooby and Cosmides (1989), and Barkow (1989a).
77. Gazzaniga (1989).
78. Marr (1982).
79. Wynn (1989).
80. Kihlstrom (1987).
81. Gardner (1983).
82. Freedman (1974).
83. E.g., see Lopreato (1984); Goldschmidt (1990).
84. Wilson (1978:5).
85. Henry (1963:11).
86. Trilling (1955:115).
87. Campbell (1975); see esp. pp. 1104 and 1119.
88. Trivers (1971). For an informed discussion of various aspects of human nature that challenges sociality, see Barkow (1989a:375 ff).
89. For a complementary view, see Dawkins (1976).
90. Meggitt (1977:110).
91. Feil (1987).

217

92. Robarchek (1989).
93. Symons (1979).
94. See Betzig (1986).
95. Chagnon (1974).
96. For a similar view, see Hallpike (1986).
97. For more detailed discussions, see LeVine (1973), Spiro (1984), and Burton (1985).
98. See Alexander (1987), Barkow (1989a,b), and Boehm (1989).
99. Edgerton (1978).

CHAPTER 4. Women and Children First: *From Inequality to Exploitation*

1. Johnson and Earle (1987:321); Roberts and Brintnall (1983).
2. Walker and Hewlett (1990).
3. Cf. Hallpike (1986).
4. Sahlins (1972).
5. Betzig (1988).
6. Ibid., p. 61. See also Chagnon (1988b) for a discussion of Yanomamo men manipulating their kinship system for their benefit.
7. Dahrendorf (1968).
8. For a summary, see Harris (1989).
9. Collier (1988).
10. Kroeber (1953).
11. Chagnon (1967:53–55).
12. Graburn (1987).
13. Turner (1894).
14. Graburn (1987); Hoebel (1954); Knauft (1987).
15. Graburn (1987).
16. Turnbull (1961:101); Singer (1978) has argued that the Mbuti beat their dogs because they could not take aggressive action against one another. Perhaps so, but the Mbuti were aggressive against people in their own camps, and sometimes they were violent.
17. Baksh (1984:99–100).
18. Korbin (1981; 1987); Graburn (1987).
19. Kilbride and Kilbride (1990).
20. Ortner (1974; Harbison, Khaleque, and Robinson (1989); Gregor (1990).
21. Shahar (1983).
22. Levinson (1989); Ember and Levinson (1991). An exception are the Wape of Papua New Guinea; a gentle people in everyday life, Wape men do not beat their wives (Mitchell 1990).
23. Simoons (1961:110).
24. Freuchen (1961:97).
25. Lumholtz (1989); Nieboer (1900:11).
26. Ross (1987).
27. Lindenbaum (1979).
28. Peacock (1990).

29. Levinson (1989).
30. Langness (1974).
31. Gilmore (1990).
32. Edgerton (fieldnotes, 1962).
33. Gregor (1990); Palmer (1989).
34. For further discussion, see Strathern (1987b).
35. LeVine (1959:966).
36. Many societies with similar problems of "marrying their enemies" have avoided these extremes of hostility. E.g., see Meggitt (1979).
37. LeVine (1959:967).
38. Ibid., p. 968.
39. Ibid., p. 970.
40. Ibid., p. 965.
41. LeVine and LeVine (1979).
42. Edgerton (1971a:101).
43. Goldschmidt (1976b:241–42).
44. Turnbull (1961).
45. Michelson (1932).
46. Cohen (1989).
47. Barkow (1989a).
48. The societies were the Lumi and Bundi (Fogel et al. 1983).
49. Cohen (1989:202).
50. Laslett (1965:220).
51. *Los Angeles Times*, August 31, 1990.
52. Ibid., September 30, 1990.
53. Pipes (1990); Andrew and Gordievsky (1990); Tucker (1990).
54. *New York Times*, August 12, 1990.
55. Service (1975).
56. Betzig (1986).
57. Rasmussen (1931).
58. Feil (1987).
59. Richards (1940:106).
60. Ruyle (1973).
61. Harris (1968:313).
62. Ruyle (1973). For a discussion of warfare to capture slaves on the Northwest Coast, see Mitchell (1984).
63. Harner (1977); Harris (1977).
64. Ortiz de Montellano (1983). Stanley M. Garn (1979) has argued that the energy costs of capturing and feeding captives were far greater than any caloric benefit gained by eating them. But he overlooks the fact that the commoners and slaves made the energy expenditure while the nobles received the calories.
65. Hassig (1988).
66. Quoted in Soustelle (1961:25).
67. Hassig (1988:116).
68. Soustelle (1961:65).
69. Omer-Cooper (1966).
70. Fynn (1950); Isaacs (1970); Walter (1969).

219

71. Fynn (1950:28–29).
72. Isaacs (1970:62).
73. Edgerton (1988).
74. McLeod (1984); Wilks (1975).
75. Anquandah (1982).
76. Wilks (1975:673).
77. Fynn (1971); Wilks (1975).
78. Bowditch (1966:31).
79. Ibid., p. 34.
80. Ibid., p. 115.
81. Ibid., p. 335–336.
82. Wilks (1975:185).
83. Ibid., p. 135.
84. Rattray (1929).
85. Bowditch (1966:250); Ramseyer and Kühne (1875).
86. Jones (1969:70).
87. Ibid., p. 71. The tribes were the Shawnees, Delawares, Kickapoos, Caddos, Comanches, and Kiowas.
88. Kuper (1981).
89. Rambo (1985).
90. Harris (1977).
91. Stannard (1989).
92. Dirks (1980).
93. Roberts and Brintnall (1983:153).
94. Perrin (1979).

CHAPTER 5.   Sickness, Suffering, and Premature Death

1. Wirsing (1985:303); Johns (1990).
2. Konner (1991). For a more even-handed approach, see Finkler (1985), who attempts to explain why only a minority of persons who receive spiritualist therapy respond positively to it.
3. Opler (1936:1374). For a lively discussion of the inadequacies of folk and Western medicine, see Foster and Anderson (1978).
4. MacLean (1971:84).
5. Meggitt (1977).
6. Holmberg (1969:229).
7. Rose (1986).
8. McMillen (1968).
9. Wirsing (1985:305).
10. Pelto (1987).
11. Scheper-Hughes (1990:546).
12. Ibid., p. 550.
13. Grant (1982); Grant (1991).
14. McCord and Freeman (1990).
15. Trovato (1988).
16. Beck (1990).

17. Beaubier (1976).
18. Cassidy (1980).
19. Cohen (1989:139).
20. Ibid., p. 140.
21. Story (1985).
22. Sahlins (1968).
23. Messer (1984).
24. Holmberg (1969).
25. Altman (1984).
26. Shostak (1981).
27. Wirsing (1985).
28. Howe (1984); Spriggs (1981); Nurse (1975).
29. Howe (1984).
30. Dennett and Connell (1988).
31. Sillitoe (1983:246).
32. Bailely (1963).
33. Neel (1970).
34. See also Grossman (1984).
35. Buchbinder (1977).
36. Dickemann (1984).
37. Alland (1970: 141–42).
38. Rosenberg (1980).
39. Simoons (1961).
40. Lindenbaum (1972).
41. Ellis (1962).
42. Ross (1987).
43. Shorter (1982).
44. McElroy and Townsend (1979).
45. Burgess and Dean (1962).
46. Barkow (1989b:304).
47. Raphael (1966).
48. Barkow (1989b).
49. McClelland (1982).
50. Barkow (1989b).
51. Trotter (1985).
52. Ibid., p. 69.
53. Needleman (1990).
54. Trotter et al. (1989).
55. Taylor et al. (1973:308).
56. Lozoff, Kamath, and Feldman (1975).
57. Lowie (1938).
58. Harris (1987:71).
59. Ibid., p. 71.
60. Katz (1987).
61. Cockburn (1971).
62. Ibid.
63. Bindon (1987).

64. Ibid.
65. Baker, Hanna, and Baker (1986).
66. Bindon (1987).
67. Mitchell and Eckert (1987).
68. *Los Angeles Times*, August 15, 1991, p. 1.
69. Edgerton (1966; 1971a).
70. *Time*, September 17, 1990.
71. Warnes and Wittkower (1982).
72. Goodman and Armelagos (1988).
73. Walker, Luther, Samloff, and Feldman (1988).
74. Ibid.
75. Shore and Stone (1973).
76. Cohen (1989).
77. Lebo (1991).
78. Dressler (1991).
79. Cohen et al. (1991).
80. Kearney (1976).
81. Maloney (1976).
82. Harris (1979). For a general discussion of the concept of taboo, see Steiner (1956).
83. Meggitt (1962:260).
84. Harris (1979).
85. Kennedy (1978).
86. Turnbull (1961).
87. Rasmussen (1931).
88. Goldschmidt (1990:190).
89. Adair, Deuschle, and McDermott (1969).
90. Kluckhohn and Leighton (1962:242).
91. Balicki (1963); Oswalt (1979).
92. Balicki (1963).
93. Quoted in Hoebel (1954:70).
94. Kennedy (1978:149). For additional discussion of irrationality and fear, see Spiro (1984).
95. Szasz (1961).
96. Rosenhan (1973).
97. Baroja (1963).
98. Plog and Edgerton (1969).
99. Jarvis (1852).
100. Torrey (1980).
101. Scheper-Hughes (1979). Ninuallain, O'Hare, and Walsh (1987) believe that the reported high rate of schizophrenia in Ireland is an artifact of hospital admission-reporting procedures.
102. Wegrocki (1948).
103. For a contrary opinion, see Lutz (1985).
104. Fabrega (1989).
105. Murphy (1982); Lin and Kleinman (1988); Fabrega (1989).
106. Breslau and Davis (1986).

107. Torrey (1980).
108. Kleinman and Good (1985); Beiser (1985).
109. Murphy (1982).
110. Ninuallain, O'Hare, and Walsh (1987).
111. Harkness (1987).
112. Stern and Kruckman (1983).
113. Harkness (1987:200–201).
114. Murphy and Taumoepeau (1980).
115. Brown and Harris (1982).
116. Brown and Harris (1978).

CHAPTER 6. From Discontent to Rebellion

1. Levy (1966:26).
2. Ibid., p. 46.
3. Ibid., p. 89.
4. Ibid., p. 128.
5. Lurie (1981).
6. Shweder (1991).
7. Stein (1988).
8. Stein (1988); Stutchbury (1982); Carey (1964).
9. Stutchbury (1982).
10. Buckland (1901, vol. 1:160).
11. Ibid.
12. Gupta (1976).
13. Stutchbury (1982).
14. Ibid.
15. Carey (1964:200).
16. Gupta (1982:62).
17. Roy (1987).
18. Singh (1989).
19. Ibid.
20. Patel and Kumar (1988).
21. McLean and Graham (1983); Gordon (1991).
22. Kennedy (1970); Hayes (1975). For a fuller discussion of the operation and whether it might be maladaptive, see the March 1991 issue of Medical Anthropology Quarterly (vol. 5, no. 1).
23. Hayes (1975).
24. Heider (1970:123).
25. Tuzin (1982).
26. Langness (1981); personal communication.
27. Howlett (1962).
28. Robbins (1982:189).
29. Van Baal (1984:137).
30. Johnson and Earle (1987).
31. Shostak (1981:316).
32. Meggitt (1977:99).

33. Tuzin (1982:349).
34. Ibid., p. 350.
35. Poole (1983:9).
36. Ibid.
37. Kroeber (1948).
38. Davenport (1969); Seaton (1974).
39. Pospisil (1971).
40. Hyde (1974).
41. For a well-known but somewhat inaccurate description of these events, see Redfield (1953).
42. Gallup (1977).
43. Campbell, Converse, and Rodgers (1976).
44. Guthrie and Tanco (1980).
45. Edgerton (1985:153).
46. For a general discussion of drinking, see Everett, Waddell, and Heath (1976); Douglas (1987).
47. Jilek (1982).
48. Roberts (1989).
49. Counts (1990).
50. Bohannan (1960); Edgerton and Conant (1964).
51. King (1982).
52. Rubinstein (1987); Hezel, Rubinstein, and White (1985).
53. Hollan (1990).
54. Naroll (1969). Naroll attempts to use suicide as the best available evidence of social pathology.
55. Poole (1985:152).
56. Ibid., p. 163.
57. Spence (1978).
58. Ibid., p. 14.
59. Wallace (1969).
60. Tambiah (1989).
61. Ross (1975).
62. Chang (1982).
63. Vail (1990). For an extended discussion of societies as unbounded populations, see Wolf (1988).
64. Adams (1974).
65. Lee (1979).
66. Woodburn (1972).
67. Kaplan and Hill (1984).
68. Gmelch (1980).
69. Plotnikov (1967).
70. Quoted in Guthrie and Tanco (1980:39). For a general discussion of migration, see Anthony (1990).
71. Graves and Graves (1974).
72. Spencer (1965).
73. Ibid., p. 149. For additional discussion of conflict and age-sets, see Almagor (1983).

74. Uzzell (1974); for an extended discussion, see Rubel, O'Nell, and Collado-Ardon (1984).
75. Hobley (1922); Harris (1957).
76. Abu-Lughod (1990).
77. Silverblatt (1987:208).
78. Ibid., p. 209. See Oakley (1991) for a discussion of Phyllis Kaberry's work on women's protest among Australian aborigines.
79. Spencer (1965:228–29).
80. Gluckman (1949); Norbeck (1963).
81. Van Allen (1972).
82. Ardener (1973).
83. Lindblom (1920).
84. Ibid.
85. Edgerton and Conant (1964).
86. Köbben (1979).
87. Kracke (1978).
88. Lee (1979); Thomas (1958).
89. Holmberg (1969).
90. Turnbull (1965:198).
91. Gluckman (1954).
92. Norbeck (1963).
93. Junod (1962).
94. Shore (1978); see also Huntsman and Hooper (1975) for a discussion of similar phenomena on Tokelau.
95. Crumrine (1969).
96. Salusbury-Jones (1939).
97. Dirks (1978).
98. Ladurie (1979).
99. Ibid.
100. Welch (1966).
101. Beals and Siegel (1966).
102. Nash (1967).
103. Huntingford (1953).
104. Fynn (1950).
105. Ritter (1935).
106. Hobsbawm (1959).
107. Crummey (1986).
108. Pospisil (1963:49).
109. Sorokin (1937).
110. Gurr (1970).
111. For a review of peasant rebellions, see Scott (1985).
112. Erofeev (1990).

CHAPTER 7. The Death of Populations, Societies, and Cultures

1. Kroeber (1961).
2. Ibid.

3. *Los Angeles Times*, November 25, 1990.
4. Mead (1956). For a discussion of the devastation brought about by European contact, see Wolf (1982).
5. Dorian (1981; 1989).
6. Laughlin and Brady (1978); Fürer-Haimendorf (1982).
7. Owusu (1978).
8. Kroeber (1948:375).
9. Isaac (1977).
10. Stearman (1984).
11. Davis (1977).
12. Hogbin (1930:65).
13. Eder (1987).
14. Mosko (1990).
15. Ferguson (1984).
16. Otterbein (1970).
17. Wright (1942, vol. 1:100).
18. Kelly (1985).
19. Ferguson (1984).
20. Kroeber and Fontana (1986).
21. Goldschmidt (1990).
22. Edgerton (1988).
23. Fynn (1971); McLeod (1981); Wilks (1975).
24. Yoffee and Cowgill (1988).
25. Pelligrino (1991).
26. Johnson and Earle (1987).
27. Tainter (1988:194).
28. Ibid., p. 195.
29. In reality, Rome not only fell to Germanic peoples, it was defended by them as well. At the time of its fall, nearly all of its soldiers, including virtually all of its high-ranking officers, were German (Adams 1983).
30. Adams (1983).
31. Tainter (1988:196).
32. Darnton (1984).
33. Kennedy (1969).
34. Knauft (1985;1987).
35. Otterbein (1987); Knauft (1987:491).
36. Burland (1973).
37. Peires (1989).
38. Ibid., p. 28.
39. Ibid., pp. 311–312.
40. Ibid., p. 245.
41. Ibid.
42. Iliffe (1979). For a discussion of a similar "crisis cult," the Ghost Dance in North America, see La Barre (1970).
43. Daly and Wilson (1988).
44. Chagnon (1988a:986). For a discussion of the allegedly positive functions of feuding, see Keiser (1986).

45. Khalaf (1990:230); Black-Michaud (1975).
46. Henry (1941:59). The Yamana of Tierra del Fuego also engaged in seemingly endless feuds (Gusinde 1961).
47. Durham (1976). Some populations, like the people of Bellona Island in the Pacific have managed to survive despite over six centuries of feuding (Kuschel 1988).
48. Tindale (1962) and Cawte (1978).
49. Cawte (1972).
50. Tindale (1962).
51. Cawte (1972).
52. Ibid., p. 102.
53. Ibid., p. 165; Cawte (1978:103).
54. Cawte (1972:166).
55. Knauft (in press); Herdt (1984:59).
56. Van Baal (1984:137).
57. Ibid.
58. Ibid., p. 139. For an extended discussion of this practice, see Knauft (in press).
59. Shkilnyk (1985).
60. Erikson (1985:xiii).
61. Ibid., p. xv.
62. Hickerson (1970); Barnouw (1978); Bishop (1978).
63. Hill (1984).
64. MacAndrew and Edgerton (1969).
65. Rozanov (1914).
66. Pearlman (1967); Silberman (1989).
67. Ienaga (1978).
68. Alletzhauser (1990:106).
69. Nitobe (1969); Dower (1986).

CHAPTER 8. Adaptation Reconsidered

1. Steward (1955).
2. See Goldschmidt (1971).
3. Edgerton (1971b).
4. McCabe (1990).
5. Lowie (1954).
6. Oliver (1962).
7. Hanson (1988).
8. Ellen (1982).
9. E.g., see Smith (1979), Hawkes, Hill, and O'Connell (1982), and Mithen (1989). Keegan (1986) has even asserted that the principles of optimal foraging can be applied to a horticultural society.
10. Woodburn (1972).
11. Hawkes (1991).
12. Freilich (1963).
13. Bailey and Aunger (1989). See also Roscoe (1990).
14. Ibid., p. 294.

15. Robarchek (1989).
16. Boehm (1978:287).
17. Chagnon (1988a).
18. Rappaport (1971:224).
19. Bennett (1976).
20. Samuels (1982); Ellen (1982); Foin and Davis (1984; 1988); LiPuma (1988).
21. Meggers (1971).
22. Harms (1987:54).
23. Biesele (1978).
24. Meggitt (1977).
25. Ortiz (1967); Boster (1984); Schneider (1974).
26. Conklin (1954).
27. Kuran (1988).
28. Nisbet and Ross (1980); Orr (1979); Shweder (1980). See also Douglas and Wildavsky (1982).
29. Lumsden and Wilson (1981).
30. Cowgill (1975).
31. Kuran (1988).
32. Shweder (1984).
33. Sperber (1985:85).
34. Rozin and Nemeroff (1990).
35. Shweder (1980:76). For a discussion of faulty heuristics and their role in evolution, see Boyd and Richerson (1985) and Greenwald (1980).
36. Wills (1990); Greeley (1989); Gallup and Castelli (1989).
37. Douglas and Wildavsky (1982).
38. *New York Times*, January 29, 1991.
39. Gilovich (1991).
40. Hallpike (1979).
41. Goldschmidt (1990:204).
42. See, e.g., Tuchman (1984).
43. Harris (1989:495).
44. Medvedyev (1991).
45. Nisbet (1973).
46. Redfield (1960).
47. Daly and Wilson (1988).
48. Leach (1965). The original was published in 1954.
49. Kimura (1983). For a discussion, see Scott (1989).
50. Gould (1989).

Bibliography

ABERLE, D. F.
   1987. "Distinguished Lecture: What Kind of Science Is Anthropology?" *American Anthropologist* 89:551–566.
ABERLE, D. F., A. K. COHEN, A. K. DAVIS, M. J. LEVY, AND F. X. SUTTON.
   1950. "The Functional Prerequisites of a Society." *Ethics* 60:100–111.
ABRAMS, E. M., AND D. J. RUE.
   1988. "The Causes and Consequences of Deforestation Among the Prehistoric Maya." *Human Ecology* 16:377–395.
ABU-LUGHOD, L.
   1990. "The Romance of Resistance: Tracing Transformations of Power Through Bedouin Women." *American Ethnologist* 17:41–55.
ACKERKNECHT, E. H.
   1971. *Medicine and Ethnology: Selected Essays.* (H. H. Walser and H. M. Koelbing, eds.). Baltimore: Johns Hopkins Press.
ADAIR, J., K. DEUSCHLE, AND W. McDERMOTT.
   1969. "Patterns of Health and Disease Among the Navahos." In L. R. Lynch (ed.), *The Cross-Cultural Approach to Health Behavior.* Rutherford, NJ: Fairleigh Dickinson University Press, pp. 83–110.
ADAMS, R. M.
   1983. *Decadent Societies.* San Francisco: North Point Press.
ADAMS, R. McC.
   1974. "Anthropological Perspectives in Ancient Trade." *Current Anthropology* 15:239–258.
ALEXANDER, J. C. (ed.).
   1985. *Neofunctionalism.* Beverly Hills, CA: Sage.

229

ALEXANDER, R. D.
1987. *The Biology of Moral Systems*. New York: Aldine de Gruyter.
1990. "Epigenetic Rules and Darwinian Algorhythms: The Adaptive Study of Learning and Development." *Ethology and Sociobiology* 11:241–303.

ALLAND, A., JR.
1967. *Evolution and Human Behavior*. Garden City, NY: Natural History Press.
1970. *Adaptation in Cultural Evolution: An Approach to Medical Anthropology*. New York: Columbia University Press.
1985. *Human Nature: Darwin's View*. New York: Columbia University Press.

ALLETZHAUSER, A. J.
1990. *The House of Nomura: The Inside Story of the Legendary Japanese Financial Dynasty*. New York: Arcade.

ALMAGOR, U.
1983. "Charisma Fatigue in an East African Generation-Set System." *American Ethnologist* 10: 635–649.

ALTMAN, J. C.
1984. "Hunter-Gatherer Subsistence Production in Arnhem Land: The Original-Affluence Hypothesis Re-examined." *Mankind* 14:179–190.

AMBLER, C. H.
1988. *Kenyan Communities in the Age of Imperialism: The Central Region in the Late Nineteenth Century*. New Haven: Yale University Press.

ANDREW, C., AND O. GORDIEVSKY.
1990. *KGB: The Inside Story*. New York: HarperCollins.

ANQUANDAH, J.
1982. *Rediscovering Ghana's Past*. London: Longmans.

ANTHONY, D. W.
1990. "Migration in Archeology: The Baby and the Bathwater." *American Anthropologist* 92:895–914.

APPELL, G. N.
1989. "Facts, Fiction, Fads, and Follies: But Where Is the Evidence?" *American Anthropologist* 91:195–198.

ARDENER, S.
1973. "Sexual Insult and Female Militancy." *Man* 8:422–440.

ARENSBERG, C.
1959. *The Irish Countryman*. Gloucester, MA: Peter Smith.

BAILELY, K. V.
1963. "Nutritional Status of East New Guinean Populations." *Tropical Geographical Medicine* 15:389–402.

BAILEY, K. G.
1987. *Human Paleopsychology: Applications to Aggression and Pathological Processes*. Hillsdale, NJ: Lawrence Erlbaum Associates.

BAILEY, R. C., AND R. AUNGER, JR.
1989. "Net Hunters vs. Archers: Variation in Women's Subsistence Strategies in the Ituri Forest." *Human Ecology* 17:273–297.

BAILEY, W. C.
1985. "Textbooks for Introductory Anthropology: Research and Commentary." *Anthropology Newsletter* (October): 18–20.

230

BAKER, P. T., J. M. HANNA, and T. S. BAKER (eds.).
   1986. *The Changing Samoans: Behavior and Health in Transition.* New York: Oxford University Press.

BAKSH, M.
   1984. *Cultural Ecology and Change of the Machiguenga Indians of the Peruvian Amazon.* Unpublished Ph.D. dissertation, University of California, Los Angeles.

BALICKI, A.
   1963. "Shamanistic Behavior Among the Netsilik Eskimo." *The Southwestern Journal of Anthropology* 19:380–396.

BANFIELD, E. C. (with the assistance of Laura Fasano Banfield).
   1958. *The Moral Basis of a Backward Society.* New York: Free Press.

BARKOW, J. H.
   1973. "Darwinian Psychological Anthropology: A Biosocial Approach." *Current Anthropology* 14:373–388.
   1989a. *Darwin, Sex, and Status: Biological Approaches to Mind and Culture.* Toronto: University of Toronto Press.
   1989b. "The Elastic Between Genes and Culture." *Ethology and Sociobiology* 10:111–129.

BARKOW, J. H., AND N. BURLEY.
   1980. "Human Fertility, Evolutionary Biology, and the Demographic Transition." *Ethology and Sociobiology* 1:163–180.

BARKOW, J. H., L. COSMIDES, AND J. TOOBY (eds.).
   1992. *Adapted Mind: Evolutionary Psychology and the Generation of Culture.* New York: Oxford University Press.

BARNETT, H. G.
   1953. *Innovation: The Basis of Cultural Change.* New York: McGraw-Hill.

BARNOUW, V.
   1978. "An Interpretation of Wisconsin Ojibwa Culture and Personality." In G. D. Spindler (ed.), *The Making of Psychological Anthropology.* Berkeley: University of California Press, pp. 64–86.

BAROJA, J. C.
   1963. "The City and the Country: Reflexions on Some Ancient Commonplaces." In J. Pitt-Rivers (ed.), *Mediterranean Countrymen.* Paris: Moulton, pp. 27–40.

BARTH, F.
   1975. *Ritual and Knowledge Among the Baktaman of New Guinea.* New Haven: Yale University Press.

BAYLISS-SMITH, T.
   1974. "Constraints on Population Growth: The Case of the Polynesian Outlier Atolls in the Pre-contact Period." *Human Ecology* 2:259–295.

BEALS, A. R., AND B. J. SIEGEL.
   1966. *Divisiveness and Social Conflict: An Anthropological Approach.* Stanford: Stanford University Press.

BEAUBIER, J.
   1976. *High Life Expectancy on the Island of Paros, Greece.* New York: Philosophical Library.

BECK, L., AND N. KEDDIE (eds.).
   1978. *Women in the Muslim World.* Cambridge: Harvard University Press.

BIBLIOGRAPHY

BECK, V.

1990. "Heaven Can Wait." *UCLA Magazine* (Spring), p. 23.

BEISER, M.

1985. "A Study of Depression Among Traditional Africans, Urban North Americans, and Southeast Asian Refugees." In A. Kleinman and B. Good (eds.), *Culture and Depression: Studies in the Anthropology and Cross-Cultural Psychiatry of Affect and Disorder.* Berkeley: University of California Press, pp. 272–298.

BELLAH, R. N., R. MADSEN, W. M. SULLIVAN, A. SWIDLER, AND S. M. TIPTON.

1985. *Habits of the Heart: Individualism and Commitment in American Life.* New York: Harper & Row.

BELO, J.

1935. "The Balinese Temper." *Character and Personality* 4:120–146.

BENEDICT, R.

1934. *Patterns of Culture.* New York: Houghton Mifflin.

BENNETT, J. W.

1976. *The Ecological Transition: Cultural Anthropology and Human Adaptation.* New York: Pergamon Press.

BENTHALL, J. (ed.).

1974. *The Limits of Human Nature.* New York: E. P. Dutton.

BERLIN, B., AND P. KAY.

1969. *Basic Color Terms: Their Universality and Evolution.* Berkeley: University of California Press.

BERNSTEIN, I. S.

1984. "The Adaptive Value of Maladaptive Behavior, or You've Got to Be Stupid in Order to Be Smart." *Ethology and Sociobiology* 5:297–303.

BETZIG, L. L.

1986. *Despotism and Differential Reproduction: A Darwinian View of History.* New York: Aldine.

1988. "Redistribution: Equity or Exploitation?" In L. Betzig, M. Borgerhoff Mulder, and P. Turke (eds.), *Human Reproductive Behavior.* New York: Cambridge University Press, pp. 49–63.

BIERSACK, M.

1989. "Local Knowledge, Local History: Geertz and Beyond." In L. Hunt (ed.), *The New Cultural History.* Berkeley: University of California Press, pp. 72–96.

BIESELE, M.

1978. "Sapience and Scarce Resources: Communication Systems of the !Kung and Other Foragers." *Social Science Information* 17:921–947.

BINDON, J.

1987. "Diabetes and Modernization in Samoa." Paper presented at the 16th annual meeting of the Association for Social Anthropology in Oceania, February 18–22, Monterey, CA.

BINNS, C. T.

1975. *The Warrior People.* London: Hale.

BISHOP, C. A.

1976. "The Emergence of the Northern Ojibwa: Social and Economic Consequences." *American Ethnologist* 3:39–54.

BLACK-MICHAUD, J.
1975. *Cohesive Force: Feud in the Mediterranean and the Middle East.* New York: St. Martin's Press.

BLOOM, A.
1987. *The Closing of the American Mind.* New York: Simon & Schuster.

BOCK, K.
1980. *Human Nature and History: A Response to Sociobiology.* New York: Columbia University Press.

BOEHM, C.
1978. "Rational Preselection from Hamadryas to *Homo Sapiens*: The Place of Decisions in Adaptive Process." *American Anthropologist* 80:265–296.
1989. "Ambivalence and Compromise in Human Nature." *American Anthropologist* 91:921–939.

BOHANNAN, P. (ed.).
1960. *African Homicide and Suicide.* Princeton: Princeton University Press.

BONWICK, J.
1870. *Daily Life and Origin of the Tasmanians.* London: Sampson, Low, Son & Marsdon.

BORGERHOFF MULDER, M.
1987a. "On Cultural and Reproductive Success: Kipsigis Evidence." *American Anthropologist* 89:617–634.
1987b. "Adaptation and Evolutionary Approaches to Anthropology." *Man* 22:25–41.

BOSTER, J.
1984. "Inferring Decision Making from Preferences and Behavior: An Analysis of Aguarano Jivaro Manioc Selection." *Human Ecology* 12:343–358.

BOSTER, J., B. BERLIN, AND J. O'NEILL.
1986. "The Correspondence of Jivaroan to Scientific Ornithology." *American Anthropologist* 88:569–583.

BOWDITCH, T. E.
1966. *Mission from Cape Coast Castle to Ashantee.* 3rd ed. (edited with Notes and an Introduction by W. E. F. Ward). London: Frank Cass and Co.

BOYD, R., AND P. J. RICHERSON.
1985. *Culture and the Evolutionary Process.* Chicago: University of Chicago Press.

BRESLAU, N., AND G. C. DAVIS.
1986. "Chronic Stress and Major Depression." *Archives of General Psychiatry* 43:309–314.

BROOKS, D. R., AND E. O. WILEY.
1986. *Evolution as Entropy: Toward a Unified Theory of Biology.* Chicago: University of Chicago Press.

BROWN, D. E.
1991. *Human Universals.* New York: McGraw-Hill.

BROWN, G. T., AND T. HARRIS.
1978. *Social Origins of Repression: A Study of Psychiatric Disorder in Women.* London: Tavistock.

233

1982. "Social Class and Affective Disorder." In I. Al-Issa (ed.), *Culture and Psychopathology*. Baltimore: University Park Press, pp. 125–156.

BRUNER, E.

1990. "The Scientists vs. the Humanists." *Anthropology Newsletter* (February), p. 28.

BUCHBINDER, G.

1977. "Nutritional Stress and Post-contact Population Decline Among the Maring of New Guinea." In L. S. Greene (ed.), *Malnutrition, Behavior, and Social Organization*. New York: Academic Press, pp. 109–141.

BUCKLAND, C. E.

1901. *Bengal Under the Lieutenant-Governors 1854–1898*. Calcutta: S. K. Lahiri and Co.

BURCH, E. S., JR.

1971. "The Non-empirical Environment of the Arctic Alaskan Eskimo." *Southwestern Journal of Anthropology* 27:148–165.

BURGESS, A., AND R. F. A. DEAN, (eds.).

1962. *Malnutrition and Food Habits*. New York: Macmillan.

BURLAND, C. A.

1973. *Montezuma: Lord of the Aztecs*. New York: Putnam.

BURTON, J. W.

1985. "Why Witches? Some Comment on the Explanation of 'Illusions' in Anthropology." *Ethnology* 24:281–296.

CAMPBELL, A., P. E. CONVERSE, AND W. L. RODGERS.

1976. *The Quality of American Life: Perceptions, Evaluations and Satisfactions*. New York: Russell Sage Foundation.

CAMPBELL, D. T.

1975. "On the Conflicts Between Biological and Social Evolution and Between Psychology and Moral Tradition." *American Psychologist* 30:1103–1126.

CARDEN, M. L.

1969. *Oneida: Utopian Community to Modern Corporation*. Baltimore: Johns Hopkins Press.

CARDOE, C.

1991. "Isolation and Evolution in Tasmania." *Current Anthropology* 32:1–21.

CAREY, W. H.

1964. *The Good Old Days of the Honourable John Company* (orig. publ. in 1882). Calcutta: Quins Book Co.

CASSIDY, C. M.

1980. "Nutrition and Health in Agriculturalists and Hunter-Gatherers: A Case Study of Two Prehistoric Populations." In N. W. Jerome, R. F. Kandel, and G. H. Pelto (eds.), *Nutritional Anthropology: Contemporary Approaches to Diet and Culture*. New York: Redgrave, pp. 117–146.

CAWTE, J.

1972. *Cruel, Poor and Brutal Nations: The Assessment of Mental Health in an Australian Aboriginal Community by Short-Stay Psychiatric Field Team Methods*. Honolulu: University Press of Hawaii.

1978. "Gross Stress in Small Islands: A Study in Macropsychiatry." In C. D.

Laughlin, Jr., and I. A. Brady (eds.), *Extinction and Survival in Human Populations.*
New York: Columbia University Press, pp. 95–121.

CAWTE, J., N. DJAGAMARA, AND M. G. BARRETT.
1966. "The Meaning of Subincision of the Urethra to Aboriginal Australians."
British Journal of Medical Psychology 39:245–253.

CHAGNON, N. A.
1967. *Yanomamo Warfare, Social Organization and Marriage Alliances.* Ph.D.
dissertation, University of Michigan, Ann Arbor.
1974. *Studying the Yanomamo.* New York: Holt, Rinehart and Winston.
1988a. "Life Histories, Blood Revenge, and Warfare in a Tribal Population."
Science 239:985–992.
1988b. "Male Yanomamo Manipulations of Kinship Classifications for Reproductive Advantage." In L. Betzig, M. Borgerhoff Mulder, and P. Turke (eds.),
Human Reproductive Behavior. Cambridge: Cambridge University Press, pp.
23–48.

CHANG, C.
1982. "Nomads Without Cattle: East African Foragers in Historical Perspective."
In E. Leacock and R. Lee (eds.), *Politics and History in Band Societies.* Cambridge: Cambridge University Press, pp. 269–282.

CHILDE, V. G.
1942. *What Happened in History.* Baltimore: Penguin Books.

CLIFFORD, J., AND G. E. MARCUS (eds.).
1986. *Writing Culture: The Poetics and Politics of Ethnography.* Berkeley: University of California Press.

COCKBURN, T. A.
1971. "Infectious Diseases in Ancient Populations." *Current Anthropology*
12:45–62.

COHEN, M. N.
1989. *Health and the Rise of Civilization.* New Haven: Yale University
Press.

COHEN, S., D. A. J. TYRRELL, AND A. P. SMITH.
1991. "Psychological Stress and Susceptibility to the Common Cold." *New England Journal of Medicine* 325:606–612.

COLBY, B. N.
1987. "Well-Being: A Theoretical Paradigm." *American Anthropologist* 87:879–
895.

COLE, M., AND S. SCRIBNER.
1974. *Culture and Thought: A Psychological Introduction.* New York: Wiley.

COLLIER, J. F.
1988. *Marriage and Inequality in Classless Societies.* Stanford: Stanford University Press.

CONKLIN, H. C.
1954. *The Relation of Hanunoo Culture to the Plant World.* Ph.D. dissertation
in anthropology, Yale University, New Haven.

COSER, L.
1956. *The Functions of Social Conflict.* New York: Free Press.

COUNT, E. W.

    1958. "The Biological Basis of Human Sociology." *American Anthropologist* 60:1049–1085.

COUNTS, D. A.

    1990. "Beaten Wife, Suicidal Woman: Domestic Violence in Kaliai, West New Britain." *Pacific Studies* 13:151–169.

COWGILL, G. L.

    1975. "On Causes and Consequences of Ancient and Modern Population Changes." *American Anthropologist* 77:505–525.

CRAPANZANO, V.

    1986. "Hermes' Dilemma: The Masking of Subversion in Ethnographic Description." In J. Clifford and G. E. Marcus (eds.), *Writing Culture: The Poetics and Politics of Ethnography*. Berkeley: University of California Press, pp. 51–76.

CRAWFORD, M. H. (ed.).

    1984. *Current Developments in Anthropological Genetics*, vol. 3. *Black Caribs: A Case Study in Biocultural Adaptation*. New York: Plenum Press.

CRUMMEY, D. (ed.).

    1986. *Banditry, Rebellion and Social Protest in Africa*. London: James Currey.

CRUMRINE, N. R.

    1969. "Capakoba, The Mayo Easter Ceremonial Impersonator: Explanations of Ritual Clowning." *Journal for the Scientific Study of Religion* 8:1–22.

DAHRENDORF, R.

    1968. *Essays in the Theory of Society*. Stanford: Stanford University Press.

DALY, M., AND M. WILSON.

    1988. *Homicide*. New York: Aldine de Gruyter.

D'ANDRADE, R.

    1990. "Some Propositions About the Relations Between Culture and Human Cognition." In J. W. Stigler, R. A. Shweder, and G. Herdt (eds.), *Cultural Psychology: Essays on Comparative Human Development*. New York: Cambridge University Press, pp. 65–129.

DARNTON, R.

    1984. *The Great Cat Massacre: And Other Episodes in French Cultural History*. New York: Basic Books.

DAVENPORT, W.

    1969. "The 'Hawaiian Cultural Revolution': Some Political and Economic Considerations." *American Anthropologist* 71:1–20.

DAVIS, S. H.

    1977. *Victims of the Miracle: Development and the Indians of Brazil*. Cambridge: Cambridge University Press.

DAVIS, W. G., AND T. C. FOIN.

    1988. "Equilibrium Unconsidered." *American Anthropologist* 90:973–976.

DAWKINS, R.

    1976. *The Selfish Gene*. Oxford: Oxford University Press.

DENING, G.

    1980. *Islands and Beaches: Discourse on a Silent Land, Marquesas 1774–1880*. Melbourne: Melbourne University Press.

DENNETT, G., AND J. CONNELL.

1988. "Acculturation and Health in the Highlands of Papua New Guinea." *Current Anthropology* 29:273–299.

DEVEREUX, G.

1980. *Basic Problems of Ethno-Psychiatry* (B. M. Gulati and G. Devereux, trans.). Chicago: University of Chicago Press.

DIAMOND, J. M.

1978. "The Tasmanians: The Longest Isolation, the Simplest Technology." *Nature* 173:185–86.

DICKEMANN, M.

1984. "Concepts and Classification in the Study of Human Infanticide: Sectional Introduction and Some Cautionary Notes." In G. Hausfarter and S. B. Hrdy (eds.), *Infanticide: Comparative and Evolutionary Perspectives*. New York: Aldine, pp. 427–438.

DIRKS, R.

1978. "Resource Fluctuations and Competitive Transformations in West Indian Slave Societies." In C. D. Laughlin and I. A. Brady (eds.), *Extinction and Survival in Human Populations*. New York: Columbia University Press, pp. 122–180.

1980. "Social Responses during Severe Food Shortages and Famine." *Current Anthropology* 21:21–44.

1988. "Annual Rituals of Conflict." *American Anthropologist* 90:856–870.

DOHRENWEND, B. S., AND B. P. DOHRENWEND (eds.).

1974. *Stressful Life Events: Their Nature and Effects*. New York: Wiley.

DORIAN, N. C.

1981. *Language Death: The Life Cycle of a Scottish Gaelic Dialect*. Philadelphia: University of Pennsylvania Press.

1989. *Investigating Obsolescence: Studies in Language Contraction and Death*. *Studies in the Social and Cultural Foundations of Language*, no. 7. New York: Cambridge University Press.

DOUGLAS, M. (ed.).

1987. *Constructive Drinking: Perspectives on Drink from Anthropology*. Cambridge: Cambridge University Press.

DOUGLAS, M., AND A. WILDAVSKY.

1982. *Risk and Culture: An Essay on the Selection of Technological and Environmental Dangers*. Berkeley: University of California Press.

DOWER, J.

1986. *War Without Mercy: Race and Power in the Pacific War*. New York: Pantheon.

DOWNING, T. E., AND G. KUSHNER (eds.).

1988. *Human Rights and Anthropology*. Cambridge, MA: Cultural Survival.

DRESSLER, W. W.

1991. *Stress and Adaptation in the Context of Culture: Depression in a Southern Black Community*. Albany: State University of New York Press.

DUPAQUIER, J., AND E. GREBENIK (eds.).

1983. *Malthus Past and Present*. London: Academic Press.

DURHAM, W. H.

1976. "Resource Competition and Human Aggression. Part 1: A Review of

Primitive War." *Quarterly Review of Biology* 51: 385–415.

1981. "Overview: Optimal Foraging Analysis in Human Ecology." In B. Winterhalder and E. A. Smith (eds.), *Hunter-Gatherer Foraging Strategies: Ethnographic and Archeological Analyses.* Chicago: University of Chicago Press, pp. 218–231.

DYSON-HUDSON, R., AND M. A. LITTLE (eds.).

1983. *Rethinking Human Adaptation.* Boulder: Westview Press.

EDER, J. F.

1987. *On the Road to Tribal Extinction: Depopulation, Deculturation, and Adaptive Well-Being Among the Batak of the Philippines.* Berkeley: University of California Press.

EDGERTON, R. B.

1966. "Conceptions of Psychosis in Four East African Societies." *American Anthropologist* 68:408–425.

1971a. "A Traditional African Psychiatrist." *Southwestern Journal of Anthropology* 68:408–425.

1971b. *The Individual in Cultural Adaptation.* Berkeley: University of California Press.

1976. *Deviance: A Cross-Cultural Perspective.* Menlo Park, CA: Cummings.

1978. "The Study of Deviance—Marginal Man or Everyman?" In G. D. Spindler (ed.), *The Making of Psychological Anthropology.* Berkeley: University of California Press, pp. 444–476.

1985. *Rules, Exceptions and Social Order.* Berkeley: University of California Press.

1988. *Like Lions They Fought: The Zulu War and the Last Black Empire in South Africa.* New York: Free Press.

EDGERTON, R. B., AND F. P. CONANT.

1964. "Kilapat: The 'Shaming Party' Among the Pokot of East Africa." *Southwestern Journal of Anthropology* 20:406–418.

EISENSTADT, S. N.

1990. "Functional Analysis in Anthropology and Sociology: An Interpretive Essay." *Annual Review of Anthropology* 19:243–260.

ELLEN, R.

1982. *Environment, Subsistence and System: The Ecology of Small-Scale Social Formations.* New York: Cambridge University Press.

ELLIS, R. W. R.

1962. *Child Health and Development.* New York: Gruen and Stratton.

ELLISON, P. T.

1990. "Human Ovarian Function and Reproductive Ecology: New Hypotheses." *American Anthropologist* 92:933–952.

EMBER, C.

1983. "A Cross-Cultural Perspective on Sex-Differences." In R. H. Munroe, R. L. Munroe, and B. B. Whiting (eds.), *Handbook of Cross-Cultural Human Development.* New York: Garland Press, pp. 531–580.

EMBER, C., AND D. LEVINSON.

1991. "The Substantive Contributions of Worldwide Cross-Cultural Studies Using Secondary Data." *Behavioral Science* (in press).

ERIKSON, K.
1985. Foreword to A. M. Shkilnyk, *A Poison Stronger than Love: The Destruction of an Ojibwa Community*. New Haven: Yale University Press.

EROFEEV, V.
1990. Review of Marquis de Custine, *Empire of the Czar: A Journey Through Eternal Russia*. New York: Anchor Books. *New York Review of Books* (June 14), pp. 23–24.

EVANS-PRITCHARD, E. E.
1940. *The Nuer: A Description of the Modes of Livelihood and Political Institutions of a Nilotic People*. Oxford: Oxford University Press.

EVERETT, M. W., J. O. WADDELL, AND D. B. HEATH (eds.).
1976. *Cross-Cultural Approaches to the Study of Alcohol: An Interdisciplinary Perspective*. The Hague: Mouton.

FABREGA, H.
1989. "Cultural Relativism and Psychiatric Illness." *Journal of Nervous and Mental Disease* 177:415–425.

FAVAZZA, A. R. (WITH B. FAVAZZA).
1987. *Bodies Under Siege: Self-Mutilation in Culture and Psychiatry*. Baltimore: Johns Hopkins University Press.

FEIL, D.
1987. *The Evolution of Highland Papua New Guinea Society*. New York: Cambridge University Press.

FERGUSON, R. B.
1984. *Warfare, Culture and Environment*. Orlando: Academic Press.
1989. "Ecological Consequences of Amazonian Warfare." *Ethnology* 28:249–264.

FINKLER, K.
1985. *Spiritualist Healers in Mexico: Successes and Failures of Alternative Therapeutics*. New York: Bergin and Garvey.

FISCHER, C.
1976. *The Urban Experience*. New York: Harcourt Brace Jovanovich.

FOGEL, R. W., ET AL.
1983. "Secular Changes in American and British Stature and Nutrition." In R. I. Rotberg and T. K. Rabb (eds.), *Hunger and History: The Impact of Changing Food Production and Consumption Patterns on Society*. Cambridge: Cambridge University Press, pp. 247–284.

FOIN, T. C., AND W. G. DAVIS.
1984. "Ritual and Self-Regulation of the Tsembaga Maring Ecosystem in the New Guinea Highlands." *Human Ecology* 12:385–412.

FONER, N.
1984. *Ages in Conflict: A Cross-Cultural Perspective on Inequality Between Old and Young*. New York: Columbia University Press.

FOSTER, G. M., AND B. G. ANDERSON.
1978. *Medical Anthropology*. New York: John Wiley & Sons.

FOUCAULT, M.
1973. *Madness and Civilization*. New York: Vintage.

FOX, R.
1971. "The Cultural Animal." In J. F. Eisenberg and W. S. Dillon (eds.), *Man*

and Beast: Comparative Social Behavior. Washington, DC: Smithsonian Institution Press, pp. 273–296.

1990. *The Violent Imagination*. New Brunswick, NJ: Rutgers University Press.

FREEDMAN, D. G.

1974. *Human Infancy: An Evolutionary Perspective*. Hillsdale, NJ: Lawrence Erlbaum.

FREILICH, M.

1963. "The Natural Experiment: Ecology and Culture." *Southwestern Journal of Anthropology* 19:21–39.

FREUCHEN, P.

1961. *Book of the Eskimo*. New York: Fawcett.

FREUD, S.

1930. *Civilization and Its Discontents*. New York: Jonathan Cape and Harrison Smith.

FROMM, E.

1955. *The Sane Society*. New York: Rinehart & Company.

FÜRER-HAIMENDORF, C. VON.

1982. *Tribes of India: The Struggle for Survival*. Berkeley: University of California Press.

FYNN, H. F.

1950. *The Diary of Henry Francis Fynn*. (comp. and ed. by J. Stuart and D. Mck. Malcolm). Pietermaritzburg: Shuter and Shooter.

FYNN, J. K.

1971. *Asante and Its Neighbors 1700–1807*. Evanston: Northwestern University.

GALLUP, G., JR., AND J. CASTELLI.

1989. *The People's Religion: American Faith in the 90s*. New York: Macmillan.

GALLUP INTERNATIONAL RESEARCH INSTITUTE.

1977. *Human Needs and Satisfactions: A Global Survey. Summary Volume*. Charles F. Kettering Foundation and Gallup International Research Institutes.

GARDNER, H.

1983. *Frames of Mind: The Theory of Multiple Intelligences*. New York: Basic Books.

GARN, S. M.

1979. "The Non-economic Nature of Eating People." *American Anthropologist* 8:902–903.

GAZAWAY, R.

1969. *The Longest Mile*. Garden City, NY: Doubleday & Co.

GAZZANIGA, M. S.

1989. "Organization of the Human Brain." *Science* 245:947–952.

GEERTZ, C.

1973. *The Interpretation of Cultures: Selected Essays*. New York: Basic Books.

1983. *Local Knowledge: Further Essays in Interpretive Anthropology*. New York: Basic Books.

1984. " 'From the Native's Point of View': On the Nature of Anthropological Understanding." In R. A. Shweder and R. A. LeVine (eds.), *Culture Theory: Essays on Mind, Self and Emotion*. Cambridge University Press, pp. 123–136.

1988. *Works and Lives: The Anthropologist as Author*. Stanford: Stanford University Press.

GELLNER, E.

1958. "Time and Theory in Social Anthropology." *Mind* 67:182–202.

1982. "Relativism and Universals." In M. Hollis and S. Lukes (eds.), *Rationality and Relativism*. Oxford: Basil Blackwell, pp. 181–256.

GILMORE, D. D.

1990. "Men and Women in Southern Spain 'Domestic Power' Revisited." *American Anthropologist* 92:953–970.

GILOVICH, T.

1991. *How We Know What Isn't So: The Fallibility of Human Reason in Everyday Life*. New York: Free Press.

GLADWIN, T.

1970. *East Is a Big Bird*. Cambridge: Harvard University Press.

GLUCKMAN, M.

1940. "The Role of the Sexes in Wiko Circumcision Ceremonies." In M. Fortes (ed.), *Social Structure: Studies Presented to A. R. Radcliffe-Brown*. Oxford: Clarendon Press, pp. 25–55.

1954. *Rituals of Rebellions in Southeast Africa*. Manchester: Manchester University Press.

1959. *Custom and Conflict in Africa*. Glencoe: Free Press.

GMELCH, G.

1980. "Return Migration." In B. J. Siegel, A. R. Beals, and S. A. Tyler (eds.), *Annual Review of Anthropology*, vol. 9. Palo Alto: Annual Reviews, pp. 135–159.

GOLDENWEISER, A.

1942. *Anthropology: An Introduction to Primitive Culture*. New York: F. S. Crofts.

GOLDSCHMIDT, W. R.

1959. *Man's Way: A Preface to the Understanding of Human Society*. Cleveland: World Publishing Co.

1966. *Comparative Functionalism*. Berkeley: University of California Press.

1971. Introduction to R. B. Edgerton, *The Individual in Cultural Adaptation*. Berkeley: University of California Press, pp. 1–22.

1976a. "Biological Versus Social Evolution." *American Psychologist* 31:355–356.

1976b. *The Culture and Behavior of the Sebei*. Berkeley: University of California Press.

1990. *The Human Career: The Self in the Symbolic World*. New York: Basil Blackwell.

GOODMAN, A. H., AND G. J. ARMELAGOS.

1988. "Childhood Stress and Decreased Longevity in a Prehistoric Population." *American Anthropologist* 90:936–943.

GORDON, D.

1991. "Female Circumcision and Genital Operations in Egypt and the Sudan: A Dilemma for Medical Anthropology." *Medical Anthropology Quarterly* 5:3–14.

241

GOULD, S. J.
　1989. *Wonderful Life: The Burgess Shale and the Nature of History.* New York: W. W. Norton.

GRABURN, N. H. H.
　1987. "Severe Child Abuse Among the Canadian Inuit." In N. Scheper-Hughes (ed.), *Child Survival: Anthropological Perspectives on the Treatment and Maltreatment of Children.* Dordrecht: D. Reidel, pp. 211–226.

GRANT, J. P.
　1982. *The State of the World's Children 1982–83.* New York: Oxford University Press.
　1991. *The State of the World's Children.* New York: Oxford University Press.

GRAVES, N. B., AND T. D. GRAVES.
　1974. "Adaptive Strategies in Urban Migration." In B. J. Siegel, A. R. Beals, and S. A. Tyler (eds.), *Annual Review of Anthropology.* Palo Alto: Annual Reviews, pp. 117–151.

GREELEY, A.
　1989. *Religious Change in America.* Cambridge: Harvard University Press.

GREENWALD, A. G.
　1980. "The Totalitarian Ego: Fabrication and Revision of Personal History." *American Psychologist* 35:603–618.

GREGOR, T.
　1977. *Mehinaku: The Drama of Daily Life in a Brazilian Indian Village.* Chicago: University of Chicago Press.
　1990. "Male Dominance and Sexual Coercion." In J. W. Stigler, R. A. Shweder, and G. Herdt (eds.), *Cultural Psychology: Essays on Comparative Human Development.* Cambridge: Cambridge University Press, pp. 477–495.

GROSSMAN, L. S.
　1984. *Peasants, Subsistence, Ecology, and Development in the Highlands of Papua New Guinea.* Princeton: Princeton University Press.

GUPTA, A. R.
　1982. *Women in Hindu Society: A Study of Tradition and Transition* (2nd ed.). New Delhi: Jyotsna Prakashan.

GURR, T. R.
　1970. *Why Men Rebel.* Princeton: Princeton University Press.

GUSINDE, M.
　1961. *The Yamana.* New Haven: Human Relations Area File.

GUTHRIE, G. M., AND P. P. TANCO.
　1980. "Alienation." In H. C. Triandis and J. D. Draguns (eds.), *Handbook of Cross-Cultural Psychology. Pathology,* vol. 6. Boston: Allyn and Bacon, pp. 9–59.

HALLPIKE, C. R.
　1972. *The Konso of Ethiopia. A Study of the Values of a Cushitic Society.* Oxford: Clarendon Press.
　1977. *Bloodshed and Vengeance in the Papuan Mountains: The Generation of Conflict in Tauade.* Oxford: Clarendon Press.
　1979. *The Foundations of Primitive Thought.* Oxford: Clarendon Press.
　1986. *The Principles of Social Evolution.* Oxford: Clarendon Press.

HALSTEAD, P., AND J. O'SHEA (eds.).
1989. *Bad Year Economics: Cultural Responses to Risk and Uncertainty.* New York: Cambridge University Press.

HAMES, R. B., AND W. T. Vickers.
1982. "Optimal Diet Breadth Theory as a Model to Explain Variability in Amazonian Hunting." *American Ethnologist* 9:358–378.

HANSON, J. R.
1988. "Age-Sex Theory and Plains Indian Age-Grading: A Critical Review and Revision." *American Ethnologist* 15:349–364.

HARAKO, R.
1976. "The Mbuti as Hunters—A Study of Ecological Anthropology of the Mbuti Pygmies (I)." *Kyoto University African Studies* 10:37–99.

HARBISON, S. F., T. M. K. KHALEQUE, AND W. C. ROBINSON.
1989. "Female Autonomy and Fertility Among the Garo of North Central Bangladesh." *American Anthropologist* 91:1005–1007.

HARKNESS, S.
1987. "The Cultural Mediation of Postpartum Depression." *Medical Anthropology Quarterly* 1:194–209.

HARMS, R.
1987. *Games Against Nature: An Eco-cultural History of the Nunu of Equatorial Africa.* New York: Cambridge University Press.

HARNER, M.
1977. "The Ecological Basis for Aztec Sacrifice." *American Ethnologist* 4:117–135.

HARRIS, G.
1957. "Possession 'Hysteria' in a Kenya Tribe." *American Anthropologist* 59:1046–1066.

HARRIS, J.
1991. "CURE: For a Bug in the Belly." *UCLA Medicine* 12:11–15.

HARRIS, M.
1960. "Adaptation in Biological and Cultural Science." *Transactions of the New York Academy of Science* 23:59–65.
1968. *The Rise of Anthropological Theory: A History of Theories of Culture.* New York: Thomas Y. Crowell.
1971. *Culture, Man and Nature.* New York: Thomas Y. Crowell.
1977. *Cannibals and Kings: The Origins of Cultures.* New York: Random House.
1979. *Cultural Materialism: The Struggle for a Science of Culture.* New York: Random House.
1981. *America Now: The Anthropology of a Changing Culture.* New York: Simon & Schuster.
1985. *Good to Eat: Riddles of Food and Culture.* New York: Simon & Schuster.
1987. "Food Ways: Historical Overview and Theoretical Prolegomenon." In M. Harris and E. B. Ross (eds.), *Food and Evolution: Toward a Theory of Human Food Habits.* Philadelphia: Temple University Press, pp. 57–90.
1989. *Our Kind: Who We Are, Where We Came From and Where We Are Going.* New York: Harper & Row.

HART, J. A., AND T. B. HART.
1986. "Ecological Basis of Hunter-Gatherer Subsistence in African Rain Forest: The Mbuti Case of Zaire." *Human Ecology* 14:29–55.

HASSIG, R.
1988. *Aztec Warfare: Imperial Expansion and Political Control.* Norman: University of Oklahoma Press.

HATCH, E.
1973. *Theories of Man and Culture.* New York: Columbia University Press.
1983. *Culture and Morality: The Relativity of Values in Anthropology.* New York: Columbia University Press.

HAUGEN, E.
1977. "Linguistic Relativity: Myths and Methods." In W. C. McCormack and S. A. Wurm (eds.), *Language and Thought: Anthropological Issues.* The Hague: Mouton, pp. 11–28.

HAUSFARTER, G., AND S. B. HRDY (eds.).
1984. *Infanticide: Comparative and Evolutionary Perspectives.* New York: Aldine.

HAWKES, K.
1991. "Showing Off: Tests of an Hypothesis About Men's Foraging Goals." *Ethology and Sociobiology* 12:29–54.

HAWKES, K., K. HILL, AND J. F. O'CONNELL.
1982. "Why Hunters Gather: Optional Foraging and the Aché of Eastern Paraguay." *American Ethnologist* 9:379–398.

HAYES, R. O.
1975. "Female Genital Mutilation, Fertility Control, Women's Roles, and the Patrilineage in Modern Sudan: A Functional Analysis." *American Ethnologist* 2:617–633.

HEIDER, K. G.
1970. *The Dugum Dani: A Papuan Culture in the Highlands of West New Guinea.* Chicago: Aldine.

HEINE, B.
1985. "The Mountain People: Some Notes on the Ik of North-eastern Uganda." *Africa* 55:3–16.

HENRY, J.
1941. *Jungle People: A Kaingáng Tribe of the Highlands of Brazil.* Richmond, VA: J. J. Augustin.
1963. *Culture Against Man.* New York: Vintage Books.

HERDT, G. H. (ed.).
1984. *Ritualized Homosexuality in Melanesia.* Berkeley: University of California Press.

HERSKOVITS, M. J.
1951. "Tender- and Tough-Minded Anthropology and the Study of Values in Culture." *Southwestern Journal of Anthropology* 7:22–31.
1972. *Cultural Relativism: Perspectives in Cultural Pluralism.* New York: Random House.

HEWLETT, B. S., AND L. L. CAVALLI-SFORZA.
1986. "Cultural Transmission Among Aka Pygmies." *American Anthropologist* 88:922–934.

HEZEL, F. X., D. H. RUBINSTEIN, AND G. H. WHITE.

1985. *Culture, Youth and Suicide in the Pacific: Papers from an East-West Center Conference.* Honolulu: East-West Center.

HIBBERT, C.

1980. *The French Revolution.* London: Allen Lane/Penguin.

HICKERSON, H.

1970. *The Chippewa and Their Neighbors: A Study in Ethnohistory.* New York: Holt, Rinehart and Winston.

HILL, T. W.

1984. "Ethnohistory and Alcohol Studies." In M. Galanter (ed.), *Recent Developments in Alcoholism,* vol. 2. New York: Plenum, pp. 313–337.

HIPPLER, A. E.

1974. "Some Alternative Viewpoints of the Negative Results of Euro-American Contact with Non-Western Groups." *American Anthropologist* 76:334–337.

1978. "Culture and Personality Perspective of the Yolngu of Northeastern Arnhem Land: Part 1—Early Socialization." *Journal of Psychological Anthropology* 1:221–244.

1981. "The Yolngu and Cultural Relativism: A Response to Reser." *American Anthropologist* 83:393–397.

HOBLEY, C. W.

1922. *Bantu Beliefs and Magic.* London: H.F. & G. Witherby.

HOBSBAWM, E. J.

1959. *Primitive Rebels: Studies in Archaic Forms of Social Movement in the 19th and 20th Centuries.* New York: W. W. Norton.

HOEBEL, E. A.

1954. *The Law of Primitive Man: A Study in Comparative Legal Dynamics.* Cambridge: Harvard University Press.

HOGBIN, I.

1930. "The Problem of Repopulation in Melanesia as Applied to Ontong Java (Solomon Islands)." *Journal of the Polynesian Society* 39:43–66.

HOLLAN, D.

1990. "Indignant Suicide in the Pacific: An Example from the Toraja Highlands of Indonesia." *Culture, Medicine and Psychiatry* 14:365–380.

HOLLIS, M., AND S. LUKES (eds.).

1982. *Rationality and Relativism.* Oxford: Basil Blackwell.

HOLMBERG, A. R.

1969. *Nomads of the Long Bow: The Sirionó of Eastern Bolivia.* Garden City, NY: Natural History Press.

HORTON, D. R.

1979. "Tasmanian Adaptation." *Mankind* 12:28–34.

HOWE, K. R.

1984. *Where the Waves Fall: A New South Seas History from First Settlement to Colonial History.* Sydney: George Allen and Unwin.

HOWLETT, D. R.

1962. *A Decade of Change in the Goroka Valley, New Guinea: Land Use and Development in the 1950s.* Unpublished Ph.D. dissertation, Australian National University, Canberra.

245

HUNTINGFORD, G. W. B.

1953. *The Southern Nilo-Hamites*. London: International African Institute.

HUNTSMAN, J., AND A. HOOPER.

1975. "Male and Female in Tokelau Culture." *Journal of the Polynesian Society* 84:415–430.

HUYDECOPER, W.

1962. *Huydecoper's Diary, Journey from Elmira to Kumasi 28 April 1816–18th May 1817* (G. Irwin, trans.; orig. publ. in 1816–1817). The Hague: Legon.

HYDE, G. E.

1974. *The Pawnee Indians*. Norman: University of Oklahoma Press.

ICHIKAWA, M.

1983. "An Examination of the Hunting-Dependent Life of the Mbuti Pygmies, Eastern Zaire." *African Study Monographs, Supplemental* 4:55–76.

IENAGA, S.

1978. *The Pacific War, 1931–1945: A Critical Perspective on Japan's Role in World War II*. New York: Random House.

ILIFFE, J.

1979. *A Modern History of Tanganyika*. Cambridge: Cambridge University Press.

1987. *The African Poor: A History*. New York: Cambridge University Press.

ISAAC, B.

1977. "The Sirionó of Eastern Bolivia: A Reexamination." *Human Ecology* 5:137–154.

ISAACS, N.

1970. *Travels and Adventures in Eastern Africa Descriptive of the Zoolus, Their Manners, Customs*. Rev. and ed. by L. Herman and P. R. Kirby. Capetown: C. Struik. Originally published in 1808.

JACKSON, K. D.

1989. *Cambodia 1975–78: Rendezvous with Death*. Princeton, NJ: Princeton University Press.

JACOBY, S.

1983. *Wild Justice: The Evolution of Revenge*. New York: Harper & Row.

JARVIE, I. C.

1984. *Rationality and Relativism: In Search of a Philosophy and History of Anthropology*. Boston: Routledge & Kegan Paul.

JARVIS, E.

1852. "On the Supposed Increase in Insanity." *American Journal of Insanity* 8:333–364.

JILEK, W. G.

1982. *Indian Healing: Shamanic Ceremonialism in the Pacific Northwest Today*. Blaine, WA: Hancock House.

JOHNS, T.

1990. *With Bitter Herbs They Shall Eat It: Chemical Ecology and the Origins of Human Diet and Medicine*. Tucson: University of Arizona Press.

JOHNSON, A. W., AND T. EARLE.

1987. *The Evolution of Human Societies: From Foraging Group to Agrarian State*. Stanford: Stanford University Press.

JOHNSON, B. B., AND V. T. COVELLO.

1987. *The Social and Cultural Construction of Risk: Essays on Risk Selection and Perception*. Boston: D. Reidel.

JOHNSON, G. A.

1983. "Decision-Making Organization and Pastoral Nomad Camp Size." *Human Ecology* 11:175–199.

JONES, R. M.

1974. "Tasmanian Tribes." In N. B. Tindale (ed.), *Aboriginal Tribes of Australia: Their Terrain, Environmental Controls, Distribution, Limits and Proper Names*. Berkeley: University of California Press, pp. 319–354.

1977. "The Tasmanian Paradox." In R. V. S. Wright (ed.), *Stone Tools as Cultural Markers: Change, Evolution and Complexity*. Canberra: Australian Institute of Aboriginal Studies, pp. 189–204.

1978. "Why Did the Tasmanians Stop Eating Fish?" In R. A. Gould (ed.), *Explorations in Ethnoarcheology*. Albuquerque: University of New Mexico Press, pp. 11–48.

JONES, W. K.

1969. "Notes on the History and Material Culture of the Tonkawa Indians." *Smithsonian Contributions to Anthropology*, vol. 2, no. 5. Washington, DC: U.S. Government Printing Office.

JUNOD, H. A.

1962. *The Life of a South African Tribe*, vol. 1. New Hyde Park, NY: University Books.

KAPLAN, H., AND K. HILL.

1984. "The Mashco-Piro Nomads of Peru." *Anthroquest: News of Human Origins, Behavior and Survival* 29:1–17.

KATZ, S. H.

1987. "Fava Bean Consumption: A Case for the Co-evolution of Genes and Culture." In M. Harris and E. B. Ross (eds.), *Food and Evolution: Toward a Theory of Human Food Habits*. Philadelphia: Temple University Press, pp. 133–159.

KEARNEY, M.

1976. "A World-View Explanation of the Evil Eye." In C. Maloney (ed.), *The Evil Eye*. New York: Columbia University Press, pp. 175–192.

KEEGAN, W. F.

1986. "The Optimal Foraging Analysis of Horticultural Production." *American Anthropologist* 88:92–107.

KEISER, R. L.

1986. " Death Enmity in Thull: Organized Vengeance and Social Change in a Kohistani Community." *American Ethnologist* 13:489–505.

1991. *Friend by Day, Enemy by Night: Organized Vengeance in a Kohistani Community*. Fort Worth: Holt, Rinehart and Winston.

KELLY, R. C.

1985. *The Nuer Conquest: The Structure and Development of an Expansionist System*. Ann Arbor: University of Michigan Press.

KENNEDY, J. G.

1969. "Psychosocial Dynamics of Witchcraft Systems." *The International Journal of Social Psychiatry* 15:165–178.

1970. "Circumcision and Excision in Egyptian Nubia." *Man* 5:175–191.

1978. "*Mushahara*: A Nubian Concept of Supernatural Danger and the Danger of Taboo." In J. G. Kennedy (ed.), *Nubian Ceremonial Life: Studies in Islamic Syncretism and Cultural Change*. Berkeley: University of California Press, pp. 125–149.

KEPHART, W. M.

1976. *Extraordinary Groups: The Sociology of Unconventional Life Styles*. New York: St. Martin's Press.

KHALAF, S. N.

1990. "Settlement of Violence in Bedouin Society." *Ethnology* 29:225–242.

KIHLSTROM, J. F.

1987. "The Cognitive Unconscious." *Science* 237:1446–1452.

KILBRIDE, P. L., AND J. C. KILBRIDE.

1990. *Changing Family Life in East Africa: Women and Children at Risk*. University Park, PA: Pennsylvania State University Press.

KIMURA, M.

1983. *The Neutral Theory of Molecular Evolution*. Cambridge: Cambridge University Press.

KING, L. M.

1982. "Suicide From a 'Black Reality' Perspective." In B. A. Bass, G. E. Wyatt, and G. J. Powell (eds.), *The Afro-American Family: Assessment, Treatment and Research Issues*. New York: Grune & Stratton, pp. 221–236.

KLASS, D.

1976. "Psychohistory and Communal Patterns: John Humphrey Noyes and the Oneida Community." In F. E. Reynold and D. Capps (eds.), *The Biographical Process: Studies in the History and Psychology of Religion*. The Hague: Mouton, pp. 273–296.

KLEINMAN, A.

1986. *Social Origins of Distress and Disease: Depression, Neurasthenia, and Pain in Modern China*. New Haven: Yale University Press.

KLEINMAN, A., AND B. GOOD (eds.).

1985. *Culture and Depression: Studies in the Anthropology and Cross-Cultural Psychiatry of Affect and Disorder*. Berkeley: University of California Press.

KLUCKHOHN, C.

1939. "The Place of Theory in Anthropological Studies." *The Philosophy of Science* 6:328–344.

1955. "Ethical Relativity: *Sic et Non*." *Journal of Philosophy* 52:663–677.

KLUCKHOHN, C., AND D. LEIGHTON.

1962. *The Navaho*. Rev. ed. Garden City, NY: Doubleday (in cooperation with the American Museum of Natural History).

KNAUFT, B. M.

1985. *Good Company and Violence: Sorcery and Social Action in a Lowland New Guinea Society*. Berkeley: University of California Press.

1987. "Reconsidering Violence in Simple Human Societies: Homicide Among the Gebusi of New Guinea." *Current Anthropology* 28:457–500.

1991. "Violence and Sociality in Human Evolution." *Current Anthropology*

248

32:1–21.

(in press) *South Coast New Guinea Cultures: History, Comparison, Dialectic.* New York: Cambridge University Press.

KNUDSEN, D., AND J. L. MILLER (eds.).

1991. *Abused and Battered: Social and Legal Responses to Family Violence.* Hawthorne, NY: Aldine de Gruyter.

KÖBBEN, A. J. F.

1979. "Unity and Disunity: Cottica Djuka Society as a Kinship System." In R. Price (ed.), *Maroon Societies: Rebel Slave Communities in the Americas.* 2nd ed. Baltimore: Johns Hopkins University Press, pp. 320–369.

KOCH, K.-F.

1974. *War and Peace in Jalémo: The Management of Conflict in Highland New Guinea.* Cambridge: Harvard University Press.

KONNER, M.

1982. *The Tangled Wing: Biological Constraints on the Human Spirit.* New York: Holt, Rinehart and Winston.

1991. "The Promise of Medical Anthropology: An Invited Commentary." *Medical Anthropology Quarterly* 5:78–82.

KORBIN, J. E. (ed.).

1981. *Child Abuse and Neglect: Cross-Cultural Perspectives.* Berkeley: University of California Press.

1987. "Child Maltreatment in Cross-Cultural Perspective: Vulnerable Children and Circumstances." In R. Gelles and J. Lancaster (ed.), *Child Abuse and Neglect: Biosocial Dimensions.* New York: Aldine, pp. 31–55.

KRACKE, W. H.

1978. *Force and Persuasion: Leadership in an Amazonian Society.* Chicago: University of Chicago Press.

KROEBER, A. L.

1948. *Anthropology.* New York: Harcourt, Brace and Company.

1953. *Handbook of the Indians of California.* San Francisco: Filmore Bros. Press.

KROEBER, C. B., AND B. L. FONTANA.

1986. *Massacre on the Gila: An Account of the Last Major Battle Between American Indians, with Reflections on the Origin of War.* Tucson: University of Arizona Press.

KROEBER, T.

1961. *Ishi in Two Worlds: A Biography of the Last Wild Indian in North America.* Berkeley: University of California Press.

KUMMER, H.

1971. *Primate Societies: Group Techniques of Ecological Adaptation.* Chicago: Aldine-Atherton.

KUPER, L.

1981. *Genocide: Its Political Use in the Twentieth Century.* New Haven: Yale University Press.

KURAN, T.

1988. The Tenacious Past: Theories of Personal and Collective Conservation. *Journal of Economic Behavior and Organization* 10:143–171.

1989. Sparks and Prairie Fires: A Theory of Unanticipated Political Revolution. *Public Choice* 61:41:74.

KUSCHEL, R.

1988. *Vengeance Is Their Reply: Blood Feuds and Homicides on Bellona Island.* Part 1: "Conditions Underlying Generations of Bloodshed." Vol. 7 of *Language and Culture of Rennell and Bellona Islands.* Copenhagen: Dansk Psykologisk Furlag.

LABARRE, W.

1945. "Some Observations on Character Structure in the Orient: The Japanese." *Psychiatry* 8:326–42.

1970. *The Ghost Dance: The Origins of Religion.* New York: Doubleday.

1984. *Muelos: A Stone Age Superstition About Sexuality.* New York: Columbia University Press.

LACK, D.

1966. *Population Studies of Birds.* Oxford: Oxford University Press.

LADURIE, L. E.

1979. *Carnival in Romans.* (M. Feeney, trans.). New York: George Braziller.

LANGNESS, L. L.

1974. "Ritual, Power, and Male Dominance in the New Guinea Highlands." *Ethos* 2:189–212.

1981. "Child Abuse and Cultural Values: The Case of New Guinea." In J. E. Korbin (ed.), *Child Abuse and Neglect: Cross-Cultural Perspectives.* Berkeley: University of California Press, pp. 13–34.

LASLETT, P.

1965. *The World We Have Lost: England Before the Industrial Age.* 2nd ed. New York: Charles Scribner's Sons.

LAUGHLIN, C. D., JR., AND I. A. BRADY (eds.).

1978. *Extinction and Survival in Human Populations.* New York: Columbia University Press.

LAUGHLIN, W. S.

1961. "Acquisition of Anatomical Knowledge by Ancient Man." In S. Washburn (ed.), *Social Life of Early Man.* New York: Viking Fund Publication in Anthropology no. 31, pp. 150–175.

LEACH, E. R.

1965. *Political Systems of Highland Burma: A Study of Kachin Social Structure* (with a new introductory note). Boston: Beacon Press.

1982. *Social Anthropology.* Oxford: Oxford University Press.

LEBO, H.

1991. "Weighing the Effects of Stress." *UCLA Magazine* (Winter), p. 18.

LEE, R. B.

1979. *The !Kung San: Men, Women and Work in a Foraging Society.* Cambridge: Cambridge University Press.

LEIS, P. E.

1965. "The Nonfunctional Attributes of Twin Infanticide in the Niger Delta." *Anthropological Quarterly* 38:97–111.

LEVINE, R. A.

1959. "Gusii Sex Offenses: A Study in Social Control." *American Anthropologist*

61:965–990.

1973. *Culture, Behavior and Personality*. Chicago: Aldine.

LeVine, R. A., and B. B. LeVine.

1979. *Nyansongo: A Gusii Community in Kenya*. Six Cultures Series, vol. 2. New York: John Wiley and Sons.

Levinson, D.

1989. *Family Violence in Cross-Cultural Perspective*. Newbury Park, CA: Sage.

Levinson, D., and M. Malone.

1980. *Toward Explaining Human Culture*. New Haven: HRAF Press.

Lévi-Strauss, C.

1964. *Tristes Tropiques*. New York: Atheneum.

Levy, H. S.

1966. *Chinese Footbinding: The History of a Curious Erotic Custom*. New York: Walton Rawls.

Levy, J. E., and S. J. Kunitz.

1974. *Indian Drinking: Navaho Practices and Anglo-American Theories*. New York: John Wiley & Sons.

Levy, M. J., Jr.

1952. *The Structuring of Society*. Princeton: Princeton University Press.

Lewis, O.

1951. *Life in a Mexican Village: Tepoztlan Restudied*. Urbana: University of Illinois Press.

Lewontin, R. C., S. Rose, and L. J. Kamin.

1984. *Not in Our Genes: Biology, Ideology and Human Nature*. New York: Pantheon.

Lin, K.-M., and A. M. Kleinman.

1988. "Psychopathology and Clinical Course of Schizophrenia: A Cross-Cultural Perspective." *Schizophrenia Bulletin* 14:555–567.

Lindblom, G.

1920. *The Akamba in British East Africa*. Uppsala: Appelbergs Boktryckeri Aktiebolag.

Lindenbaum, S.

1972. "Sorcerers, Ghosts and Polluting Women: An Analysis of Religious Belief and Population Control." *Ethnology* 11:241–253.

1979. *Kuru Sorcery: Disease and Danger in the New Guinea Highlands*. Palo Alto: Mayfield.

Linton, R.

1952. "Universal Ethical Principles: An Anthropological View." In R. N. Anshen (ed.), *Moral Principles of Action: Man's Ethical Imperative*. New York: Harper.

LiPuma, E.

1988. "Ethnographic Equilibrium." *American Anthropologist* 90:970–973.

Lizot, J.

1985. *Tales of the Yanomami: Daily Life in the Venezuelan Forest*. (Ernest Simon, trans.). Cambridge: Cambridge University Press.

Lockard, J. S., and D. L. Paulhus (eds.).

1988. *Self-Deception: An Adaptive Mechanism?* Englewood Cliffs, NJ: Prentice Hall.

LOPREATO, J.

1984. *Human Nature and Biocultural Evolution*. Boston: Allen and Unwin.

LOWIE, R. H.

1920. *Primitive Society*. New York: Boni and Liveright.

1938. "Subsistence." In F. Boas (ed.), *General Anthropology*. New York: D.C. Heath, pp. 282–326.

1954. *Indians of the Plains*. New York: American Museum of Natural History.

LOZOFF, B., K. R. KAMATH, AND R. A. FELDMAN.

1975. "Infection and Disease in South Indian Families: Beliefs About Childhood Diarrhea." *Human Organization* 34:353–358.

LUMHOLTZ, C.

1889. *Among Cannibals*. London: John Murray.

LUMSDEN, C. J.

1989. "Does Culture Need Genes?" *Ethology and Sociobiology* 10:11:28.

LUMSDEN, C. J., AND E. O. WILSON.

1981. *Genes, Mind and Culture*. Cambridge: Harvard University Press.

LURIE, A.

1981. *The Language of Clothes*. New York: Random House.

LUTZ, C. A.

1985. "Depression and the Translation of Emotional Worlds." In A. Kleinman and B. Good (eds.), *Culture and Depression: Studies in the Anthropology and Cross-Cultural Psychiatry of Affect and Disorder*. Berkeley: University of California Press, pp. 63–100.

1988. *Unnatural Emotions: Everyday Sentiments on a Micronesian Atoll and Their Challenge to Western Theory*. Chicago: University of Chicago Press.

MACANDREW, C., AND R. B. EDGERTON.

1969. *Drunken Comportment: A Social Explanation*. Chicago: Aldine.

MACLEAN, V.

1971. *Magical Medicine: A Nigerian Case-Study*. Harmondsworth, Middlesex: Penguin Books.

MAGNARELLA, P. J.

1982. "Cultural Materialism and the Problem of Probabilities." *American Anthropologist* 84:138–142.

MALINOWSKI, B.

1936. "Anthropology." In *Encyclopaedia Britannica*. 1st supp. vol., pp. 131–140.

1944. *A Scientific Theory of Culture*. Chapel Hill, NC: University of North Carolina Press.

MALONEY, C. (ed.).

1976. *The Evil Eye*. New York: Columbia University Press.

MALOTKI, E.

1983. *Hopi Time: A Linguistic Analysis of the Temporal Concepts in the Hopi Language*. Berlin: Mouton.

MAQUET, J.

1964. "Objectivity in Anthropology." *Current Anthropology* 5:47–55.

MARCUS, G. E., AND M. M. J. FISCHER.
1986. *Anthropology as Cultural Critique: An Experimental Movement in the Human Sciences*. Chicago: University of Chicago Press.

MARR, D.
1982. *Vision: A Computational Investigation into the Human Representation and Processing of Visual Information*. San Francisco: Freeman.

MARSHALL, E. M.
1959. *The Harmless People*. New York: Knopf.

MARTIN, J. F.
1983. "Optimal Foraging Theory: A Review of Some Models and Their Applications." *American Anthropologist* 85:612–629.

MARTINDALE, D.
1965. *Functionalism in the Social Sciences: The Strength and Limits of Functionalism in Anthropology, Economics, Political Science, and Sociology*. Philadelphia: American Academy of Political and Social Science, Monograph No. 5.

MASTERS, R. D.
1989. *The Nature of Politics*. New Haven: Yale University Press.

McCABE, J. T.
1990. "Turkana Pastoralism: A Case Against the Tragedy of the Commons." *Human Ecology* 18:81–103.

McCLELLAND, D. B. L.
1982. "Antibodies in Milk." *Journal of Reproduction and Fertility* 65:519–86.

McCORD, C., AND H. P. FREEMAN.
1990. "Excess Mortality in Harlem." *New England Journal of Medicine* 322:173–178.

McELROY, A., AND P. TOWNSEND.
1979. *Medical Anthropology in Ecological Perspective*. North Scituate, MA: Duxbury Press.

McGOVERN, T. H., G. BIGELOW, T. AMORASI, AND D. RUSSELL.
1988. "Northern Islands, Human Error, and Environmental Degradation: A View of Social and Ecological Change in the Medieval North Atlantic." *Human Ecology* 16:227–270.

McGREGOR, G.
1946. *Warriors Without Weapons: A Study of the Society and Personality Development of the Pine Ridge Sioux*. Chicago: University of Chicago Press.

McLEAN, S., AND S. E. GRAHAM (eds.).
1983. *Female Circumcision, Excision and Infibulation: The Facts and Proposals for Change*. New York: Minority Rights Group.

McLEOD, M. D.
1984. *The Asante*. London: British Museum.

McMILLEN, S.
1968. *None of These Diseases*. Old Tappan, NJ: Fleming H. Revell.

McNEILL, W. H.
1976. *Plagues and Peoples*. Garden City, NY: Anchor/Doubleday.

MEAD, M.
1956. *New Lives for Old: Cultural Transformation—1928–1953*. New York: Morrow.

MEGGERS, B.

1971. *Amazonia: Man and Culture in a Counterfeit Paradise*. Chicago: University of Chicago Press.

MEGGITT, M. J.

1962. *Desert People: A Study of the Walbiri Aborigines of Central Australia*. Chicago: University of Chicago Press.

1977. *Blood Is Their Argument: Warfare Among the Mae Enga Tribesmen of the New Guinea Highlands*. Palo Alto: Mayfield.

MESSER, E.

1984. "Anthropological Perspectives on Diet." *Annual Review of Anthropology*. 13:205–249.

MICHELSON, T.

1932. *The Narrative of a Southern Cheyenne Woman*. Washington, DC: Smithsonian Miscellaneous Collections, vol. 87, no. 9.

MILLER, B. D.

1981. *The Endangered Sex: Neglect of Female Children in Rural North India*. Ithaca: Cornell University Press.

MILLS, C. W.

1950. *The Sociological Imagination*. New York: Oxford University Press.

MITCHELL, D.

1984. "Predatory Warfare, Social Status, and the North Pacific Slave Trade." *Ethnology* 23:39–48.

MITCHELL, J. E., AND E. D. ECKERT.

1987. "Scope and Significance of Eating Disorders." *Journal of Consulting Clinical Psychology*. 55:628–634.

MITCHELL, W. E.

1990. "Why Wape Men Don't Beat Their Wives: Constraints Toward Domestic Tranquility in a New Guinea Society." *Pacific Studies* 13:141–150.

MITHEN, S. J.

1989. "Modeling Hunter-Gatherer Decision-Making: Complementing Optimal Foraging Theory." *Human Ecology* 17:59–83.

MOORE, B., JR.

1978. *Injustice: The Social Bases of Obedience and Revolt*. White Plains, NY: M. E. Sharpe.

MOORE, O. K.

1957. "Divination—A New Perspective." *American Anthropologist* 50:69–74.

MOSKO, M. S.

1990. "The Symbols of 'Forest': A Structural Analysis of Mbuti Culture and Social Organization." *American Anthropologist* 89:896–913.

MOSLEY, W. H., AND L. C. CHEN (eds.).

1984. *Child Survival: Strategies for Research. Population and Development Review*. Supp. to vol. 10. New York: Cambridge University Press.

MURDOCK, G. P.

1965. *Culture and Society*. Pittsburgh: University of Pittsburgh Press.

MURPHY, H. B. M.

1982. *Comparative Psychiatry: The International and Intercultural Distribution of Mental Illness*. New York, Berlin, Heidelberg: Springer-Verlag.

254

MURPHY, H. B. M., AND B. M. TAUMOEPEAU.
1980. "Traditionalism and Mental Health in the South Pacific: A Reexamination of the Old Hypothesis." *Psychological Medicine* 10:471–482.

NAROLL, R.
1969. "Cultural Determinants and the Concept of the Sick Society." In S. C. Plog and R. B. Edgerton (eds.), *Changing Perspectives in Mental Illness*. New York: Holt, Rinehart and Winston, pp. 128–154.
1983. *The Moral Order: An Introduction to the Human Situation*. Beverly Hills: Sage Publications.

NASH, J.
1967. "Death as a Way of Life: The Increasing Resort to Homicide in a Maya Indian Community." *American Anthropologist* 69:455–470.

NEEDHAM, R.
1972. *Belief, Language and Experience*. Oxford: Basil Blackwell.

NEEDLEMAN, H. L., A. SCHEU, D. BELLINGER, A. LEVITON, AND E. N. ALLRED.
1990. "The Long-Term Effects of Exposure to Low Doses of Lead in Childhood: An 11-Year Follow-up Report." *New England Journal of Medicine* 322:83–88.

NEEL, J. V.
1962. "Diabetes Mellitus: A 'Thrifty' Genotype Rendered Detrimental by 'Progress'?" *American Journal of Human Genetics* 14:353–362.
1970. "Lessons from a 'Primitive' People." *Science* 170:815–822.

NIEBOER, H.
1900. *Slavery as an Industrial System*. The Hague: Martinas Nijhoff.

NINUALLAIN, M., A. O'HARE, AND D. WALSH.
1987. "Incidence of Schizophrenia in Ireland." *Psychological Medicine* 17:943–948.

NISBET, R.
1973. *The Social Philosophers: Community and Conflict in Western Thought*. New York: Thomas Y. Crowell.

NISBET, R., AND L. ROSS.
1980. *Human Inference: Strategies and Shortcomings of Social Judgment*. Englewood Cliffs, NJ: Prentice-Hall.

NISSAM-SABAT, C.
1987. "On Clifford Geertz and His 'Anti-Anti-Relativism.'" *American Anthropologist* 89:935–943.

NITOBE, I.
1969. *Bushido: The Soul of Japan*. New York: Rutland.

NOBLE, D. G. (ed.).
1984. *New Light on Chaco Canyon*. Santa Fe, NM: School of American Research Press.

NORBECK, E.
1961. *Religion in Primitive Society*. New York: Harper & Row.
1963. "African Rituals of Conflict." *American Anthropologist* 65:1254–1279.

NOYES, P.
1937. *My Father's House: An Oneida Boyhood*. New York: Farrar and Rinehart.

NUCKOLLS, C.
1991. "Culture and Causal Thinking: Diagnosis and Prediction in a South Indian Fishing Village." *Ethos* 19:3–51.

NURSE, G. T.
1975. "Seasonal Hunger Among the Ngoni and Ntumba of Central Malawi." *Africa* 45:1–11.

OAKLEY, J.
1991. "Defiant Moments: Gender, Resistance and Individuals." *Man* 26:3–22.

OLIVER, S. C.
1962. *Ecology and Cultural Continuity as Contributing Factors in the Social Organizations of the Plains Indians.* University of California Publications in American Archeology and Ethnology, 48(1).

O'MEARA, J. T.
1989. "Anthropology as Empirical Science." *American Anthropologist* 91:354–369.

OMER-COOPER, J. D.
1966. *The Zulu Aftermath: A Nineteenth Century Revolution in Bantu Africa.* Evanston, IL: Northwestern University Press.

O'NELL, C. W., AND A. J. RUBEL.
1980. "The Development and Use of a Gauge to Measure Social Stress in Three Meso-American Communities." *Ethnology* 19:111–127.

OPLER, M. E.
1936. "Some Points of Comparison and Contrast Between Treatment of Functional Disorders by Apache Shamans and Modern Psychiatric Practice." *American Journal of Psychiatry* 92:1371–1387.

ORR, D. W.
1979. "Catastrophe and Social Order." *Human Ecology* 7:41–52.

ORTNER, S.
1974. "Is Female to Male as Nature Is to Culture?" In M. Z. Rosaldo and L. Lamphere (eds.), *Women, Culture and Society.* Stanford: Stanford University Press, pp. 67–87.

ORTIZ, S.
1967. "The Structure of Decision Making Among Indians in Columbia." In R. Firth (ed.), *Themes in Economic Anthropology.* London: Tavistock, pp. 191–228.

ORTIZ DE MONTELLANO, B. R.
1983. "Counting Skulls: Comment on the Aztec Cannibalism Theory of Harner-Harris." *American Anthropologist* 85:403–406.

OSWALT, W. H.
1973. *Habitat and Technology: The Evolution of Hunting.* New York: Holt, Rinehart and Winston.
1979. *Eskimos and Explorers.* Novato, CA: Chandler and Sharp.

OTTERBEIN, K. F.
1970. *The Evolution of War: A Cross-Cultural Study.* New Haven: HRAF Press.
1987. Comment on "Reconsidering Violence in Simple Human Societies: Homicide Among the Gebusi of New Guinea." *Current Anthropology* 28:484–485.

OWUSU, M.
1978. "Ethnography of Africa: The Usefulness of the Useless." *American Anthropologist* 80:310–334.

256

PALMER, C.
  1989. "Is Rape a Cultural Universal? A Re-examination of the Ethnographic Data." *Ethnology* 28:1–16.
PARDOE, C.
  1991. "Isolation and Sociality in Human Evolution." *Current Anthropology* 32:391–428.
PARSONS, T.
  1964. "Evolutionary Universals in Society." *American Sociological Review* 29:339–357.
PATEL, S., AND K. KUMAR.
  1988. "Defenders of Sati." *Economic and Political Weekly* 23:129–130.
PEACOCK, N. R.
  1990. "Rethinking the Sexual Division of Labor: Reproduction and Women's Work Among the Efe." In M. DiLeonardo (ed.), *Gender at the Crossroads of Knowledge: Feminist Anthropology in the Post-Modern Era.* Berkeley: University of California Press, pp. 339–360.
PEARLMAN, M.
  1967. *The Zealots of Masada: Story of a Dig.* New York: Scribner's.
PEIRES, J. B.
  1989. *The Dead Will Arise: Nongqawuse and the Great Xhosa Cattle-Killing Movement of 1856–7.* London: James Curry.
PELLIGRINO, C.
  1991. *Unearthing Atlantis: An Archeological Odyssey.* New York: Random House.
PELTO, G. H.
  1987. "Social Class and Diet in Contemporary Mexico." In M. Harris and E. B. Ross (eds.), *Food and Evolution: Toward a Theory of Human Food Habits.* Philadelphia: Temple University Press, pp. 517–540.
PERRIN, N.
  1979. *Giving Up the Gun: Japan's Reversion to the Sword, 1543–1879.* Boston: D. R. Godine.
PIPES, R.
  1990. *The Russian Revolution.* New York: Alfred A. Knopf.
PLOG, S. C., AND R. B. EDGERTON (eds.).
  1969. *Changing Perspectives in Mental Illness.* New York: Holt, Rinehart and Winston.
PLOMLEY, N. J. B.
  1966. *Friendly Mission: The Tasmanian Journals and Papers of George Augustus Robinson, 1829–1834.* Hobart: Tasmanian Historical Research Association.
PLOTNIKOV, L.
  1967. *Strangers to the City: Urban Man in Jos, Nigeria.* Pittsburgh: University of Pittsburgh Press.
POOLE, F. P.
  1983. "Cannibals, Tricksters, and Witches: Anthropophagic Images Among Bimin-Kuskusmin." In P. Brown and D. Tuzin (eds.), *The Ethnography of Cannibalism.* Washington, DC: Society for Psychological Anthropology, pp. 6–32.

BIBLIOGRAPHY

1985. "Among the Boughs of the Hanging Tree: Male Suicide Among the Bimin-Kuskusmin of Papua New Guinea." In F. X. Hezel, D. H. Rubenstein, and G. H. White (eds.), *Culture, Youth and Suicide in the Pacific: Papers from the East-West Center Conference*. Honolulu: East-West Center, pp. 152–181.

POSPISIL, L.

1958. *Kapauku Papuans and Their Law*. New Haven: Yale University Publications in Anthropology, no. 67.

1963. *The Kapauku Papuans of West New Guinea*. New York: Holt, Rinehart and Winston.

1971. *Anthropology of Law: A Comparative Theory*. New York: Harper and Row.

PRICE, T. D., AND J. A. BROWN.

1984. *Prehistoric Hunter-Gatherers: The Emergence of Cultural Complexity*. Orlando: Academic Press.

QUINE, W. V.

1960. *Word and Object*. Cambridge: MIT Press.

RADCLIFFE-BROWN, A. R.

1949. "Functionalism: A Protest." *American Anthropologist* 51:320–323.

RAGIN, C. C.

1984. *The Comparative Method: Moving Beyond Qualitative and Quantitative Strategies*. Berkeley: University of California Press.

RAMBO, A. T.

1985. "Primitive Polluters: Semang Impact on the Malaysian Tropical Rain Forest Ecosystem." Anthropological Papers, no. 76. Ann Arbor: Museum of Anthropology, University of Michigan.

RAMENOFSKY, A. F.

1987. *Vectors of Death: The Archaeology of European Contact*. Albuquerque: University of New Mexico Press.

RAMSEYER, F. A., AND J. KÜHNE.

1875. *Four Years in Ashantee*. (Mrs. Weitbrecht, ed.). New York: Robert Carter and Bros.

RAPHAEL, D. L.

1966. *"The Lactation-Suckling Process Within a Matrix of Supportive Behavior."* Ph.D. thesis, Columbia University, New York.

RAPPAPORT, R. A.

1968. *Pigs for the Ancestors: Ritual in the Ecology of a New Guinea People*. New Haven: Yale University Press.

1971. "Ritual, Sanctity and Cybernetics." *American Anthropologist* 73:59–76.

1984. *Pigs for the Ancestors: Ritual in the Ecology of a New Guinea People*. 2nd ed. New Haven: Yale University Press.

RASMUSSEN, K.

1931. *The Netsilik Eskimos: Social Life and Spiritual Culture*. Copenhagen: Gyldendalske Boghandel, Nordisk Forlag.

RATTRAY, R. S.

1929. *Ashanti Law and Constitution*. Oxford: Clarendon Press.

REDFIELD, R.
    1947. "The Folk Society." *American Journal of Sociology.* 52:293–308.
    1953. *The Primitive World and Its Transformations.* Ithaca: Cornell University Press.
    1960. *The Little Community.* Chicago: University of Chicago Press.

RENTELN, A. D.
    1988. "Relativism and the Search for Human Rights." *American Anthropologist* 90:56–72.

RESER, J. P.
    1982. "Cultural Relativity or Cultural Bias: A Response to Hippler." *American Anthropologist* 84:399–406.

RICHARDS, A. I.
    1940. "The Political System of the Bemba Tribe—North-eastern Rhodesia." In M. Fortes and E. E. Evans-Pritchard (eds.), *African Political Systems.* London: Oxford University Press, pp. 83–120.

RICHERSON, P. J., AND R. BOYD.
    1989. "The Role of Evolved Predispositions in Cultural Evolution: Or, Human Sociobiology Meets Pascal's Wager." *Ethology and Sociobiology* 10:195–219.

RICHES, D. (ed.).
    1986. *The Anthropology of Violence.* New York: Basil Blackwell.

RITTER, E. A.
    1935. *Shaka Zulu: The Rise of the Zulu Empire.* London: Allen Lane.

ROBARCHEK, C. A.
    1989. "Primitive Warfare and the Ratomorphic Image of Mankind." *American Anthropologist* 91:903–920.

ROBBINS, S.
    1982. *Auyana: Those Who Held onto Home.* Seattle: University of Washington Press.

ROBERTS, R. E., AND D. BRINTNALL.
    1983. *Reinventing Inequality: An Inquiry into Society and Stratification.* Cambridge: Schenkman.

ROBERTS, S. S.
    1989. "Indians Battle Fetal Alcohol Syndrome." *Journal of NIH Research* 1:32–36.

ROGERS, A. R.
    1988. "Does Biology Constrain Culture?" *American Anthropologist* 90:819–831.
    1990. "Evolutionary Economics of Human Reproduction." *Ethology and Sociobiology* 11:479–495.

ROGERS, E. M., AND F. F. SHOEMAKER.
    1971. *The Communication of Innovations: A Cross-Cultural Approach.* New York: Free Press.

ROGERS, S. L.
    1985. *Primitive Surgery: Skills Before Science.* Springfield, IL: Charles C. Thomas.

ROMANUCCI-ROSS, L.
    1973. *Conflict, Violence and Morality in a Mexican Village.* Palo Alto: National Press Books.

RORTY, R.
1980. *Philosophy and the Mirror of Nature*. Princeton: Princeton University Press.

ROSALDO, R.
1984a. "Grief and a Headhunter's Rage: On the Cultural Force of Emotions." In E. Branner (ed.), *Text, Play and Story*. Washington, DC: Proceedings of the American Ethnological Society, pp. 178–195.

1984b. "Toward an Anthropology of Self and Feeling." In R. Shweder and R. LeVine (eds.), *Culture Theory: Essays on Mind, Self and Emotion*. Cambridge: Cambridge University Press, pp. 137–157.

ROSCOE, P. B.
1990. "The Bow and Spreadnet: Ecological Origins of Hunting Technology." *American Anthropologist* 92:691–701.

ROSE, L.
1986. *The Massacre of the Innocents: Infanticide in Britain 1800–1939*. London: Routledge & Kegan Paul.

ROSENBERG, E. M.
1980. "Demographic Effects of Sex-Differential Nutrition." In N. W. Jerome, R. F. Kandel, and G. H. Pelto (eds.), *Nutritional Anthropology: Contemporary Approaches to Diet and Culture*. New York: Redgrave, pp. 181–204.

ROSENBERG, H.
1990. "The Mother of Invention: Evolutionary Theory, Territoriality, and the Origins of Agriculture." *American Anthropologist* 92:399–415.

ROSENHAN, D. L.
1973. "On Being Sane in Insane Places." *Science* 179:250–258.

ROSS, E. B.
1985. "The 'Deceptively Simple' Racism of Clark Wissler." *American Anthropologist* 87:390–393.

1987. "An Overview of Trends in Dietary Variation from Hunter-Gatherer to Modern Capitalist Societies." In M. Harris and E. B. Ross (eds.), *Food and Evolution: Toward a Theory of Human Food Habits*. Philadelphia: Temple University Press, pp. 7–55.

ROSS, J.-K.
1975. "Social Borders: Definitions of Diversity." *Current Anthropology* 46:53–72.

ROTH, H. L.
1899. *The Aborigines of Tasmania*. 2nd ed. Halifax: F. King & Sons.

ROTBERG, R. I., AND T. K. RABB (eds.).
1985. *Hunger and History: The Impact of Changing Food Production and Consumption Patterns on Society*. New York: Cambridge University Press.

ROY, D. B.
1987. *Socioeconomic Impact of Sati in Bengal and the Role of Raja Rammohun Roy*. Calcutta: Naya Pradesh.

ROZANOV, V. V.
1914. *Anokolipsicheskaya Sekta (Knisti and Skoptsi)*. Petersburg: T. V. Vaisberga and P. Gershunina.

ROZIN, P., AND C. NEMEROFF.
1990. "The Laws of Sympathetic Magic: A Psychological Analysis of Similarity and Contagion." In J. W. Stigler, R. A. Sweder, and G. Herdt (eds.), *Cultural Psychology: Essays on Comparative Human Development*. New York: Cambridge University Press, pp. 205–232.

RUBEL, A. J., C. W. O'NELL, AND R. COLLADO-ARDON.
1984. *Susto: A Folk/Illness*. Berkeley: University of California Press.

RUBINSTEIN, D. H.
1987. "Cultural Patterns and Contagion: Epidemic Suicide Among Micronesian Youth." In A. B. Robillard and A. J. Marsella (eds.), *Contemporary Issues in Mental Health Research in the Pacific Islands*. Honolulu: Social Science Research Institute, pp. 127–148.

RUYLE, E. E.
1973. "Slavery, Surplus, and Stratification on the Northwest Coast: The Ethnoenergetics of an Incipient Stratification System." *Current Anthropology* 14:603–631.

RYAN, L.
1982. *The Aboriginal Tasmanians*. St. Lucia, Queensland, Australia: University of Queensland Press.

SAGAN, E.
1985. *At the Dawn of Tyranny: The Origins of Individualism, Political Oppression, and the State*. New York: Knopf.

SAHLINS, M. D.
1968. *Tribesmen*. Englewood Cliffs, NJ: Prentice Hall.
1972. *Stone Age Economics*. Chicago: Aldine.
1976. *The Uses and Abuses of Biology: An Anthropological Critique of Sociobiology*. Ann Arbor: University of Michigan.
1985. *Islands of History*. Chicago: University of Chicago Press.

SALE, KIRKPATRICK.
1991. Letter to the Editor. *New York Times* (July 25).

SALISBURY, R. F., AND E. TOOKER (eds.).
1984. *Affluence and Cultural Survival: 1981 Proceedings of the American Ethnological Society*. Washington, DC: American Ethnological Society.

SALUSBURY-JONES, G. T.
1939. *Street Life in Medieval England*. London: Pen-in-Hand.

SAMUELS, M. L.
1982. "POPREG I: A Simulation of Population Regulation Among the Maring of New Guinea." *Human Ecology* 10:1–45.

SANDAY, P. R.
1981. *Female Power and Male Dominance: On the Origins of Sexual Inequality*. Cambridge: Cambridge University Press.

SANSOM, G. B.
1962. *Japan: A Short Cultural History*. New York: Appleton-Century-Croft.

SAPIR, E.
1924. "Culture, Genuine and Spurious." *American Journal of Sociology* 29:401–429.

BIBLIOGRAPHY

SCHAPERA, I.

1930. *The Khoisan Peoples of South Africa: Bushmen and Hottentots*. London: George Routledge & Sons.

SCHEPER-HUGHES, N.

1979. *Saints, Scholars, and Schizophrenics: Mental Illness in Rural Ireland*. Berkeley: University of California Press.

1988. "The Madness of Hunger: Sickness, Delirium, and Human Needs." *Culture, Medicine, and Psychiatry* 12:429–458.

1990. "Mother Love and Child Death in Northeast Brazil." In J. W. Stigler, R. A. Shweder, and G. Herdt (eds.), *Cultural Psychology: Essays on Comparative Human Development*. Cambridge: Cambridge University Press, pp. 542–565.

SCHNEIDER, D. M.

1984. *A Critique of the Study of Kinship*. Ann Arbor: University of Michigan Press.

SCHNEIDER, H. K.

1974. *Economic Man: The Anthropology of Economics*. New York: Free Press.

SCHOLTE, R.

1984. "Reason and Culture: The Universal and the Particular Revisited." *American Anthropologist* 86:960–965.

SCHWARTZ, T.

1974. "Cult and Context: The Paranoid Ethos in Melanesia." *Ethos* 2:154–174.

SCOTT, J. C.

1985. *Weapons of the Weak: Everyday Forms of Peasant Resistance*. New Haven: Yale University Press.

SCOTT, J. P.

1989. *The Evolution of Social Systems*. New York: Gordon and Breach.

SEATON, S. L.

1974. "The Hawaiian *Kapu* Abolition of 1819." *American Ethnologist* 1:193–206.

SERVICE, E. R.

1975. *Origins of the State and Civilization*. New York: W. W. Norton.

SHAHAR, S.

1983. *The Fourth Estate: A History of Women in the Middle Ages*. (Chaya Galai, trans.). London: Methuen.

SHAW, P.

1985. "Civilization and Its Malcontents: Responses to *Typee*." *New Criterion* (January), pp. 23–33.

SHKILNYK, A. M.

1985. *A Poison Stronger than Love: The Destruction of an Ojibwa Community*. New Haven: Yale University Press.

SHORE, B.

1978. "Ghosts and Government: A Structural Analysis of Alternative Institutions for Conflict Management in Samoa." *Man* 13:175–199.

SHORE, J. H., AND D. L. STONE.

1973. "Duodenal Ulcer Among Northwest Coastal Indian Women." *American Journal of Psychiatry* 130:774–777.

SHORTER, E.
1982. *A History of Women's Bodies*. Harmondsworth: Penguin.

SHOSTAK, M.
1981. *Nisa: The Life and Words of a !Kung Woman*. Cambridge: Harvard University Press.

SHWEDER, R. A.
1980. "Rethinking Culture and Personality Theory. Part III. From Genesis and Typology to Hermeneutics and Dynamics." *Ethos* 8:60–94.
1984. "Anthropology's Romantic Rebellion Against the Enlightenment, or There's More to Thinking than Reason and Evidence." In R. A. Shweder and R. A. LeVine (eds.), *Culture Theory: Essays on Mind, Self and Emotion*. New York: Cambridge University Press, pp. 27–66.
1990. "Post-Nietzschean Anthropology: The Idea of Multiple Objective Worlds." In M. Kransz (ed.), *Relativism, Interpretation and Confrontation*. Notre Dame: University of Notre Dame Press, pp. 99–139.
1991. *Thinking Through Cultures: Expeditions in Cultural Psychology*. Cambridge: Harvard University Press.

SHWEDER, R. A., AND R. A. LeVINE (eds.).
1984. *Culture Theory: Essays on Mind, Self, and Emotion*. Cambridge: Cambridge University Press.

SIEBERS, T.
1983. *The Mirror of Medusa*. Berkeley: University of California Press.

SILBERMAN, N. A.
1989. *Between Past and Present*. New York: Henry Holt.

SILLITOE, P.
1983. *Roots of the Earth: Crops in the Highlands of Papua New Guinea*. Sydney: New South Wales Press.

SILVERBLATT, I.
1987. *Moon, Sun, and Witches: Gender Ideologies and Class in Inca and Colonial Peru*. Princeton, NJ: Princeton University Press.

SIMOONS, F. J.
1961. *Eat Not This Flesh: Food Avoidances in the Old World*. Madison: University of Wisconsin Press.

SINGER, M.
1978. "Pygmies and Their Dogs: A Note on Culturally Constituted Defense Mechanisms." *Ethos* 6:270–277.

SINGH, I.
1989. *Women, Law and Social Change in India*. New Delhi: Radiant Publishers.

SMITH, E. A.
1979. "Human Adaptation and Energetic Efficiency." *Human Ecology* 7:53–74.

SOFFER, O.
1987. *The Pleistocene Old World: Regional Perspectives*. New York: Plenum Press.

SOLWAY, J. S., AND R. B. LEE.
1990. "Foragers, Genuine or Spurious: Situating the Kalahari San in History." *Current Anthropology* 31:109–146.

263

SOROKIN, P. A.

1937. *Social and Cultural Dynamics.* New York: American Book Co.

SOUSTELLE, J.

1961. *The Daily Life of the Aztecs: On the Eve of the Spanish Conquest.* London: Weidenfeld and Nicolson.

SPENCE, J. D.

1978. *The Death of Woman Wang.* New York: Viking Press.

SPENCER, P.

1965. *The Samburu: A Study of Gerontocracy in a Nomadic Tribe.* Berkeley: University of California Press.

1988. *The Maasai of Matapato: A Study of Rituals of Rebellion.* Bloomington, IN: Indiana University Press.

SPERBER, D.

1982. "Apparently Irrational Beliefs." In M. Hollis and S. Lukes (eds.), *Rationality and Relativism.* Oxford: Basil Blackwell, pp. 149–180.

1985. "Anthropology and Psychology: Towards an Epidemiology of Representations." *Man* 20:73–89.

SPIRO, M. E.

1968. "Religion, Personality, and Behavior in Burma." *American Anthropologist* 70:359–363.

1979. "Whatever Happened to the Id?" *American Anthropologist* 81:5–13.

1984. "Some Reflections on Cultural Determinism and Relativism with Special Reference to Emotion and Reason." In R. A. Shweder and R. A. LeVine (eds.), *Culture Theory: Essays on Mind, Self, and Emotion.* New York: Cambridge University Press, pp. 323–346.

1986. "Cultural Relativism and the Future of Anthropology." *Cultural Anthropology* 1:259–285.

1990. "On the Strange and Familiar in Recent Anthropological Thought." In J. W. Stigler, R. A. Shweder, and G. Herdt (eds.), *Cultural Psychology: Essays on Comparative Human Development.* New York: Cambridge University Press, pp. 47–61.

SPRIGGS, M.

1981. *Vegetable Kingdoms: Taro Irrigation and Pacific Prehistory.* Ph.D. dissertation, Australian National University, Canberra.

STANNARD, D. E.

1989. *Before the Horror: The Population of Hawaii on the Eve of Western Contact.* Honolulu: Social Science Research Institute, University of Hawaii.

STEARMAN, A. M.

1984. "The Yuquí Connection: Another Look at Sirionó Deculturation." *American Anthropologist* 86:630–650.

1987. *No Longer Nomads: The Sirionó Revisited.* Lanham, MD: Hamilton Press.

STEIN, D.

1988. "Burning Widows, Burning Brides: The Perils of Daughterhood in India." *Pacific Affairs* 61:465–485.

STEINER, F.

1956. *Taboo.* London: Cohen and West.

STERN, G., AND L. KRUCKMAN.

264

1983. "Multi-Disciplinary Perspectives on Post-partum Depression." *Social Science and Medicine* 17:1027–1041.

STEWARD, J.
1955. *The Theory of Culture Change*. Urbana: University of Illinois Press.

STIGLER, J. W., R. A. SHWEDER, AND G. HERDT (eds.).
1990. *Cultural Psychology: Essays on Comparative Human Development*. New York: Cambridge University Press.

STORY, R.
1985. "An Estimate of Mortality in a Pre-Columbian Urban Population." *American Anthropologist* 87:519–535.

STRATHERN, M.
1987a. "The Persuasive Fictions of Anthropology." *Current Anthropology* 28:251–281.

STRATHERN, M. (ed.).
1987b. *Dealing with Inequality: Analyzing Gender Relations in Melanesia and Beyond*. Cambridge: Cambridge University Press.

STUTCHBURY, E. L.
1982. "Blood, Fire and Meditation: Human Sacrifice and Widow Burning in Nineteenth Century India." In M. Allen and S. N. Mukherjee (eds.), *Women in India and Nepal*. Canberra: Australian National University Monographs on South Asia, no. 8, pp. 21–75.

SUMNER, W. G.
1906. *Folkways*. Boston: Ginn and Co.

SYMONS, D.
1979. *The Evolution of Human Sexuality*. New York: Oxford University Press.
1989. "A Critique of Darwinian Anthropology." *Ethology and Sociobiology* 10:131–144.
1990. "Adaptiveness and Adaptation." *Ethology and Sociobiology* 11:427–444.
(in press). "On the Use and Misuse of Darwinism in the Study of Human Behavior." In J. Tooby, L. Cosmides, and J. Barkow (eds.), *The Adapted Mind*. Oxford: Oxford University Press.

SZASZ, T. S.
1961. *The Myth of Mental Illness: Foundations of a Theory of Personal Conduct*. New York: Hoeber-Harper.

SZTOMPKA, P.
1974. *System and Function: Toward a Theory of Society*. New York: Academic Press.

TAINTER, J. A.
1988. *The Collapse of Complex Societies*. Cambridge: Cambridge University Press.

TAMBIAH, S. J.
1989. "Ethnic Conflict in the World Today." *American Ethnologist* 16:335–349.
1990. *Magic, Science, Religion, and the Scope of Rationality*. New York: Cambridge University Press.

TANZER, M.
1971. *The Sick Society: An Economic Examination*. New York: Holt, Rinehart and Winston.

265

TAYLOR, C. E., ET AL.
1973. "Asian Medical Systems: A Symposium on the Role of Comparative Sociology in Improving Health Care." *Social Science and Medicine* 7:307–318.

THOMAS, E. M.
1958. *The Harmless People*. New York: Random House.

TINDALE, N. B.
1962. "Some Population Changes Among the Kaiadilt People of Bentinck Island, Queensland." *Records of the South Australian Museum of Adelaide* 14:297–336.

TOOBY, J., AND L. COSMIDES.
1989. "Evolutionary Psychology and the Generation of Culture, Part I: Theoretical Considerations." *Ethology and Sociobiology* 10:29–49.

TORREY, E. F.
1980. *Schizophrenia and Civilization*. New York: Jason Aronson.

TRILLING, L.
1955. *Beyond Culture: Essays on Literature and Learning*. New York: Viking Press.

TRIVERS, R. L.
1971. "The Evolution of Reciprocal Altruism." *Quarterly Review of Biology* 46:35–57.
1985. *Social Evolution*. Menlo Park: Benjamin/Cummings.

TROTTER, R. T., II.
1985. "Greta and Azarcon: A Survey of Episodic Lead Poisoning from a Folk Remedy." *Human Organization* 44:64–72.
1991. "A Survey of Four Illnesses and Their Relationship to Intracultural Variation in a Mexican-American Community." *American Anthropologist* 93:115–125.

TROTTER, R. T., II, AND M. S. MICOZZI.
(in press). "Persistent Maladaptive Behavior and Abuse of Ethnomedical Substances." *Medical Anthropology*.

TROTTER, R. T., II, B. ORTIZ DE MONTELLANO, AND M. H. LOGAN.
1989. "Fallen Fontanelle in the American Southwest: Its Origin, Epidemiology, and Possible Organic Causes." *Medical Anthropology* 10:211–221.

TROVATO, F.
1988. "Mortality Differentials in Canada, 1951–1971: French, British, and Indians." *Culture, Medicine, and Psychiatry* 12:459–477.

TUCHMAN, B. W.
1984. *The March of Folly: From Troy to Vietnam*. New York: Knopf.

TUCKER, R. C.
1990. *The Revolution from Above*. New York: W. W. Norton.

TURKE, P. W.
1990. "Which Humans Behave Adaptively, and Why Does it Matter?" *Ethology and Sociobiology* 11:305–339.

TURNBULL, C.
1961. *The Forest People*. New York: Simon & Schuster.
1965. *Wayward Servants: The Two Worlds of the African Pygmies*. Garden City, NY: Natural History Press.

266

1972. *The Mountain People*. New York: Simon & Schuster.

1978. "Rethinking the Ik: A Functional Non-social System." In C. D. Laughlin, Jr., and I. A. Brady (eds.), *Extinction and Survival in Human Populations*. New York: Columbia University Press, pp. 49–75.

TURNER, L. M.

1894. *Ethnology and the Ungava District*. Washington, DC: Bureau of American Ethnology, 11th Annual Report, pp. 167–350.

TUZIN, D. F.

1982. "Ritual Violence Among the Ilahita Arapesh: The Dynamics of Moral and Religious Uncertainty." In G. H. Herdt (ed.), *Rituals of Manhood: Male Initiation in Papua New Guinea*. Berkeley: University of California Press, pp. 321–355.

TYLER, S. A.

1984. "The Poetic Turn in Post-Modern Anthropology: The Poetry of Paul Friedrich." *American Anthropologist* 86:328–336.

1986. "Post-Modern Ethnography: From Document of the Occult to Occult Document." In J. Clifford and G. E. Marcus (eds.), *Writing Culture: The Poetics and Politics of Ethnography*. Berkeley: University of California Press, pp. 122–140.

TYLOR, E. B.

1871. *Primitive Culture: Researches into the Development of Mythology, Philosophy, Religion, Language, Art and Custom*. London: J. Murray.

UZZELL, D.

1974. "Susto Revisited: Illness as a Strategic Role." *American Ethnologist* 1:369–378.

VAIL, L. (ed.).

1990. *The Creation of Tribalism in Southern Africa*. Berkeley: University of California Press.

VAN ALLEN, J.

1972. "Sitting on a Man: Colonialism and the Lost Political Institutions of Igbo Women." *Canadian Journal of African Studies* 6:165–181.

VAN BAAL, J.

1984. "The Dialectics of Sex in Marind-anim Culture." In G. H. Herdt, (ed.), *Ritualized Homosexuality in Melanesia*. Berkeley: University of California Press, pp. 128–166.

VAYDA, A. P.

1967. "Maori Warfare." In P. Bohannan (ed.), *Law and Warfare: Studies in the Anthropology of Conflict*. Garden City, NY: Natural History Press, pp. 359–380.

1969. "Expansion and Warfare Among Swidden Agriculturalists." In A. P. Vayda (ed.), *Environment and Cultural Behavior: Ecological Studies in Cultural Anthropology*. New York: Natural History Press, pp. 202–220.

1987. "Explaining What People Eat: A Review Article." *Human Ecology* 15:493–510.

VINING, D. R.

1990. "Social Versus Reproductive Success—the Central Theoretical Problem of Human Sociobiology." *Behavior and Brain Sciences* 9:167–260.

VOLLWEILER, L. G., AND A. B. SANCHEZ.

1983. "Divination—'Adaptive' from Whose Perspective?" *Ethnology* 22:193–210.

WAGLEY, C.

1951. "Cultural Influences on Population: A Comparison of Two Tupi Tribes." *Revista do Museu Paulista*–5:95–104.

1977. *A Welcome of Tears: The Tapirape Indians of Central Brazil*. New York: Oxford University Press.

WALKER, P., J. LUTHER, M. SAMLOFF, AND M. FELDMAN.

1988. "Life Events Stress and Psychosocial Factors in Men with Peptic Ulcer Disease: II. Relationships with Serum Pepsinogen Concentrations and Behavioral Risk Factors." *Gastroenterology* 94:323–330.

WALKER, P. L., AND B. S. HEWLETT.

1990. "Dental Health, Diet and Social Status Among Central African Foragers and Farmers." *American Anthropologist* 92:383–398.

WALLACE, A. F. C.

1960. *Culture and Personality*. New York: Random House.

1969. *The Death and Rebirth of the Seneca*. New York: Random House.

WALTER, E. V.

1969. *Terror and Resistance: A Study of Political Violence*. New York: Oxford University Press.

WARNES, H., AND E. D. WITTKOWER.

1982. "Culture and Psychosomatics." In I. Al-Issa (ed.), *Culture and Psychopathology*. Baltimore: University Park Press, pp. 387–414.

WASHBURN, W. E.

1987. "Cultural Relativism, Human Rights and the AAA." *American Anthropologist* 89:939–943.

WEGROCKI, H.

1948. "A Critique of Cultural and Statistical Concepts of Abnormality." In C. Kluckhohn and H. A. Murray (eds.), *Personality in Nature, Society and Culture*. New York: Knopf, pp. 691–701.

WEISS, G.

1981. "The Tragedy of Ethnocide: A Reply to Hippler." *American Anthropologist* 83:899–900.

WELCH, C. E.

1966. " 'Oh Dem Golden Slippers': The Philadelphia Mummers Parade." *Journal of American Folklore* 79:533–535.

WHITE, D. R.

1989. "Questioning the Correlational Evidence for Kipsigis Wealth as a Cause of Reproductive Success Rather than Polygyny as a Cause of Both Extra Children and Extra Wealth." *American Anthropologist* 91:175–178.

WIERZBICKA, A.

1987. "Soul and Mind: Linguistic Evidence for Ethnopsychology and Cultural History." *American Anthropologist* 91:41–58.

1988. "Emotions Across Culture: Similarities and Differences." *American Anthropologist* 90:982–983.

Bibliography

WILKIE, D. S., AND B. CURRAN.
1991. "Why Do Mbuti Hunters Use Nets? Ungulate Hunting Efficiency of Archers and Net Hunters in the Ituri Rain Forest." *American Anthropologist* 93:680–689.

WILKS, I.
1975. *Asante in the Nineteenth Century: The Structure and Evolution of a Political Order.* Evanston, IL: Northwestern University Press.

WILLIAMS, G. E.
1947. "Anthropology for the Common Man." *American Anthropologist* 49:84–90.

WILLS, G.
1990. *Under God: Religion and American Politics.* New York: Simon & Schuster.

WILMSEN, E. N., AND J. R. DENBOW.
1990. "Paradigmatic History of San-speaking Peoples and Current Attempts at Revision." *Current Anthropology* 31:489–524.

WILSON, E. O.
1978. *On Human Nature.* Cambridge: Harvard University Press.

WILSON, P. J.
1988. *The Domestication of the Human Species.* New Haven: Yale University Press.

WINDOM, C. S.
1989. "The Cycle of Violence." *Science* 244:160–166.

WIRSING, R.
1985. "The Health of Traditional Societies and the Effects of Acculturation." *Current Anthropology* 26:303–22.

WIRTH, L.
1938. "Urbanism as a Way of Life." *American Journal of Sociology* 44:1–24.

WOCKLER, R.
1978. "Perfectible Apes in Decadent Cultures: Rousseau's Anthropology Revisited." *Deadalus* (Summer), pp. 107–134.

WOLF, E. R.
1982. *Europe and the People Without History.* Berkeley: University of California Press.
1988. "Inventing Society." *American Ethnologist* 15:752–761.

WOODBURN, J. C.
1972. "Ecology, Nomadic Movement and the Compositions of the Local Group Among Hunters and Gatherers: An East African Example and Its Implications." In P. J. Ucko, R. Tringham, and G. W. Dimbleby (eds.), *Man, Settlement and Urbanism.* London: Gerald Duckworth, pp. 192–206.

WRIGHT, Q.
1942. *A Study of War.* 2 vols. Chicago: University of Chicago Press.

WYNN, T.
1989. *The Evolution of Spatial Competence.* Illinois Studies in Anthropology, no. 17. Urbana: University of Illinois Press.

WYNNE-EDWARDS, V. C.
1962. *Animal Dispersion in Relation to Social Behavior.* London: Oliver and Boyd.

269

1986. *Evolution Through Group Selection*. Boston: Blackwell Scientific.

YOFFEE, N., AND G. H. COWGILL.

1988. *The Collapse of Ancient States and Civilization*. Tucson: University of Arizona Press.

YOUNG, A.

1976. "Some Implications of Medical Beliefs and Practices for Social Anthropology." *American Anthropologist* 78:5–24.

Index

Aberle, D., 42, 215n.
Abrams, E. M., 217n.
Abu-Lughod, L., 215n.
Adair, J., 222n.
Adams, R. M., 224n., 226n.
Adaptivism, 12, 30–32; *see also* Functionalism
Alexander, J. C., 213n.
Alexander, R. D., 32, 213–14n., 217–18n.
Alland, A., Jr., 114, 213n., 215n., 221n.
Alletzhauzer, A. J., 227n.
Almagor, V., 224n.
Altman, J. C., 221n.
Amorasi, T., 217n.
Anderson, B. G., 220n.
Andrew, C., 219n.
Anquandah, J., 220n.
Appell, G. N., 212n.
Ardner, S., 225n.
Aristophanes, 3, 17
Aristotle, 198
Aunger, R., Jr., 193, 227n.

Bailely, K. V., 221n.
Bailey, K. G., 67, 217n.
Bailey, R. C., 193, 227n.
Baker, P. T., 222n.
Baker, T. S., 222n.
Baksh, M., 80, 218n.
Balicki, A., 128, 222n.

Banfield, E. C., 14, 212n.
Barkow, J. H., 39, 41, 87, 117, 215–19n., 221n.
Baroja, J. C., 222n.
Barrett, M. G., 211n.
Beals, A. R., 225n.
Beck, V., 220n.
Beiser, M., 222n.
Bellah, R. N., 65, 217n.
Belo, J., 3, 211n.
Benedict, R., 25, 33, 90, 179, 214n.
Bennett, J. W., 228n.
Bentham, J., 76
Berlin, B., 29, 213n.
Bernstein, I. S., 213n.
Betzig, L. L., 77, 216n., 218–19n.
Biersack, M., 212n.
Biesele, M., 228n.
Bigelow, G., 217n.
Bindon, J., 221n.
Birdsell, J., 112
Black-Michaud, J., 227n.
Bloom, A., 212n.
Boas, F., 25, 90
Bock, K., 215n.
Boehm, C., 44, 194, 215–16n., 218n., 228n.
Bohannan, P., 224n.
Borgerhoff Mulder, M., 41, 213n., 215n.
Boster, J., 228n.

271

Bowditch, T. E., 96, 98–99, 220n.
Boyd, R., 39, 63, 213–15n., 217n.,
    228n.
Brady, I. A., 226n.
Breslau, N., 222n.
Brintnall, D., 218n., 220n.
Brooks, D. R., 215n.
Brown, D. E., 212–13n.
Brown, G. T., 132, 223n.
Bruner, E., 213n.
Buchbinder, G., 113, 221n.
Buckland, C. E., 223n.
Burch, E. S., Jr., 217n.
Burgess, A., 221n.
Burland, C. A., 173, 226n.
Burton, J. W., 218n.

Campbell, A., 224n.
Campbell, D. T., 12, 30–31, 42–43, 57–
    58, 70, 213n., 215n., 217n.
Cannibalism, 91–93, 100, 141
Carden, M. L., 212n.
Cardoe, C., 215n.
Carey, W. H., 136, 223n.
Cassidy, C. M., 110, 221n.
Castelli, J., 228n.
Cawte, J., 211n., 227n.
Chagnon, N. A., 79, 179, 194, 218n.,
    228n.
Chang, C., 224n.
Child abuse, 80–81
Childe, V. G., 217n.
Clifford, J., 213n.
Cockburn, T. A., 221n.
Cohen, M. N., 87, 110, 212n., 219n.,
    221–22n.
Cohen, S., 124, 222n.
Colby, B. N., 38, 214–15n.
Cole, M., 213n.
Collado-Ardon, R., 225n.
Collapse of societies, 161–87
  and belief systems, 171–78
    and prophecy, 173–78
    and religion, 172–73
    and witchcraft, 171–72
  and catastrophes, 169–70
  and choosing death, 185–87
    in battle, 186–87
    by martyrs, 186
  colonial intervention halting, 181–82
  and decision not to reproduce, 185
  and dissatisfaction with culture, 163–64,
    170–71
  and external forces, 161–63, 164, 165
    colonial intervention, 182–83
  and failure to reproduce, 164–65, 182
  and feuding, 178–81

and inadequate technology for defense,
    166
and loss of technology, 163
and military conquest, 165–69
and population decreases, 161–62, 164–
    65, 177, 180
and ritualized killings, 172
Collier, J. F., 218n.
Conant, F. P., 224–25n.
Conklin, H. C., 196, 228n.
Conklin, J. C., 196, 228n.
Connell, J., 113, 221n.
Converse, P. E., 224n.
Cosmides, L., 41, 213n., 215n., 217n.
Count, E. W., 217n.
Counts, D. A., 224n.
Covello, V. T., 216n.
Cowgill, G. L., 226n., 228n.
Crapanzano, V., 212n.
Crummey, D., 225n.
Crumrine, N. R., 225n.
Cultural relativism, 2, 10, 22–39, 205–
    207
  antirelativistic sentiment, 34–39
Culture; see also Traditional beliefs and
    practices
  attempts to eliminate certain aspects of,
    142–43
  and colonial contact, 140–41
  discontentment with, 45, 133–49, 158–
    59
  objections to certain aspects of, 141–
    43
  response to discontentment with, 144–
    48
    alienation as, 144
    drunkenness as, 144–45, 183–85
    emigration as, 148
    revitalization movements as, 147–48
    suicide as, 145–47, 185

Dahrendorf, R., 77–78, 218n.
Daly, M., 204, 216n., 226n., 228n.
D'Andrade, R., 213n.
Darnton, R., 226n.
Davenport, W., 224n.
Davis, G. C., 222n.
Davis, K., 77
Davis, S. H., 226n.
Davis, W. G., 228n.
Dawkins, R., 217n.
Dean, R. F. A., 221n.
Decision making, 194–201
  and identifying problems, 199–200
  and irrationality, 196–99
  by leaders, 200
  and rationality, 196–200

and reluctance to change, 200–201
and unconscious problem-solving, 194–96
Demarist, A. M., 60
Dennett, G., 112–13, 221n.
Deuschle, K., 222n.
Dickemann, M., 221n.
Dirks, R., 220n., 225n.
Divination, 54
Djagamara, N., 211n.
Dorian, N. C., 226n.
Douglas, M., 198, 224n., 228n.
Dower, J. 227n.
Dressler, W. W., 124, 222n.
Drunkenness, 144–45, 183–85
Dunkel-Schetter, C., 124
Durham, W. H., 227n.
Dyson-Hudson, R., 226n.

Earle, T., 218n., 228n.
Eckert, E. D., 222n.
Eder, J. F. 164, 226n.
Edgerton, R. B., 212n., 218–20n., 222n., 224–27n.
Eisenstadt, S. N., 213n.
Ellen, R., 55, 211n., 216n., 227–28n.
Ellis, R. W. R., 221n.
Ember, C., 218n.
Epistemological relativism, 26, 27, 28, 30
Erikson, K., 183, 227n.
Erofeev, V., 225n.
Ethnocentrism, 55
Evans-Pritchard, E. E., 11–12, 30, 36, 54, 212–13n.
Everett, M. W., 224n.
Exploitation, 79–104; see also Male dominance; Political exploitation
  child abuse as, 80
  cruelty to animals as, 80
  infanticide as, 79, 80

Fabrega, H., 222n.
Favazza, A. R., 211n.
Favazza, B., 211n.
Feil, D., 217n., 219n.
Feldman, R. A., 220–21n.
Ferguson, R. B., 55, 216n., 226n.
Feuding, 11, 51–52, 57, 179
Finkler, K., 220n.
Fischer, C., 212n.
Fogel, R. W., 219n.
Folk societies
  decision making in, 194–200
  defined, 4
  effects of external forces on, 8, 59, 140–41, 161–63, 164, 165
  idealization of, 5–9

Folk-urban comparison, 5, 203
  and mental illness, 129
Fontana, B. L., 226n.
"Foodways"; see Maladaptive health beliefs and practices
Footbinding, 134–35
Foster, G. M., 220n.
Foucault, M., 9, 128
Fox, R., 3, 66, 211n., 217n.
Freeman, H. P., 220n.
Freedman, D. G., 68, 217n.
Freilich, M., 193, 227n.
Freuchen, P., 81, 218n.
Freud, S., 34, 37, 121, 214n.
Fromm, E., 34, 122
Functionalism, 22, 26, 31–32, 42, 77, 126
Fynn, H. F., 94–95, 219–20n., 225n.
Fynn, J. K., 226n.

Gallup, G., Jr., 224n., 228n.
Gardner, H., 217n.
Garn, S. M., 219n.
Gazaway, R., 19–21, 212n.
Gazzaniga, M. S., 217n.
Geertz, C., 26, 28–29, 34, 62, 212–14n., 217n.
Gellner, E., 28–29, 58, 213n., 216n.
Genital mutilation, 9–10, 139
Gilmore, D. D., 219n.
Gilovich, T., 198–99, 228n.
Gladwin, T., 33, 214n.
Gluckman, M., 94, 154, 225n.
Gmelch, G., 224n.
Goldenweiser, A., 33, 214n.
Goldschmidt, W. R., 10, 43, 86, 211–12n., 215n., 217n., 219n., 222n., 226–28n.
Good, B., 223n.
Goodman, A. H., 123, 222n.
Gordievsky, O., 219n.
Gordon, D., 223n.
Gould, S. J., 32, 205, 208, 228n.
Graburn, N. H. H., 79, 218n.
Graham, S. E., 223n.
Grant, J. P., 220n.
Graves, N. B., 224n.
Graves, T. B., 224n.
Greeley, A., 228n.
Greenwald, A. G., 228n.
Gregor, T., 11–12, 212n., 218–19n.
Grossman, L. S., 221n.
Gupta, A. R., 223n.
Gurr, T. R., 225n.
Gusinde, M., 227n.
Guthrie, G. M., 224n.

Hallowell, A. R., 34
Hallpike, C. R., 37–38, 42, 53, 199, 213–
    16n., 218n., 228n.
Hanna, J. M., 222n.
Hanson, J. R., 227n.
Harako, R., 211n.
Harbison, S. F., 218n.
Harkness S., 130, 222n.
Harms, R., 195, 228n.
Harner, M., 92, 219n.
Harris, G., 223n., 225n.
Harris, M., 12, 30, 32, 36–37, 66, 90, 92,
    118, 124, 126, 200, 212–15n., 217–
    22n., 228n.
Harris, T., 132, 233n.
Hassig, R., 219n.
Hatch, E., 212–15n.
Haugen, E., 212n.
Hawkes, K., 192, 227n.
Hayes, R. O., 211n., 223n.
Heath, D. B., 224n.
Heider, K. G., 140, 223n.
Heine, B., 7, 211n.
Henry, J., 69–70, 179, 217n., 227n.
Herdt, G. H., 227n.
Herskovits, M. J., 25, 33, 35, 37,
    214n.
Hewlett, B. S., 218n.
Hezel, F. X., 224n.
Hickerson, H., 227n.
Hill, K., 224n., 227n.
Hill, T. W., 227n.
Hippler, A. E., 37, 214n.
Hobley, C. W., 225n.
Hobsbawm, E. J., 225n.
Hoebel, E. A., 218n., 222n.
Hogbin, I., 226n.
Hollan, D., 224n.
Hollis, M., 26, 212n.
Holmberg, A. R., 13, 107, 112, 212n.,
    220–21n., 225n.
Hooper, A., 225n.
Horton, D. R., 216n.
Howe, K. R., 112, 221n.
Howlett, D. R., 223n.
Human nature, 43–44, 61–74
    adaptive value of interpersonal strategies
        and, 67
    biological predispositions and, 66–69
    cognitive ability and, 68
    cultural controls on, 69–73
    culturally constituted needs and, 64–65
    irrationality of, 198
    psychological mechanisms and, 68
Human sacrifice, 95–100, 142–43
Hume, D., 73
Huntingford, G. W. B., 225 n.

Huntsman, J., 225n.
Hyde, G. E., 224n.

Ienaga, S., 227n.
Iliffe, J., 226n.
Ill health, 105–112; see also Mental ill-
        ness; Mortality
    among hunter-gatherers, 111–12
    in ancient urban areas, 111
    and external forces, 109
    and subsistence practices, 110
Inequality, 75–79, 103–104
    based on ability, 76, 78
    based on age, 76
    based on sex, 76
    in folk societies, 76–79
    leading to exploitation, 79
    universality of, 76–79, 103–104
Isaac, B., 163, 226n.
Isaacs, N., 95, 219–20n.

Jarvis, E., 222n.
Jefferson, T., 129
Jilek, W. G., 224n.
Johns, T., 220n.
Johnson, A. W., 218n., 223n., 226n.
Johnson, B. B., 216n.
Jones, R. M., 49, 51, 215–16n.
Jones, W. K., 220n.
Junod, H. A., 225n.

Kaberry, P., 225n.
Kamath, K. R., 221n.
Kamin, L. J., 40, 215n.
Kanwar, R., 138
Kaplan, H., 224n.
Katz, S. H., 221n.
Kay, P., 29, 213n.
Kearney, M., 222n.
Keddie, N., 232n.
Keegan, W. F., 227n.
Keiser, R. L., 226n.
Kennedy, J. G., 36, 124, 128, 214n., 222–
        23n., 226n.
Kephart, W. M., 212n.
Khalaf, S. N., 179, 227n.
Khaleque, M. K., 218n.
Kihlstrom, J. F., 217n.
Kilbride, J. C., 218n.
Kilbride, P. L., 218n.
Kimura, M., 205n.
King, L. M., 224n.
Kleinman, A. M., 222n.
Kluckhohn, C., 10–11, 26, 36, 128, 211–
        12n., 222n., 227n.
Knauft, B., 172, 218n., 226–27n.
Köbben, A. J. F., 153, 225n.

Koch, K. F., 10, 211*n.*
Konner, M., 67, 217*n.*, 220*n.*
Korbin, J. E., 218*n.*
Kracke, W. H., 153, 225*n.*
Kroeber, A. L., 35–36, 142, 214*n.*, 218*n.*, 224*n.*, 226*n.*
Kroeber, C. B., 226*n.*
Kroeber, T., 225*n.*
Kruckman, L., 222*n.*
Kumar, K., 223*n.*
Kummer, H., 52–53, 216*n.*
Kuper, L., 220*n.*
Kuran, T., 228*n.*
Kuschel, R., 227*n.*
Kwashiorkor, 112, 115–16

LaBarre, W., 34, 53, 64, 214*n.*, 216*n.*, 226*n.*
Lack, D., 213*n.*
Ladurie, L. E., 155, 225*n.*
Langness, L. L., 56, 216*n.*, 219*n.*, 223*n.*
LaRochefoucauld, F. de, 67
Laslett, P., 219*n.*
Laughlin, C. D., Jr., 226*n.*
Leach, E. R., 23, 30, 205, 212–13*n.*, 228*n.*
Lebo, H., 222*n.*
Lee, R. B., 149, 211*n.*, 224–25*n.*
Leighton, D., 10–11, 128, 211*n.*, 222*n.*
Leis, P. E., 68, 216*n.*
LeVine, B. B., 219*n.*
LeVine, R. A., 84, 213*n.*, 218–19*n.*
Levinson, D., 212*n.*, 218–19*n.*
Levy, H. S., 223*n.*
Levy, M. J., Jr., 215*n.*
Lewis, O., 6, 211*n.*
Lewontin, R. C., 40, 215*n.*
Life expectancy, 110–11
Lin, K.-M., 222*n.*
Lindblom, G., 225*n.*
Lindenbaum, S., 218*n.*, 221*n.*
Linton, R., 35–36, 73, 214*n.*
LiPuma, E., 228*n.*
Lobel, M., 124
Lockard, J. S., 217*n.*
Lopreato, J., 58, 213*n.*, 215–17*n.*
Los Angeles Times, 217*n.*, 219*n.*, 222*n.*, 225*n.*
Lowie, R. H., 118, 213*n.*, 221*n.*, 227*n.*
Lozoff, B., 221*n.*
Lubbock, J., 31
Lukes, S., 26, 212*n.*
Lumholtz, C., 218*n.*
Lurie, A., 223*n.*
Luther, J., 222*n.*
Lutz, C. A., 213*n.*, 222*n.*

MacAndrew, C., 227*n.*
MacLean, V., 220*n.*
Maladaptation, 39–54
defined, 16, 45
Maladaptation criteria, 40–45
failure to meet human needs as, 43
functional prerequisites of society and, 42–43
and group selection, 43
personal satisfaction as, 44–45, 102
reproductive success as, 40–42, 44–45, 102
and social imperatives, 43
and sociobiology, 40–42
and terminal conditions for a society, 42
Maladaptive health beliefs and practices, 112–21
harmful diets as, 118–20
and fava beans, 119–19
and "foodways," 118–20
inadequate diets as, 113–17
for children, 114–16
from denial of colostrum to infants, 116–17
for pregnant or lactating women, 114–15
and medical treatments, 117–18, 121
and physical beauty, 120, 133–35
Male dominance, 81–86
of division of labor, 82
and hostility between the sexes, 84–86
and rape, 83, 85
of women's diet, 81–82
Malinowski, B., 31, 43, 66, 213*n.*, 215*n.*
Malone, M., 212*n.*
Maloney, C., 222*n.*
Malotki, E., 212*n.*
Malthus., T., 44
Maquet, J., 212*n.*
Marcus, G. E., 212–13*n.*
Marr, Dr., 68
Martindale, D., 213*n.*
Marwick, M. G., 36
Marx, K., 3, 76, 87.
McCabe, J. T., 227*n.*
McClelland, D. B. L., 221*n.*
McCord, C., 220*n.*
McDermott, W., 222*n.*
McElroy, A., 221*n.*
McGovern, T. H., 217*n.*
McGregor, G., 217*n.*
McLean, S., 223*n.*
McLeod, M. D., 220*n.*, 226*n.*
McMillen, S., 220*n.*
Mead, M., 4, 25, 162, 226*n.*

Meggers, B., 195, 228*n*.
Meggitt, M. J., 106, 124, 217*n*., 219–
  20*n*., 222–23*n*., 228*n*.
Mental illness, 128–32; *see also* Ill health;
  Mortality
  and depression, 132
  and postpartum depression (dysphoria),
    130–31
  and schizophrenia, 129–30
  and stressors, 130–32
Messer, E., 221*n*.
Michelson, T., 219*n*.
Miller, B. E., 42, 215*n*.
Mills, C. W., 211*n*.
Mitchell, D., 219*n*.
Mitchell, J. E., 222*n*.
Mitchell, W. E., 218*n*.
Mithen, S. J., 227*n*.
Montezuma, 173
Moore, O. K., 54, 216*n*.
Mortality, 105–12, 184; *see also* Ill health;
  Mental illness
Mosko, M. S., 226*n*.
Murdock, G. P., 35–37, 214*n*.
Murphy, H. B. M., 131, 222*n*.
Murray, H. A., 43

Naroll, R., 212*n*., 214–15*n*., 224*n*.
Nash, J., 224*n*.
Needham, R., 24–25, 212–13*n*.
Neel, J. V., 221*n*.
Nemeroff, C., 228*n*.
"Neutral theory," 205
New York Times, 219*n*., 228*n*.
Nieboer, H., 218*n*.
Ninuallain, M., 222*n*.
Nisbet, R., 211*n*., 228*n*.
Nissam-Sabat, C., 27, 212*n*.
Nitobe, I., 227*n*.
Norbeck, E., 36, 154, 214*n*., 225*n*.
Noyes, J. H., 17–18
Noyes, P., 212*n*.
Nurse, G. T., 221*n*.

Oakley, J., 225*n*.
O'Hare, A., 222*n*.
Oliver, S. C., 227*n*.
O'Meara, J. T., 213*n*.
Omer-Cooper, J. D., 219*n*.
O'Nell, C. W., 225*n*.
Opler, M. E., 106, 220*n*.
Opler, M. K., 34
Orr, D. W., 228*n*.
Ortner, S., 218*n*.
Ortiz, S., 228*n*.
Ortiz de Montellano, B. R., 219*n*.
Oswalt, W. H., 213*n*., 222*n*.

Otterbein, K. F., 172, 226*n*.
Owusu, M., 226*n*.

Palmer, C., 219*n*.
Parsons, T., 77, 215*n*.
Patel, S., 223*n*.
Paulhus, D. L., 217*n*.
Peacock, N. R., 218*n*.
Pearlman, M., 227*n*.
Peires, J. B., 173, 226*n*.
Pelligrino, C., 226*n*.
Pelto, G. H., 220*n*.
Peptic ulcers, 123–24
Peron, R., 48
Perrin, N., 220*n*.
Pipes, R., 219*n*.
Plog, S. C., 222*n*.
Plomley, N. J. B., 215–16*n*.
Plotnikov, L., 224*n*.
Political exploitation, 86–101
  and commoners, 92–93, 95
  by controlling wealth, 90–93, 94–95,
    96–99
  by an individual's coercive force, 88–89
  by secret societies, 89–90
  and self-interest of elites, 87, 102
  by use of terror, 88, 90, 94–95, 97
  by warfare, 89, 91–94, 96
Poole, F. P., 141, 146, 224*n*.
Population growth, 44–45, 102
Pospisil, L., 67, 142, 217*n*., 224–25*n*.
Postmodernism, 28–30
Pregnancy and food taboos, 113–14
Primitive harmony, 2, 3, 6, 8–9, 203
Protest; *see* Rebellion

Quine, W. V., 213*n*.

Rabb, T. K., 215*n*.
Radcliffe-Brown, A. R., 31, 126, 213*n*.
Ragin, C. C., 212*n*.
Rambo, A. T., 220*n*.
Ramseyer, F. A., 220*n*.
Rape, 85, 141
Raphael, D. L., 117
Rappaport, R. A., 32, 194–95, 213*n*.
Rasmussen, K., 128, 219*n*., 222*n*.
Rattray, R. S., 220*n*.
Rebellion, 149–59
  and generational conflict, 150–51
  by killing, 155–57
    elites, 156–57
    leaders, 155–56
    witches, 155–56
  and peasant uprisings, 157–58
  by refusing to share food, 154
  and ritual protest, 153–55

carnivals, 155
  of clowns and jesters, 154–55
  slave, 157
  by women, 151–53
    ridiculing, 152
    shaming, 153
    spirit possession, 151
    susto, 151
Redfield, R., 3, 5, 35–36, 211n., 214n., 224n., 228n.
Renteln, A. D., 212n.
Reproductive success, 41–42, 102
Reser, J. P., 214n.
Richards, A. I., 90, 219n.
Richerson, P. J., 39, 63, 213–14n., 217n., 228n.
Ritter, E. A., 225n.
Robarchek, C. A., 218n., 228n.
Robbins, S., 140, 223n.
Roberts, R. E., 224n.
Rogers, A. R., 42, 215n., 217n.
Rogers, E. M., 216n.
Rorty, R., 24, 212n.
Rosaldo, R., 27, 212–13n.
Roscoe, P. B., 227n.
Rose, L., 40, 215n., 220n.
Rosenberg, E. M., 221n.
Rosenhan, D. L., 128, 222n.
Ross, E. B., 213n., 218n., 221n.
Ross, J.-K., 224n.
Ross, L., 228n.
Rotberg, R. I., 215n.
Roth, H. L., 215–16n.
Rousseau, J. J., 4, 76
Roy, D. B., 223n.
Rozanov, V. V., 227n.
Rozin, P., 228n.
Rubel, A. J., 225n.
Rubinstein, D. H., 224n.
Rue, D. J., 217n.
Russell, D., 217n.
Ruyle, E. E., 91, 219n.
Ryan, L., 216n.

Sahlins, M., 77, 213n., 218n., 221n.
Sale, K., 3, 211n.
Salusbury-Jones, G. T., 225n.
Samloff, M., 222n.
Samuels, M. L., 228n.
Sanchez, A. B., 54, 216n.
Sapir, E., 27
Sapir-Whorf hypothesis, 27
Sarhili, King, 173, 176–77
Schapera, I., 211n., 216n.
Scheper-Hughes, N., 109, 129, 220n., 222n.
Schneider, D. M., 26, 212n.

Schneider, H. K., 228n.
Scholte, R., 212n.
Schwartz, T., 36, 124, 214n.
Scott, J. C., 225n.
Scott, J. P., 215n., 228n.
Scribner, S., 213n.
Scrimshaw, S., 124
Seaton, S. L., 224n.
Semmelweis, I., 107–108
Service, E. R., 88, 219n.
Shahar, S., 218n.
Shaka Zulu, 167
Shaw, P., 211n.
Shkilnyk, A. M., 183–84, 227n.
Shoemaker, F. F., 216n.
Shore, B., 124, 222n., 225n.
Shorter, E., 221n.
Shostak, M., 221n., 223n.
Shweder, R. A., 197, 213n., 216n., 223n., 228n.
"Sick" societies, 34
  and stress, 122
Siegel, B. J., 225n.
Silberman, N. A., 227n.
Sillitoe, P., 113, 221n.
Silverblatt, I., 225n.
Simoons, F. J., 81, 218n., 221n.
Singer, M., 218n.
Singh, I., 223n.
Small-scale societies; see Folk societies
Smith, E. A., 227n.
Social and cultural inadequacy, 21
Sorokin, P. A., 225n.
Soustelle, J., 219n.
Speck, F., 54
Spence, J. D., 147, 224n.
Spencer, P., 151, 224–25n.
Sperber, D., 28, 53, 197, 213n., 216n., 218n.
Spiro, M. E., 28, 36, 56, 212–14n., 216n., 218n., 222n.
Spriggs, M., 221n.
Stannard, D. E., 220n.
Stearman, A. M., 212n., 226n.
Stein, D., 223n.
Stern, G., 222n.
Steward J., 188, 227n.
Stone, D. L., 124, 222n.
Story, R., 221n.
Strathern, M., 213n., 219n.
Stress, 121–28
  defined, 124
  effects on life expectancy, 123
  in folk societies, 125–28
    from taboos, 125–27, 128
    from witchcraft, 125, 127–28
  mental illness and, 131

Stress (*cont.*)
  in New York City, 122
  and psychosomatic illness, 123–24
    peptic ulcers, 123–24
  and susceptibility to illness, 124–25
Stutchbury, E. L., 223*n.*
Suicide, 145–47
Sumner, W. G., 25, 212*n.*
Susto, 151
Suttee, 136–39
Symons, D., 41, 71, 215*n.*, 217–18*n.*
Sztompka, P., 213*n.*

Tainter, J. A., 171–72, 226*n.*
Tambiah, S. J., 216*n.*, 224*n.*
Tanco, P. P., 224*n.*
Taumoepeau, B. M., 131, 223*n.*
Taylor, C. E., 118, 221*n.*
Thomas, E. M., 6, 211*n.*, 225*n.*
Time, 222*n.*
Tindale, N. B., 180, 227*n.*
Tooby, J., 41, 213*n.*, 215*n.*, 217*n.*
Torrey, E. F., 129, 222*n.*
Townsend, P., 221*n.*
Traditional beliefs and practices; *see also*
    Culture
  adaptive value of, 53–55, 194
  and biological predispositions, 61–69
  defined, 17–21
  failing to address as maladaptive, 11–12
  and human nature, 69–74
  interpreted as adaptive, 7–11, 12
  irrationality of, 196–99
  labeling as harmful, 13–14
  persistence of, 57–61, 197–99, 201
Traditional medicine, 105–108
  negative functions of, 106–108
  positive functions of, 105
Trilling, L., 69, 217*n.*, 219*n.*
Trivers, R. L., 79, 217*n.*
Trotter, R. T., II, 117, 221*n.*
Trovato, F., 220*n.*
Tuchman, B. W., 200, 228*n.*
Tucker, R. C., 219*n.*
Turke, P. W., 41–42, 215*n.*
Turnbull, C., 6–8, 80, 148, 154, 211*n.*,
    218–19*n.*, 222*n.*, 225*n.*

Turner, L. M., 79
Tuzin, D. F., 223–24*n.*
Tylor, E. B., 31, 213*n.*

Uzzell, D., 225*n.*

Vail, L., 224*n.*
Van Allen, J., 225*n.*
Van Baal, J., 141, 182, 223*n.*, 227*n.*
Vining, D. R., 42, 215*n.*
Vollweiler, L. G., 54, 216*n.*

Wagley, C., 217*n.*
Walker, P., 222*n.*
Walker, P. L., 218*n.*
Wallace, A. F. C., 29, 213*n.*, 224*n.*
Walsh, D., 222*n.*
Walter, E. V., 219*n.*
Warfare, 55, 70–71, 89, 140–41, 165–89
Warnes, H., 222*n.*
Washburn, W. E., 213–14*n.*
Wegrocki, H., 222*n.*
Welch, C. E., 225*n.*
White, D. R., 215*n.*, 224*n.*
Whiting, B., 36
Whorf, B., 27
Wildavsky, A., 198, 228*n.*
Wiley, E. D., 215*n.*
Wilks, I., 220*n.*, 226*n.*
Wills, G., 228*n.*
Wilson, E. O., 41, 69, 217*n.*, 228*n.*
Wilson, M., 204, 216*n.*, 226*n.*, 228*n.*
Wirsing, R., 220–21*n.*
Wirth, L., 211*n.*
Wissler, C., 31
Witchcraft, 10–11, 71–72, 125, 155, 171–73
Wittgenstein, L., 24, 29
Wittkower, E. D., 222*n.*
Wockler, R., 211*n.*
Wolf, E. R., 224*n.*, 226*n.*
Woodburn, J. C., 192, 224*n.*, 227*n.*
Wright, Q., 165
Wynn, T., 68, 217*n.*
Wynne-Edwards, V. C., 32, 213*n.*

Yoffee, N., 226*n.*